Arab Village

KUFR AL-MA FROM ITS OUTSKIRTS FACING SOUTH
TOWARD THE NEIGHBORING VILLAGE OF KHANSIRI

Arab Village

A SOCIAL STRUCTURAL STUDY OF A TRANS-JORDANIAN PEASANT COMMUNITY

by Richard T. Antoun

INDIANA UNIVERSITY PRESS

BLOOMINGTON · LONDON 1972

Published in Canada by Fitzhenry & Whiteside, Ltd., Don Mills, Ontario
Library of Congress Catalog Card No. 70-633555   ISBN 0-253-38429-X

This volume is No. 29 in the Indiana University Social Science Series.

MANUFACTURED IN THE UNITED STATES OF AMERICA

TO MY MOTHER AND FATHER
AND MY FRIENDS IN JORDAN

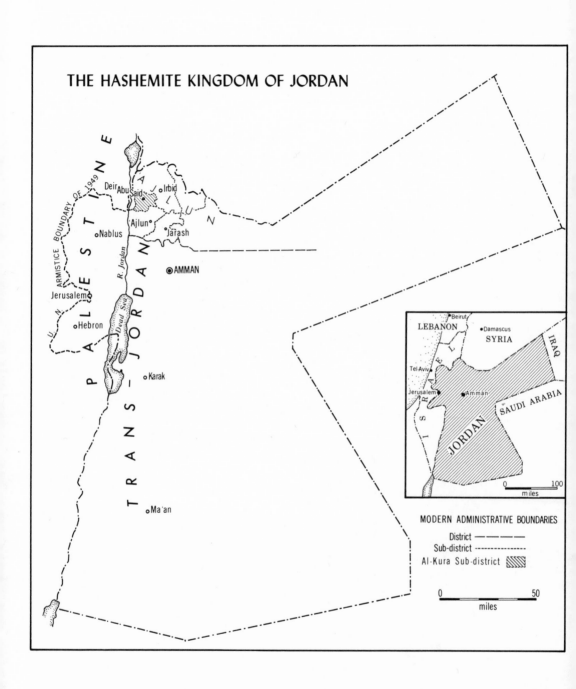

THE HASHEMITE KINGDOM OF JORDAN

PALESTINE

ARMISTICE BOUNDARY OF 1949
U. N.

Deir Abu Said
Irbid
Ajlun
Nablus
Jarash
R. Jordan
AMMAN
Jerusalem
Dead Sea
Hebron
TRANS-JORDAN
Karak
Ma'an

LEBANON
Beirut
Damascus
SYRIA
IRAQ
Tel-Aviv
ISRAEL
Jerusalem
Amman
JORDAN
SAUDI ARABIA
0   100
miles

MODERN ADMINISTRATIVE BOUNDARIES
District ———
Sub-district ------------
Al-Kura Sub-district [hatched]

0   50
miles

Preface

In June of 1959, I was the recipient of a grant from the Anthropology Department and Middle East Center of Harvard University to carry out an ethnographic study of a Sunni Muslim Arab village in the Fertile Crescent. Up to that time few studies of peasant villages had been undertaken there. Of those undertaken few had been published. Travelers and anthropologists, alike, had focused their attention on fascinating nomadic peoples such as the Bedouin or on religious minorities such as the Druzes, Shi'a, Greek Orthodox, and Maronites of Lebanon, the Alawis of Syria, or the Mandaeans, Shi'a, and Yezidis of Iraq. The Sunni Muslim Arab peasant, representing the social (villages) and religious (orthodox Muslims) majority in the area, had been the subject of published monographs by only one professional anthropologist, Hilma Granqvist. Granqvist's studies of a Palestinian village focused on infancy, childhood, and marriage. Since the completion of my field work, professional anthropologists have contributed two additional monographs. Abner Cohen has analyzed an Arab border village in Israel and Abdullah Lutfiyya has described a Palestinian village in the Hashemite Kingdom of Jordan. Cohen makes a remarkable and pioneering attempt to relate changes in village social structure to changes in national social structure while Lutfiyya records valuable information for students interested in the relationship between local custom and belief and Islamic law and ethics. However, none of the above mentioned studies has sought to assess, sociologically, the significance of the village community as such.[1]

The factors governing my selection of a host country (Jordan) and a particular research area within it (Ajlun) were partly pragmatic, partly theoretical, and partly personal. The revolution of 1958 in Iraq and the civil war of 1959 in Lebanon had produced an uncertain political situation in Syria as well as in Iraq and Lebanon. Jordan, by contrast, remained comparatively tranquil. Moreover, the prevailing amicable relations between the United States and Jordan made the climate for research by Americans in Jordan particularly favorable. Before my arrival in Jordan in October, 1959, I had already decided to confine my search for a village to the area east of the Jordan River formerly known as Transjordan. The area west of the river, Palestine, had undergone considerable political, economic, and social upheaval as a result of the British Mandate, the growth of Zionism, and the Arab-Israeli War of 1948−49. I wished in a first study to select a traditional village, one which had been relatively untouched by the upheavals in Palestine and which would provide a baseline for subsequent studies of social change. With the cooperation of the Department of Agriculture of Jordan I was able to accompany the agricultural inspectors on their daily trips to the villages of the Ajlun District in northwestern Transjordan. After visiting twenty villages I finally selected Kufr al-Ma as the locus of study and moved there early in November, 1959.

The reasons for the selection of Kufr al-Ma rather than other villages in Transjordan or the Ajlun District were, again, partly pragmatic, partly theoretical, and partly personal. I was particularly interested in the relationship between Islamic law, ethics and ritual on the one hand and local custom on the other; I wished, therefore, to select a village large enough to have a mosque and a permanent religious specialist, the *imām*. Kufr al-Ma, with a population of two thousand, fulfilled these requirements. As far as I was able to discern from my brief visit, the village was traditional not only in its religious orientation but also in its agricultural regime and social life. Because of the roughness of the terrain, mechanized ploughs were not suitable for working the land, and the peasants used oxen and donkeys to draw the ancient wooden plough. I attended a wedding celebration on the evening of my visit and received the impression that marriage was contracted and celebrated in the traditional manner. I was impressed with the hospitality and consideration shown our party, above all by the mayor, *mukhtār*, of the village who, I sensed, would cooperate with me in my study. Finally, I had tired of tramping from one village to the next and, anxious to begin my work, felt that, after all, having satisfied the general requirements of the study, one village was probably as suitable as the next.

In some respects my fondest hopes were more than realized while in others they were disappointed. The mukhtar and the imam became my close friends and, being respected men in the village, were instrumental in my acceptance as a temporary member of the community. But I soon discovered that the village, however traditional in its religious beliefs, social life, and agricultural regime, was characterized by considerable occupational mobility and economic differentiation. In fact, only a minority of the employed men worked in agriculture. Moreover I found that the very size of the village presented a formidable problem. I spent nearly all of the first month drawing a sketch map of the village, and the census of households was still incomplete after a full year of study due to the absence from the village of a considerable proportion of the male labor force who worked in towns.

I came to the village without specific hypotheses regarding social change, peasant communities, Islam, politics, or social structure that I wished to validate or invalidate and without having had the benefit of a course in methods or techniques of fieldwork. The only dictum which I followed in the collection of data was of considerable generality: to live in the village as a participant-observer for a full year and to collect any data that might shed light on the social life of the village. Besides drawing maps, taking a household census, and collecting genealogies, kinship terminologies, stories, songs, and life histories, I recorded daily observations of agricultural methods, family life, and village disputes. In addition, I translated the pertinent records of the civil and religious courts in the adjoining village and of the land registry office.

Finally, I transliterated eighteen sermons delivered by the imam in the mosque on the occasion of the Friday congregational prayer.

This brief account of my theoretical orientation, or lack of it, my fieldwork techniques, or lack of them, and the procedures by which I selected a village for study may horrify social scientists who cannot conceive of conducting research without the elaboration of hypotheses in advance of fieldwork, careful sampling, the precise stipulation of operational procedures during data collection, and the statistical validation of relationships claimed to exist among the phenomena investigated.

Such a view reflects a misunderstanding of the aims and the methods of social and cultural anthropologists engaged in community studies. It may not be out of place here in a social science monograph series to state briefly for fellow social scientists the aims of social anthropological study in small communities. Social anthropologists are primarily interested in studying the "nature" of the community: its structure, its functions, its ideology and values, and the forces which maintain its cohesiveness or, coversely, lead to change of functions and the succession of one community type for another. Unless specifically stated otherwise, the social anthropologist does not study the community as "sample." That is, he does not claim to have selected a representative community of the region or the nation or the culture except in a very broad and general sense. Thus Kufr al-Ma probably shares many cultural traits with other Arab villages located on the rim of the desert and other Sunni Muslim villages, and comparatively few traits with Arab villages located in the heart of fertile river valleys or with villages that are Shi'a Muslim or Christian in religion. It does not follow, however, that the political process, the rapidity of social change, rural-urban migration, social control, or the mode of marriage is more similar in Sunni Muslim villages as a class than in Shi'a Muslim villages as a class. The structures and processes above-mentioned may be shaped by factors that crosscut cultural and geographical similarities and that vary independently from them, e.g., size of village, distance from towns, level of income, and number of competing groups within the community. In short, superficial cultural similarity on the one hand and geographical similarity on the other may disguise fundamental differences in structure and process.

The primary importance of the community study for the social anthropologist, then, is not in its status as a representative sample but, as Arensberg has phrased it, in its "referral [of problems and questions] to empirical reality." In his words, "Merely carrying the search for factors in a problem to concrete data in the events of real lives in a real time and place has often been empirical referral enough to cut away misconceptions and assure rewarding discoveries."[2]

The "problem" which the social anthropologist studies is not necessarily—not even usually—the type of problem which many sociologists, social psychologists, and political scientists regard as of primary importance when they undertake community studies, e.g., social stratification, social mobility, power politics, culture and personality, deviance, and the nature of elites. The problem for him is none other than the description and analysis of the total community in terms of its basic ecological, structural, functional, and ideological attributes. This kind of description and analysis cannot be undertaken without a prior knowledge of the way of life, the design for living (i.e., the culture) of the community. To know this way of life requires the full participation of the investigator in the community life over an extended period of time and the gathering of such diverse kinds of data as those enumerated above. Sociologists, political scientists, geographers, economists, and psychologists, absorbed in the particular theoretical and applied problems of their own disciplines and working in the culturally familiar communities of the western world, often view with a mixture of impatience, boredom, and condescension the standard ethnography or structural study produced by the social and cultural anthropologist. They are anxious to get on with what they consider the important work at hand, the formulation of particular hypotheses related to the theoretical problems of their own discipline and the testing of such hypotheses in controlled comparisons in particular field situations. They sense that the social and cultural anthropologist can help them for they know that he too is interested in politics, social control, deviance, markets, and ecology. But they are disappointed that after such a long period of field research he spends so much time writing ethnography and talking about social structure, values, and cultural patterns. In this view they fail to recognize the necessity for the basically descriptive and ethnographic job of reporting—the necessity of the social anthropologist to be, in addition, a "cultural" anthropologist. It is this "cultural" anthropology that lays the essential foundation for all attempts to deal with particular theoretical problems (e.g., social change, modernization, peasant conservatism, politics, deviance) in nonwestern societies. It is only after the full involvement of the social anthropologist in the day-to-day complexities of community life and the systematic and detailed recording of cases over time that he is able to assess which particular theoretical problems should be studied. And it is only after he has thoroughly familiarized himself with the distinctive way of life of the community that he has the corrected vision to be able to describe and analyze such problems. The writer, therefore, makes no apologies for the basically ethnographic and structural approach followed in this monograph. It is the approach most suited to analyzing the "nature" of the community, and it is the approach that lays the soundest basis for the study of particular theoretical problems posed by other disciplines.

I would be very much remiss at this point if I did not thank all those individuals, institutions and foundations who have helped and encouraged me in my research. They are in no way responsible for the errors and deficiencies of the present work, but they have contributed in large measure to its merits. After leaving Kufr al-Ma in November, 1960, I had the good fortune of being offered a post as Research Associate in the Department of Social Anthropology and Sociology at the University of Manchester. Many of the cases that appear in this monograph were first presented there in seminars to the members of the department. Professor Max Gluckman, whose own work focuses on the sociology of dispute, took a personal interest in the analysis of cases and led the stimulating discussion after the seminar. I wish to thank him here for his cooperation in every way to make my stay in Manchester a rewarding intellectual and personal experience.

During the twenty months in which I served as Research Associate, Dr. Emrys L. Peters was the source of continuing intellectual stimulation and friendship. As a social anthropologist who had studied both tribal and peasant communities in the Arab world, his observations on my own material were always valuable as the body of this monograph attests in a number of places. Dr. Peters called my attention to the importance of propinquity and matrilaterality for Arab peasants, and he read the first draft of the first two chapters of the monograph meticulously, offering many criticisms and suggestions for which I wish here to express my gratitude.

Although this monograph was first written at the University of Manchester, its inception and initial revision were related to work pursued in the Department of Anthropology and the Center for Middle Eastern Studies of Harvard University. A joint grant from the department and the center enabled me to go to Jordan and a later grant from the Milton Fund allowed me to remain there for a full year. Mr. Derwood Lockard, Associate Director of the center, acted as a good and patient counselor during the harrowing days which preceded the completion of my formal course work at Harvard and, on my return from the field, made a number of important suggestions in regard to the form and content of the thesis which was finally submitted to Harvard University in February, 1963.

Professor Douglas Oliver acted as my advisor in the Anthropology Department at Harvard from the time I first entered as a graduate student. His insistence on conceptual clarity in the description and analysis of social groups has, I hope, been reflected in what follows. His formulation of a method for describing social relations (see article listed in bibliography, p. 177) has influenced my own thinking about social structure to a considerable degree.

I was able to return to Kufr al-Ma for further research in the winter of 1965–66, the summer of 1966, and the spring of 1967. Although the focus of my interest on these field trips was on village politics, Islamic and tribal law, and rural-urban migration, I collected further information about the general social structure of the village which has been incorporated in the present monograph. I wish to thank Indiana University for granting me a one-year leave of absence and for extending that leave of absence a second year, allowing me to complete my fieldwork. I wish also to thank the International Affairs Center of Indiana University for providing grants to cover transportation costs to and from Jordan and the Joint Committee on the Near and Middle East of the Social Science Research Council for a grant to cover my expenses while in the field. Finally, I wish to thank the Office of Research and Advanced Studies of Indiana University for a grant-in-aid to cover part of the publication expenses, as well as the Indiana University Press, particularly its Monograph Editor, Walter Albee, and his editorial assistant, Sandy Mathai, for guiding the manuscript to its final form. I owe special thanks to Harvey Frye, of the Audio Visual Department, who drafted all the charts, and to John Hollingsworth, of the Geography Department, who spent many hours on preparation of some difficult maps.

During my leave of absence from Indiana, I had the privilege of teaching part time in the Department of Sociology and Anthropology and the Department of Cultural Studies of the American University of Beirut. I wish to thank the chairmen of these departments, Samir Khalaf and James M. Peet, for their full cooperation in arranging my academic schedule so as to make my research trips possible.

Finally, I would like to express my thanks to those Jordanians who facilitated my task at every turn. Mr. Salih Suheimat of the Department of Interior gave me the necessary introductions to local government officials. Mr. Nur al-Din al-Sabbagh, director of agricultural activities in the Ajlun District, and Mr. Abd al-Tel, agricultural inspector of the area, aided me in the selection of a village. Mr. Khalil Haddad, Land Registry Officer at Deir Abu Said, aided me in the translation of land records. The judges of the local religious courts, their excellencies Shaykh Muhammad al-Mutliq and Shaykh Muhammad al-As'ad al-Imam, allowed me to attend the trials of numerous cases and were extremely cooperative in helping me to understand the application of Islamic law in its local setting.

To the people of Kufr al-Ma and, in particular, to Muflih al-Hakim and Shaykh Luqman al-Muhammad I wish to express my sincere thanks for accepting me as a "son of the village," opening their doors to me at all times of the day and night, and answering my interminable questions with candor and good humor.

Bloomington, Indiana   R. T. A.
September, 1968

Contents

Tables

Illustrations

Genealogical Charts

List of Cases

Glossary

Arabic Words and Anthropological Terms Frequently Used

affine
: a relative traced through marriage.

aggregate
: a category of individuals classified together by fact of sharing some common cultural trait, e.g., descent. The individuals composing the aggregate do not interact on a day-to-day basis, and the aggregate does not perform critical economic or political functions. Examples of aggregates referred to in the text are the sib, the subsib, and "the peoples of Tibne."

agnate
: a member of the father's descent group

'amm
: the father's brother; this term is also extended to other members of ego's descent group of a senior generation.

'ashīra
: the term used to refer to the clan or sib depending on the context.

bint 'amm
: the father's brother's daughter; this term is also extended to the daughters of other members of ego's clan.

cognate
: any relative with whom blood relationship is claimed traced through any line.

conflict
: inherent opposition whether structural, normative, or ideological. That is, the individuals involved must, at some time or another, be drawn into opposition by the very fact of occupying certain positions, applying certain norms, or holding certain beliefs.

cross cousin
: a cousin traced through two linking relatives of opposite sex, i.e., father's sister's child or mother's brother's child.

descent
: affiliation of an individual at birth with a particular group of relatives with whom he is especially intimate and from whom he can expect certain kinds of services that he cannot expect from nonrelatives or other kinsmen. Examples of descent groups are the clan, lineage, and luzum.

dispute
: a particular verbal controversy.

dunum	approximately one-quarter of an acre.
fandi	the lineage or the subsib depending on the context.
fellāH	an individual owning his own land, owning and tilling his own land, or sharecropping another's land for at least one-half of the crop; also, a villager possessing the cultural attributes of peasantry, e.g., distinctive clothing, speech, manner, diet, and world view.
group	individuals bound together in a social unit that is characterized by regular face-to-face relationships, residential contiguity, and important political and/or economic functions, e.g., the household, the close consultation group, the lineage, and the clan.
Harrāth	an individual sharecropping land for less than one half of the crop.
Humūla	the term used by local government officials to refer to the clan.
ideology	beliefs about what the nature of social relationships "are" in any particular situation and in respect to any particular group or individual; the patrilineal genealogy and the idiom of matrilaterality are examples of ideologies discussed in the text.
imām	the religious specialist of the village.
khāl	the mother's brother; this term is also extended in address and reference to other adult male members of ego's mother's clan.
kindred	that group of near kinsmen related on both the mother's and father's side who are expected to be present and to participate in the important social occasions of any individual's life.
kinship	blood relationship, actual or claimed, traced through any line.
luzum	the close consultation group.
maDāfa	the guest house.
mahr	the Islamic marriage payment which is given by the bridegroom to the bride.
makhwal	matrilateral relationship.
matrilateral	pertaining to relatives traced through the mother.
mukhtār	the village mayor.
mushā'	the system of customary communal tenure by which land is held inalienably by the village and redistributed annually or bienially among its residents.

norm	a statement that can be elicited from an informant as to what behavior "ought" to be in any particular situation and in relation to any particular person.
Palestine	a geographical area, being the land west of the Jordan River whose boundaries coincide with those of the former mandated territory of the same name.
parallel cousin	a cousin traced through two linking relatives of the same sex, i.e., father's brother's child or mother's brother's child.
patrilateral	pertaining to relatives traced through the father.
patrilineal	pertaining to the father's line; more particularly, to membership in the father's group.
Jordan	a political unit including the original Hashemite Kingdom of Jordan as well as the land annexed to it on the West Bank by Amir Abdullah in 1949.
pattern	the arrangement of parts in a given universe of social relations.
shaykh	any old man; also, any man noted for religious learning; most commonly, as used in this monograph, the traditional political leader of the village or the subdistrict.
social control	the process by which an individual is led to subordinate his own desires for the interests of the group or community of which he is a member; it also refers to the institutions which bring about internalization of and conformity to cultural norms, e.g., mediation, courts, gossip, boycott.
social network	the persons, be they friends, neighbors, or kinsmen, who interact with one another most frequently— on the basis of social equality. The social network is defined with respect to a particular individual and, therefore, its composition differs for every individual.
social unit	a general descriptive term including both groups and aggregates but not networks. The social unit refers to a discrete social group whose membership is fixed and delimited.
SulHa	reconciliation or, more specifically, a formal meeting for that purpose.
Transjordan	a geographical area, being the land east of the Jordan River whose boundaries coincide with the former Amirate of Transjordan.
wasiTa	a go-between; also, the process of mediation carried on by the go-between.

Transliteration of Arabic Letters and Symbols

Consonants

ا	a
ب	b
ت	t
ث	th
ج	j
ح	H
خ	kh
د	d
ذ	Th
ر	r
ز	z
س	s
ش	sh
ص	S
ض	D
ط	T
ظ	TH
ع	ʻ
غ	gh
ف	f
ق	q
ك	k
ل	l
م	m
ن	n
ه	h
و	w
ي	y

Vowels

	(short)	(long)
◌َ	a	ā
◌ِ	i	ī
◌ُ	u	ū

Other Symbols

◌ّ indicated by the doubling of the letter

◌ indicated by the doubling of the letter followed by a vowel

The voiced velar stop characteristic of Transjordanian (but not classical) Arabic and pronounced as the "g" in the English word "goat" will be transliterated by the letter "g".

Key Arabic words frequently repeated in the course of the text will not be italicized and their long vowel marks will not be transliterated after first mention. Place names will be spelled according to the most common usage found on maps. Proper names will be transliterated with vowel marks in Tables 9 and 10 but not in the text.

Introduction

The organization of any book, and its manner of presentation, is to a large degree a reflection of the prevailing fashions within a particular discipline. Within the field of cultural and social anthropology there have been two trends in presentation and organization reflecting two very different points of view. One view, that connected with the pioneering work of Bronislaw Malinowski, stresses the well-documented field report in which many aspects of the culture observed are described, related to one another and presented to the public in a rather bulky monograph filled with charts, diagrams, illustrations, and appendices. Even when, exceptionally, Malinowski wrote a book guided by a particular hypothesis, e.g., *Sex and Repression in a Savage Society*, the hypothesis was not formulated prior to or during fieldwork but long after the author had left the field of investigation. In recent years, with the growth of cross-cultural studies in the United States and the development of "models" for structural analysis on both sides of the Atlantic, monographs on particular societies, — primitive, peasant, and industrial — have been guided by more precise rules of relevance which exclude data if it is not directly pertinent to the theoretical problem area that is the subject of the book, e.g., social control, social change, politics, enculturation, ethnoscience, the relationship of ecology to social structure. Malinowski's dictum that all data collected in the field milieu are relevant has been repudiated by many social scientists and even, as suggested above, by some social anthropologists engaged in community studies. The trend toward the selection of problem areas and the selection of facts related to these areas cannot but be praised by social scientists who hope eventually to generate laws about human behavior.

There are, however, three substantial arguments for continuing along the well-trod Malinowskian path. When, as suggested above, the "problem" is nothing less than the understanding of the life of the entire community, and the "model" must explain events not only at a moment in time but also as they develop and change structures and functions through time, the net of the fieldworker must be just as wide as the variety of community life. It must include not only demographic, ecological, and economic data but also genealogical, terminological, and ideological data; it must cover the suppositional, normative, and historical aspects of behavior (see Oliver, "An Ethnographer's Method") as well as the details of the particular case studies that are the key to the understanding of process.

The very strength of the post-Malinowskian school of social anthropology—its elegant and pithy monographs—is also its greatest weakness: it is impossible to criticize the author's conclusions because all contrary evidence has been selected out.[1] Such a charge never could have been made against Malinowski or his disciples, who furnished so much evidence that some of it could be, and was, used against them.[2] In this monograph I have attempted to follow the Malinowskian dictum and have retained the evidence in the hope that those who disagree with the conclusions will have some independent basis for formulating their own. Indeed, if one accepts the twentieth century view of science that knowledge lies as much in the knower as the thing known, retaining the evidence for another "knower" to examine is the only course to follow. Therefore, whatever the problem being considered in this monograph and whatever the conclusion arrived at, the evidence will be presented, mainly, in the form of "trouble cases." These cases represent as full and unedited an account of certain key events as good literary form allows. In all, nine cases have been described and analyzed. They have been presented in a certain style. That is, each case is described fully as I witnessed it or, in a few instances, as it was reported to me, without stinting on what might seem repetitious and extraneous detail; then each case is analyzed and conclusions are drawn regarding the structure and function of the group concerned. Certain details of each case, while not germane to the analysis immediately following, are referred to later in the monograph. For ease of reference, I have presented each case in its entirety in one place.

There is a third and equally compelling reason for retaining the evidence in the form of trouble cases. For the author, the study of social structure is not an arid endeavor, wanting in interest or life. Its delineation is based on the observation of real people in real situations exercising choice and making decisions. I have attempted to convey the "flesh and blood" nature of anthropological study based on fieldwork in the description and analysis of cases.[3]

I have defined in the glossary, in the body of the monograph, and in the footnotes a number of terms that refer to particular social units, e.g., "sib," "clan," *luzum*, and "household." In addition, I have used terms that involve a higher degree of abstraction such as "group," "aggregate," and "network." These latter terms are introduced as a shorthand for the sake of clarity of reference and at no point should be taken as a point of departure for a general theoretical discussion of their sociological meaning. The term "social unit" is a comprehensive term meant to include "groups" and "aggregates" but not "networks" (see glossary). The terms "norm" and "ideology" appear again and again in the text, and their referrents should be understood from the beginning. By "norm" I do not mean normal in the sense of statistically dominant (unless explicitly stated so) or ideal in the sense of Weber's ideal type. Rather, I mean a statement that can be elicited verbally from an individual regarding behavior that *OUGHT* to or *SHOULD* occur in any given situation. By an "ideology" I do not mean thinking or theorizing of an abstract or impractical nature or beliefs about the way men should relate to one another under optimum conditions. I mean a statement or statements that can be elicited from an informant verbally regarding what he actually believes the nature of social relationships to *BE*. A genealogy which stipulates relationships of kinship or descent is, therefore, as much an ideology as a document such as the Declaration of Independence which describes the natural basis of political relationships. Finally, the term "conflict" refers to inherent opposition, whether structural, normative, or ideological. That is, the individuals involved must at some time or another, be drawn into opposition by the very fact of occupying certain positions, applying certain norms, or holding certain beliefs. A "dispute" is a particular verbal controversy. Thus a particular dispute may or may not involve "conflict."

The purpose of this monograph, as stated above, is to describe and analyze the social structure of a Transjordanian village. Since this village is organized in terms of propinquity as well as kinship, it has been necessary to analyze the nature of the groups based on these principles: the household, the close consultation group, the lineage, the clan, the village, and the subdistrict. The organization of these groups reflects both principles. Indeed, one of the central problems of social structural analysis in agricultural communities is, as Raymond Firth saw long ago in his pioneering work, *We The Tikopea*, to isolate the working of the two principles and then to note their interpenetration or conflict in particular situations. Because social anthropologists have been weaned on the classic studies of tribal societies, e.g., *The League of the Ho-de-no sau-nee or Iroquois* (1851), *The Todas* (1906), *The Life of a South African Tribe* (1927), *The Nuer* (1940), *The Web of Kinship Among the Tallensi* (1949), *Political Systems of Highland Burma* (1954), they have given undue weight to descent and kinship in their analyses of peasant societies whose members, after all, are "land-mates" and neighbors as well as kinsmen.[4] This structural coincidence, widespread in Middle Eastern peasant life—that one's neighbors are also one's kinsmen—has led me to pay particular attention to instances in which men have moved away from their kinsmen but remained within the village. It is the analysis of these crucial cases that allows the investigator to make statements about the relative importance of different structural principles.

There is a second and related problem of structural analysis: the examination of the relationship between the ideologies of descent, kinship, and propinquity on the one hand and the actual behavior of groups based on these principles on the other. The specific problem that presents itself in Kufr al-Ma is the following: To what degree does the ideology of descent (patrilineality) found at the consultation group, lineage, and clan levels explain the actual day-to-day behavior of these groups as well as the means and personnel utilized to resolve their outstanding difficulties? If it does not explain such behavior, which additional principles must be introduced to do so? Finally, what is the function of the continued adherence to an ideology of patrilineal descent when many of the functions attached to patrilineal descent groups have lapsed?

The third problem of structural analysis investigated throughout this monograph relates to social change. What kinds of accommodations, adjustments, or, in their absence, conflicts, occur between kinsmen when occupational mobility and economic differentiation result in specific challenges to the pertinence and validity of certain norms of kinship? For instance, how can traditional claims to the marriage of the patrilateral parallel cousin be reconciled with differences in wealth which make the preferred spouses and their respective families occupy widely differing economic statuses?

The fourth and final problem of structural analysis, related to all the others and, in a way, summarizing them, is the problem of the nature of the village as "community." That is, to what degree can the village be regarded as a social isolate with fixed boundaries? To what degree are its component social units integrated in a larger delimited and cohesive whole? Is this larger whole distinguished from the social units that compose it by a distinct set of functions and an appropriate ideology? Is membership in the "community" by fact of residence or by a more complex process of social adhesion? The sections devoted to the subdistrict, the village itself, and particularly, the sections devoted to the analysis of marriage attempt to answer these questions.

CHAPTER ONE

The Ecological and Historical Background

1. THE SETTING

Kufr al-Ma is an Arab village located in the denuded eastern foothills of the Jordan Valley. It is one of 200 cereal-growing villages of the Ajlun district of northwestern Transjordan. Its population of two thousand is composed entirely of orthodox Muslims. Approaching the village along a dirt road from its eastern side, one sees that only a few ancient olive trees soften the unrelieved bleakness of the stone-strewn soil. Nothing in the outer aspect of the village itself suggests that it differs from the hill settlements which surround it—neither its close-jammed, brown, clay-covered houses, its dusty paths, nor its gardens and orchards.

Unless the traveler passed through the rolling foothills in the late spring or early summer when the verdure of the winter crops covers the landscape, he would never suspect that peasants could eke out a subsistence in these surroundings. No streams exist to resuscitate crops from the summer heat and the blasts of desert wind. Although a number of ravines and gullies dissect the landscape, no springs provide water for wells from which men or animals might drink. Each family in the village has dug a cistern to catch the precious winter rains. In July, when these cisterns run dry, the peasants of Kufr al-Ma must trudge to the nearest spring in the adjoining village of Deir Abu Said (see Map 1, p. 3). There they purchase water from the residents, load it on their donkeys, and return along the dusty track to their village.

However barren its outer aspect, Kufr al-Ma lies in the center of a populated cereal-growing region. Located in the northwestern corner of the Transjordanian plateau, its manner of sedentary subsistence agriculture is, apparently, of some antiquity as evidenced by the ancient ruins of towns such as Jerash and Pella. An estimate of the population per square mile of cultivated area is about 780, making the northwestern corner of Transjordan one of the most densely settled areas in the Middle East.[1]

The village itself, like its sister villages, is located on the side of a hill. The visitor approaches from the main road at the bottom and, traversing a rough dirt road bordered by prickly pear and fig orchards (see Map 2A, p. 74), gradually makes his way up to a wide open area at the center of the village on which front four village shops. As he ascends, the proximity of the houses increases until at the top, below the cemetery and three-eighths of a mile from the entrance to the village, he is surrounded by houses abutting one on the other on either side of the narrow lane (see photograph, p. ii).

Each of the surrounding hill villages — namely, Khanzira, Abu el-Qein, and Tibne — present the same aspect. They stand at a distance of between one and two miles from Kufr al-Ma (see Map 1) and are separated from it by an expanse of cultivated land and one or more dry ravines. But significant differences in altitude exist between villages as the traveler moves from the northwest to the southeast (see Map 1). Tibne, for instance, at 2,080 feet above sea level and surrounded by treacherous ravines, stood as a refuge against the depredations of the Bedouins and extortion by Ottoman Turks while other villages not so fortunately situated were victimized. Deir Abu Said presents much the same picture as the adjoining villages. However, it contains a larger population (3,000) and is the administrative center of the subdistrict, Al Kura. As such, it houses the offices of the subdistrict officer, the forest ranger, the land registrar, the religious judge, the civil judge, the tax official, and the doctor. Although its main street is paved and its coffee house caters to the government officials who are forced to reside there, Deir Abu Said resembles an overgrown village rather than an administrative center. Although vegetable stands adorn its main street and the weekly livestock fair takes place within its environs, Deir Abu Said can hardly be considered a market town.

The inhabitants of Kufr al-Ma along with those of several adjoining villages—namely, Deir Abu Said, Tibne, Abu el-Qein, Inbe, Rehaba, Irkheim, Marhaba, Jenin, Zemal, and Es Samt (see Map 1)—refer to themselves and are referred to by others as "the people of Tibne" (*ahāli tibnah*) or "the clans of Tibne" (*Hamā'il tibnah* or *'ashā'ir tibnah*). They state that about one hundred years ago their ancestors who lived in Tibne began to settle Kufr al-Ma and other villages. In the main, these villages were held to have been uninhabited but occasionally the peoples of Tibne displaced settlers from their native villages. Most of the peoples of Tibne claim to be descended from a single ancestor. Whether this claim is true or not, numerous kinship and affinal ties distinguish the inhabitants of these villages from the other villages of the Al Kura subdistrict (see Map 1).

2. VEGETATION, SOIL TYPE, RAINFALL, WIND, AND ALTITUDE

Geographers have classified the vegetation of Transjordan into four types.[2] They are, in order of plant size and soil deterioration, maquis, garigue, batha, and rocky soil steppe. Each of these types of vegetation is found in the vicinity of Kufr al-Ma.

Maquis is a secondary growth of shrubs that follows the destruction of forest. In Jordan the trees are usually a drought-resisting species of evergreen oak. They may grow taller than a man with semidwarf shrubs growing in the intervening spaces. The woodland of Kufr al-Ma (see Map 1) consists largely of maquis. Garigue appears as a result of soil deterioration or continued destruction of trees. Shrubs are smaller and fewer while underscrub increases. Rocky soil appears between plants. The woodland of Kufr al-Ma is interspersed with garigue. Batha

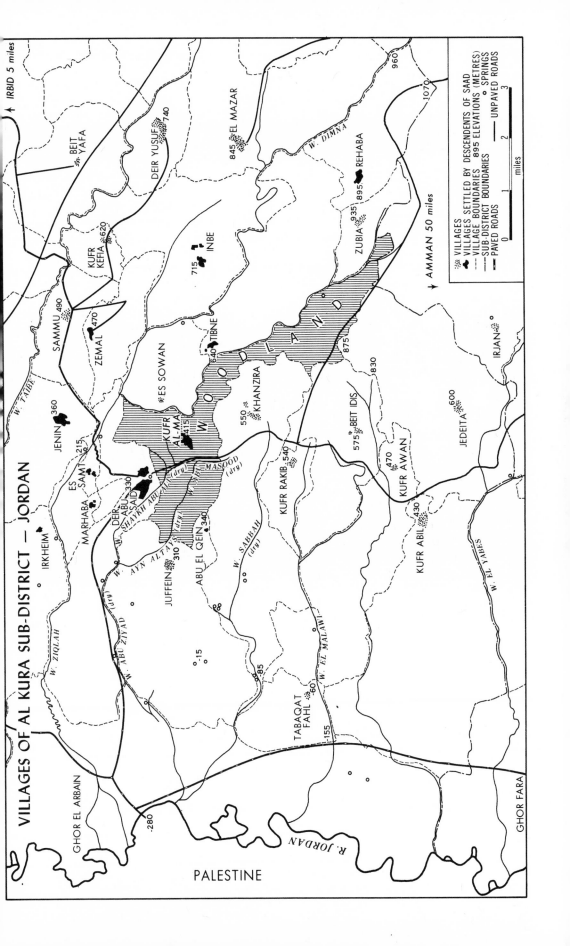

VILLAGES OF AL KURA SUB-DISTRICT — JORDAN

← IRBID 5 miles

PALESTINE

R. JORDAN

GHOR EL ARBAIN

GHOR FARA

IRKHEIM

MARHABA

ES SAMT 215

JENIN 360

DEIR ABU SAID 330

BEIT YAFA

DEIR YUSUF 740

KUFR KEFIA 620

SAMMU 490

ZEMAL 470

ES SOWAN

INBE 715

KUFR AL MA 415

W. SHAYKH ABU ALI (dry)

W. ABU MASOOD (dry)

JUFFEIN 310

ABU EL QEIN 340

W. AYN ALTAY (dry)

W. ABU ZIYAD (dry)

W. SABBAH (dry)

W. ZIQLAH

W. TAIBE

W. DIMNA

EL MAZAR 845

REHABA 895

ZUBIA 935

TIBNE 640

KHANZIRA 550

KUFR RAKIB 540

BEIT IDIS 575

KUFR AWAN 470

KUFR ABIL 430

JEDEITA 600

IRJAN

TABAQAT FAHL 60

W. EL MALAWI

W. EL YABES

-15

-85

-155

-280

830

875

960

1070

W O O D L A N D

→ AMMAN 50 miles

VILLAGES
VILLAGES SETTLED BY DESCENDENTS OF SAAD
VILLAGE BOUNDARIES   895 ELEVATIONS (METRES)
SUB-DISTRICT BOUNDARIES   ○ SPRINGS
PAVED ROADS   —— UNPAVED ROADS

miles
0   1   2   3

is the vegetation found on the sides of hills and ravines. It occurs as a result of still worse soil and moisture conditions. Shrubs here are very scanty with dwarf shrubs (mainly shrubby burnet) and herbs common. Batha is found increasingly as one proceeds westward from Kufr al-Ma through Abu el-Qein and Juffein (see Map 1) toward the Jordan Valley. Finally, as the traveler descends the deep ravines entering the Jordan Valley nothing but rocky soil and stones remain with vegetation very scattered.

The soils of Transjordan have been classified into five[3] types: Steppe, hammada, terra rosa, sandy, and harra. Only the first and third are found in the region of Kufr al-Ma. Steppe soil is produced from weathered limestone. It is soft and light gray. It is without humus, and water and air penetrate easily. Terra rosa is a reddish-brown soil with a lime content of ten to forty percent and some humus. It is more compact, less aerated, less permeable but moister and more adhesive than steppe soil. Both soils are of moderately high fertility.

The barrenness of the Jordanian landscape and the paucity of its natural vegetation is associated with the dearth of rainfall. But it is not only the total annual precipitation but also the interval between rainfalls, the total amount of any given rainfall, and the seasonal occurrence of the rain that are critical ecologically. Table 1 shows the incidence of rainfall in Kufr al-Ma from 1955 to 1961 as recorded in the agricultural inspector's office in the nearby village of Deir Abu Said. Precipitation varied from about eight inches in 1959–60 to about twenty-four inches in 1956–57. The fluctuation of the annual rainfall is matched by the contingent nature of monthly precipitation. In November of 1959, there was

TABLE 1

ANNUAL PRECIPITATION IN AL KURA SUBDISTRICT,
JORDAN 1954–1961 AS RECORDED AT THE AGRICULTURAL
STATION IN DEIR ABU SAID

Year	Nov.	Dec.	Jan.	Feb.	March	April	May	Annual Total
1954–55	39.7*	97.5	2	46	75.5	16	6	284.7
1955–56	143.5	123	113	33	109	26		558
1956–57	8.5	132	87	133	149.5	26	6.5	595
1957–58	66	172.5	197	11	6	14		475.5
1958–59	2	34.5	86.5	148.5	41	10		322.5
1959–60		4.5	63	21	84	19		204.5
1960–61	52.5	52	82	134	36.5	71.5	10	438.5

*All figures are in millimeters—one inch equals 25.4 millimeters.

no rain at all while in November of 1960 two inches fell. In April of 1960, four-fifths of an inch fell while in April of 1961, three inches fell. Frequently, these early winter and late spring rains are the critical factors in making for a successful agricultural year. The early rains cause the crops to germinate and the late rains carry them into the summer. Thus the 1960—61 season was exceptional not so much for its heavy rainfall as for its early November and its late April rains. The 1959—60 season, despite its negligible annual total rainfall (only eight inches, the amount generally regarded by geographers as the absolute minimum for cereal cultivation) was saved by a late March downpour of over three inches. The main winter rains, on the other hand, fill the wells and cisterns, feed the springs, and supply the valleys with water.

Even during January and February, at the height of the precipitation, the rains are not continuous. A storm may last for several days or a week and be followed by a week of sunshine, followed again by a storm. Thunderstorms occur, particularly in the spring, but the rain falls only in gentle showers.

The amount of a given rainfall is also important, particularly at the time of planting. The peasant of Kufr al-Ma makes a critical decision at the beginning of every planting season. He must decide whether to sow his seed before the first winter rains in hope of their quick arrival or to delay until after the rains have fallen. If he ploughs and sows his seed before the rains and the rains do not come, he has wasted precious seed and considerable effort. If a light November rain does come, the seed germinates; but unless this light rain is followed by a heavier downfall in the next month, the crop will still be lost. On the other hand, if the peasant postpones sowing until after the first rains have fallen to insure germination, the crop will mature later and may be struck in the late spring and early summer by the scorching desert wind or by the scourge of locusts. Such an event occurred in the winter of 1959—60. The first heavy rains occurred in January (see Table 1, p. 4). The crop was only half matured when it was struck in May by a dry eastern wind. In a few days the green blades of wheat and barley had turned a parched yellow.

The particular seasonal occurrence of the rain is differentially critical for certain crops. An early November rain, while it may be beneficial for the farmer who has already sown his wheat, will be disastrous for the peasant who is harvesting an autumn stand of tomatoes. A late spring or early summer thunderstorm may guarantee a bumper crop of wheat or barley while ruining a young summer crop of sesame seed or maize.

In Jordan, the importance of the winter rains is intensified by the nature of the landscape:

> . . . with so much of the plateau cut by wadis [valleys] draining to very low levels, the water-table generally is far below the surface. Thus ground water cannot be used to any appreciable extent to supplement inadequate rainfall, nor are there any perennial streams.[4]

Kufr al-Ma, for instance, was entirely dependent on the winter rains to fill the cisterns of the village since there was no spring from which the villagers might draw water if the cisterns ran dry. In 1960, most of the cisterns of the village had run dry by mid-July and the village women were forced to make the daily trek to Deir Abu Said (which has a spring) where they had to buy water from the inhabitants. The situation became so desperate that in August the central government began transporting water in trucks to fill the cisterns.

The long summer drought, which usually lasts from April until November, also affects building activity. Kufr al-Ma, a village possessing too little land in relation to its expanding population, exports labor in the form of builders. These builders construct houses in the area out of native rough-hewn rock. This rock is cemented by mud clay and overlaid with the same clay to present a tan stucco-like appearance. When water is unavailable for moistening the clay, all building ceases.

The type of soil and the amount and distribution of rainfall may be less important in a given season than other micro-ecological factors such as the slope of the land, the presence or absence of stones, and slight altitudinal differences. In Kufr al-Ma, for instance, land neighbors may not reap an equivalent return at harvest time (see p. 8). In a drought season a man with a hillside plot littered with stones may raise a better crop than a man with richer soil on level ground.

Even small differences in altitude affect crop growth. Kufr al-Ma is surrounded by other hill villages which lie at a distance of between one and five miles. Each of these villages stands at a slightly different altitude. Deir Abu Said stands at 1,072 feet above sea level; Kufr al-Ma stands at 1,348 feet; Khanzira stands at 1,787 feet; Juffein stands at 1,007 feet; and Tibne stands at 2,080 feet (see Map 1, p. 3). The higher more easterly villages receive more of the winter rains (rains that come from a southwesterly direction across Palestine) than the lower western villages (of which Kufr al-Ma is one). Moreover, mountain dews sustain summer crops during the long hot summer in the higher villages while they are not so effective in the western villages. In the spring of 1960, Rehaba, an eastern village standing at 2,908 feet, harvested a bumper crop of wheat; Kufr al-Ma only salvaged half of its crop after the passing of the easterly wind; and Juffein, the lowest lying and westernmost of the villages, lost its entire crop.

3. AGRICULTURAL REGIME

The Transjordanian plateau is the center of Jordan's grain production. The bulk of Transjordan's population, living in some 226 towns and villages of the Ajlun District, is engaged in cultivating most of the million acres devoted to rain-fed cereals. Wheat, barley, and legumes (for fodder) are the chief winter crops and maize and sesame seed are the chief summer crops.

In Kufr al-Ma and its adjoining villages these cereals are grown for subsistence. Only the straw from the winter crops and the sesame seed are sold. Trucks pick up these commodities in the village and transport them to Palestine for sale. In a bumper year some peasants will harvest much more grain than they can consume. This surplus is used to pay off their previous debts at the village shops; it is stored against future purchases; and it is expended for marriage payments. The leguminous crops are mainly vetches, kersenneh, chickpeas, and lentils (see Table 2). All of these crops are grown in Kufr al-Ma, but only kersenneh takes up substantial acreage. In the hills of southern Ajlun, where rainfall is greatest, vineyards produce grapes and raisins. Tobacco is also grown there for home consumption.

The particular crops planted in any given year depend on the amount and type of land available, the layout of the land, and the peculiar needs of the individual farmer in relation to his production in previous years. After a series of poor agricultural years when straw for animals has been exhausted, fodder crops are planted. Maize may be planted instead of sesame seed to supplement both fodder and cereal crops. Maize can be used to feed animals or men since its flour can be used to bake bread in the absence of wheat flour. On the other hand, in bountiful years the abundance of straw from cereal crops permits a reduction in the amount of acreage devoted to fodder.

TABLE 2

PRODUCTION OF PRINCIPAL CROPS IN THE HASHEMITE KINGDOM OF JORDAN—1953 CENSUS OF AGRICULTURE

Production in Tons

Crop	Total	Irrigated Lands	Unirrigated Lands
Wheat	94,032	10,763	83,269
Barley	29,847	2,522	27,325
Maize*	9,648	1,543	8,105
Broad Beans	1,163	550	613
Chick Peas	1,775	25	1,750
Lentils	5,250	50	5,200
Kersenneh	5,088	9	5,079
Sesame	3,895	285	3,610
Tobacco	273	7	266
Potatoes	1,192	980	212
Vegetables and Melons	70,400	40,300	30,100

*Yellow and white.

There are various degrees of bounty and dearth. The wheat may not have matured on the blade, but the plant may be uprooted and its straw used for fodder. In a very bad year neither wheat nor straw will be harvested, but still, enough rain comes for the growth of herbage and weeds which can be fed to animals. In some years (1960, for instance) neither wheat, straw, nor herbage grew in many areas.

I have already mentioned the differential crop yields in separate villages owing to altitude differences and the differential crop yields in the same village caused by micro-ecological differences in landscape and soil. In 1960, a dearth year, one of the village mayors reaped only half the seed that he had planted. A second peasant planted one sack of grain and harvested two. A third planted one sack and harvested six. A fourth planted a sack and harvested twelve (a twelvefold return on seed is considered bounty). Micro-ecological differences may bring bounty to an individual peasant when all of his neighbors are suffering dearth. Moreover, Jordan's grain production fluctuates widely from year to year due to the unpredictable variation in the amount and seasonal occurrence of the annual rains. Production in a good year may be seven times that of a bad one.

The peasants of Kufr al-Ma are engaged in what geographers have termed "dry land farming." This can be defined as "crop production under conditions of deficient rainfall."[5] In Jordan, dry farming is associated not only with low rainfall, but also with uneven falls of rain, long intervals between rains, scorching winds, and daily oscillations in temperature. Since water is the overall limiting factor in crop production, efforts are centered around the conservation of moisture. Ploughing, fallowing, and weeding are three aspects of this conservation effort.

The peasant initiates the ploughing season in August and September after the wheat harvest has been completed. He ploughs widely spaced furrows in order to open up the hard-crusted land to wind, rain, and sun. This first ploughing is referred to as "cleaving open" (*shgāg*). Some agronomists believe that ploughing reduces capillary action and evaporation by breaking up lumps of soil and increasing interstitial space between them.[6] Others contend that such scratch ploughing serves only to "discourage the formation of deep cracks up which moisture from the lower depths could readily escape in the form of water vapour."[7] The peasant himself is firmly convinced that ploughing serves to conserve moisture in the soil. The proverb, "He who has tilled his soil twice has watered it once," is always on the tip of his tongue. Ploughing also serves the purpose of allowing greater water penetration, destroying weeds, turning stubble into the soil, and encouraging bacteriological action.

If the cultivator wishes to plant winter wheat, he broadcasts his seed by hand in November and ploughs over the land in close furrows. This second winter ploughing is referred to as "planting" (*zara'*). In the second ploughing the furrows are closer together than the first in order to cover up the seed. The term for such close ploughing is *sināni* ("like teeth").

If the cultivator wishes to plant a summer crop, he usually ploughs three times. His second (*thanni*) ploughing will not take place until

February and the third ploughing for planting will take place in March or April. In planting the summer crops—maize, sesame seed and vegetables—the seeds are not scattered over the terrain, but dropped one by one through a funnel into the prepared furrow. Often the peasant's daughter will drop the seeds into the furrow while he follows with the plough to cover them. The difference in planting technique may be related to the higher return on each seed of maize as compared with wheat, on the necessity to plant the seed more deeply in the ground to take advantage of moisture during the hot summer, and on the frail nature of the wheat plant which requires other plants close about it for support against strong winds. Thus, the winter crops—wheat, barley, kersenneh, broad beans, and chickpeas—are ploughed once before planting (though some farmers do in fact neglect this ploughing) and the summer crops—sesame and maize—are ploughed twice before planting. The soil on which certain summer vegetables such as tomatoes and watermelons are planted may even be ploughed thrice before planting.

The ploughing and planting of crops is a task which a single individual can handle. But wives and daughters often accompany their menfolk to the fields, bring them tea, hoe behind the plough for winter crops, and may even plant the seed for summer crops. Cooperation does not usually stretch beyond the extended parental family (parents, unmarried children, married sons and their wives and children).

Donkeys, oxen, and horses are used for ploughing, the first and second working in yoked pairs. Oxen are generally regarded as the best plough animals, being the strongest and the steadiest, while the donkeys are regarded as the worst. The latter, however, are cheaper to buy (fourteen dollars to the ox's 112) and cheaper to maintain. They subsist on barley rather then kersenneh. The possession of plough animals allows a landless peasant to sharecrop for half a share of the harvest while the sharecropper without animals receives only a fourth.

The basic agricultural instrument used by the peasant in Kufr al-Ma is the nail-plough. It is made by the peasant himself out of wood gathered in the woodlands of the village while the ploughshare is made in the forge of the local blacksmith. This plough has been criticized by western agronomists for its failure to invert the furrow slice and because it leaves untilled ridges between successive furrows. Other observers have found it suitable for the Middle Eastern environment:

> The Arab plough is like the ancient Hebrew plough . . . Its distinguishing characteristic is that it cuts the surface soil and does not turn it up. It performs very slowly it is true, but very thoroughly all the functions for which a combination of modern machines is required— a plough, a roller and a harrow. Its great virtues are that it does not bring up clods, that it does not press or crush the moist earth, but flits as it were over the ground with its coulter which resembles a duck's foot in its base, and that it penetrates the ground with its point which is sharp and long like the head of a spear. It produces the requisite broken crust by itself, without the aid of other implements. [8]

The nail-plough is eminently suitable for working the calcereous, hilly, and rock-strewn soil of Kufr al-Ma, and it is questionable whether the modern tractor and mould-board plough could be used efficiently here, although they have been used successfully in less rough terrain in other areas of Jordan. The only other tools used by the peasant with any frequency are a sickle and a simple dibble which is often used by women who follow the ploughman and dig up patches missed by the plough.

The cultivator in Kufr al-Ma recognizes three types of land according to its position in the crop cycle. *Būr* is unploughed fallow or land that has remained unploughed for several years. *Hasīd* is land in stubble after the wheat harvest. This land is regarded as exhausted and must remain in fallow for six months (from September to March). But it should be ploughed twice (*shgag* and thanni) before spring planting. After it has been planted with a soil-enriching summer crop—sesame, kersenneh, or vegetables—the land is termed *krāb* (enriched soil ready for cereal planting).

The cultivator must decide either to delay sowing wheat until after the first winter rain (*wasm*) or to anticipate it and plant beforehand. The decision to plant before the rains (*'afīr*) or after the rains (*rayy*) depends on several factors. If the land is bur and is hard after several years of fallow, it cannot be ploughed until after the first rains have fallen. Men with much land prefer to plant 'afir. If they wait, they will not have enough time to till all their lands or tend them properly (by weeding) in the shortened agricultural season imposed by their postponement of sowing. Villages at high altitudes such as Rehaba and Zubia (see Map 1, p. 3) prefer to plant 'afir since the crops planted late in the winter may be affected adversely by the cold. And, as has been mentioned, postponement of planting exposes the crop to the danger of locusts and the late spring desert wind. By planting rayy, on the other hand, the farmer ploughs under the weeds (which have grown after the rains) at the same time as he plants. Agronomists have only lately come to recognize what the peasant has known for some time—that weed control in the early stages of growth may be more important than cultivation methods for crop yields. [9] Of course, as one proceeds farther south and east in Jordan the number of cultivators who are willing to risk 'afir crops declines with the diminution in rainfall.

The crops are usually planted in the following order: wheat and barley are planted at the end of November, through December and into January. Broad beans may also be planted in December. Kersenneh, lentils, and chickpeas, crops which require a shorter growing season and more warmth, are planted in February. At the end of March and throughout April the summer crops—sesame and maize—are planted. Last of all, in late April, the vegetables—tomatoes, snake cucumber, and watermelon—are planted. Onions and potatoes may be planted after any one of the winter rainfalls. By May planting ceases.

Kersenneh, broad beans, and lentils have a growing season of about forty days from their first watering as do the summer crops, maize and sesame. Barley takes about sixty-five days to mature and

Fellah ploughing before the planting of spring crops

wheat seventy-five. Thus, kersenneh, broad beans, and lentils are harvested beginning in the middle of April, barley twenty days later, and
wheat ten days following.

Most of the summer is spent harvesting, threshing, and winnowing
the various crops. After the grain is transported from the field on
donkeyback to the threshing ground, it is winnowed and sifted. Harvesting is usually carried out by an extended parental family or a stem
family (a man, his wife, one of his married sons together with the
son's wife and children, as well as his own unmarried children). But
the harvesting group may also include good friends or neighbors. A
man with large land holdings (twenty-five acres or more) may hire one
or two harvesters to reap for him in return for a sack of grain. The
harvester may be a kinsman, an affine, or any other villager. Or he
may hire a number of village women for a daily wage to uproot the
crops. According to village custom, only men handle the sickle during
harvest; women may uproot while children follow behind, picking up
stray blades. Young shepherds (between the ages of eleven and twenty)
bring in their flocks immediately behind the harvesters to graze on the
stubble. All harvested land becomes public grazing area where any
shepherd may graze his flocks.

The various threshing grounds on the outskirts of the village are
individually owned. A man may use his relative's threshing ground
after that relative has finished threshing his own crops. Or alternatively, a man may rent a threshing ground from another for fifty
piastres (about two dollars) a season.

On the threshing grounds wheat is separated into four piles:
(1) seed, (2) fine straw for sheep fodder, (3) longer firmer blades of
straw (*qasal*) used in making mats, and (4) short qasal used for fuel,
bedding, and feed for plough animals. The seed is taken to the mill and
ground for home consumption, or it is used to pay the annual accumu-
lated debts at the village grocery shop. Besides the sharecropper and
storekeeper, the village mayors (there are two in Kufr al-Ma), the
village religious official, and the blacksmith collect the portions due
them annually on the threshing grounds. Most of the crops are con-
sumed in the village or used to pay local debts with the exception of
sesame and some straw which is sold to middlemen from Palestine.

By early September, most of the year's work is done. There remains the trek into the woodlands and the three-day encampment there
to gather the winter's supply of firewood and the still longer trek to the
village of Tibne at the end of September to pick the ripe olives. The
inhabitants of Kufr al-Ma own thousands of olive trees in Tibne (for
that is their village of origin), and olive oil constitutes an important
item in their diet. Not enough, however, is grown for sale. The grind-
ing and pressing of the olives back in the village bring to an end the
yearly agricultural cycle.

All of the peasants in Kufr al-Ma with the exception of one follow a
two-crop rotation system (see Table 3).

The method on which the average cereal farm of the fellah is
worked is that the holding is divided into two areas. In one of the

areas he sows his winter crops [wheat, barley, and kersenneh]
while the other lies fallow. In this fallow portion, in the spring,
the summer crop [sesame, maize, and vegetables] is sown; in the
former portion, after reaping the winter crops in May and June,
the land lies fallow until the following spring when the summer
crops are sown. In the latter portion after reaping of the summer
crop, the winter crop is at once sown. Thus in each portion two
crops, one summer and one winter, are taken in two years.[10]

Under this rotation system, the land remains in fallow for about
seven months after the winter harvest and three months after the summer harvest. Goats and sheep are brought in to graze on the stubble
and to enrich the soil with their droppings.

TABLE 3

TYPES OF CROP ROTATION

Two Year Crop Rotation Followed by One Peasant in Kufr al-Ma

	1955	1956	1957	1958	1959
1/2 of Land Plot	Sesame Lentils Kersenneh Maize	Wheat	Kersenneh	Wheat	Watermelon
1/2 of Land Plot	Wheat	Sesame Lentils Kersenneh Broad Beans	Wheat	Sesame Lentils Broad Beans	Wheat

Three Year Crop Rotation Followed by Peasants in the Irbid District

	First Year	Second Year	Third Year
1/3 of Land Plot	Wheat	Chick Peas Broad Beans Kersenneh Lentils	Sesame or Maize
1/3 of Land Plot	Chick Peas Broad Beans Kersenneh Lentils	Sesame or Maize	Wheat
1/3 of Land Plot	Sesame or Maize	Wheat	Chick Peas Broad Beans Kersenneh Lentils

Government agents have always encouraged the Jordanian peasant
to follow a three-crop agricultural regime such as that followed in the
flat agricultural land near Irbid in northwestern Jordan (see Table 4).
There a peasant divides his land into three plots and plants different
crops on each in successive years, the full cycle taking three years.
Not only does this regime enrich the soil, but it also destroys the wheat
worm (which dies if it finds no wheat in the soil for two consecutive
years). Only one man in Kufr al-Ma practices the three-crop system.
The explanation seems to be twofold. For a cultivator to follow a three-
crop system while other villagers were following a two-crop system
would be to court disaster, for the whole area is thrown open to grazing
after the general harvest. The man who did not follow the village planting regime would run the risk of having his crops eaten by grazing
animals. More important, growing three crops simultaneously pre-
sumes a large enough piece of land to allow this division. Most land
holdings in Kufr al-Ma are under twenty-five dunums (six acres) and do
not permit this division. Most peasants in Kufr al-Ma are primarily
concerned with producing enough wheat to assure a year's supply of
flour for bread, the peasant staple. Even under the two-crop rotation
system peasants do not fulfill their yearly bread requirements. It is
this same necessity to produce enough bread that prevents the peasant
in Kufr al-Ma from fallowing for a longer period than seven months. A
three-crop regime would only reduce the acreage devoted to wheat production. Certain prosperous farmers in Kufr al-Ma could undoubtedly
afford to work a three-crop system. But their sharecroppers are reluctant to work for them unless a substantial portion of the acreage is
devoted to wheat. The major factor in preventing the adoption of a
three-crop system in Kufr al-Ma, then, is the small size of the land
plots. In the Irbid area where three-crop rotation is practiced, land
parcels are much larger. The only farmer in Kufr al-Ma who practices
the three-year rotation has over twenty-five acres of land; he is exceptional also in that he lives apart from the village on his plot of land
where he can guard it from animal depredation.

The peasants of Kufr al-Ma are, to be sure, more fortunate than
those of the Beersheeba district (see Table 4), who are not even able to
maintain a two-crop system. But the economy of the latter is semi-
pastoral. The accepted limit of cereal growing in the United States,
Canada, and Australia is within the twelve-inch rainfall zone.[11] The
tillers of Kufr al-Ma often cultivate with eight inches of rainfall. The
two-crop regime which they maintain is indicative of the subsistence
nature of their agriculture. Such a regime places a very low ceiling on
economic differentiation within the village for those who till the soil.
Agriculture in Kufr al-Ma does not even provide a sufficient basis of
subsistence for the peasant, who, as we shall see in Chapter 2, has
been forced to seek employment in nonagricultural pursuits.

TABLE 4

TYPES OF AGRICULTURAL REGIME AS RELATED TO RAINFALL AND SOIL FERTILITY*

Annual Number of Crops	Amount of Rainfall	Crop Rotation				Geographical Area
One Winter Crop	4 inches Minimum	Barley	Barley	Barley	Barley	Southern Beersheba
One Winter Crop	8 inches Minimum	Barley	Wheat	Barley	Wheat	Northwestern Beersheba
One Crop Winter or Summer	8 inches Minimum	Barley	Summer Millet		Wheat	Extreme Northern Beersheba
Two Crops Winter and Summer	12 inches Minimum	Kersenneh Wheat Barley	Sesame Vegetables Maize	Kersenneh Wheat Barley	Sesame Vegetables Maize	Ajlun District (Kufr Al-Ma)
Three Crops	16 inches Minimum	Winter Wheat	Winter Legumes	Sesame or Summer Maize		Ajlun District (Irbid)
Mixed Farming		Milch Cows Vegetables Cereals	Fruit Poultry			Jezreel Valley (Israel)

*This chart is based on ethnographic data collected by the author as well as the information available in *The Proceedings of the Conference on Middle East Agricultural Development.*

4. A HISTORICAL SKETCH OF AJLUN IN THE LATE NINETEENTH AND THE TWENTIETH CENTURIES

Although Transjordan was part of the Ottoman Empire and lay along the caravan route from Damascus to Medina, the Ottoman government paid little attention to the area in the nineteenth century. To be sure, the government paid the Bedouins a stipend to allow the caravans safe passage, but frequent defaults in payments were followed by the sacking of caravans. Villagers were forced to pay the *khawa*, a tax on wheat or animals levied by the neighboring tribes in return for protection and allowance to till their soil.

In response to these depredations, villagers united under the leadership of the strongest family among them to protect their crops and sheep. Disorder was so widespread in the region of Ajlun at the end of the nineteenth century that the inhabitants were prevented from emigrating only by the Ottoman government's dispatch of an expedition which, joining with the villagers, drove the Bedouins out of the Jordan Valley into southeastern Jordan.

Al Kura, the subdistrict in which Kufr al-Ma lies, was one of the few areas in Ajlun that was not subjugated by Bedouin tribes.[13] This was due, in large part, to the development of a district organization centering in Tibne and led by the Wazir family. Wazir Rabbā''s grandfather (see Chart One, p. 38) had originally settled in Tibne after coming from the Hauran in Syria. He had married the daughter of Amir al-Mahaydi and had succeeded his father-in-law as the leader (shaykh) in Al Kura subdistrict. As the Shaykh of the area he not only exercised political authority, but also judged between villagers in the settlement of their disputes.[14] Disputants would go to the Shaykh's guest house "to demand justice" (*li Talab al haqq*) in the presence of the assembled elders. In return for protection, the Shaykh demanded economic contributions from the villagers as a mark of their allegiance. He would appoint members of his family as headmen in the villages of the area. Frequently, the villagers would welcome a member of the Wazir family to the village and even grant him a piece of land if he would settle there and become their shaykh.[15]

Although the Shaykh's important day-to-day function was arbitral, his role was essentially political. The authority of the Shaykh extended beyond the acceptance of his decision in arbitration. The Shaykh made war and peace and collected taxes (see below). The villagers in his district constituted a potential military following that could be called upon in any crisis. His principal political function was protection; it was offered in return for economic contributions on the occasion of the harvest and often in return for permanent land grants (see discussion below (pp.17–18).The Shaykh also constituted a redistribution point for economic surplus. He earned his reputation as a wise man by his skill in settling disputes and his reputation as a good man by slaughtering sheep for the guests who came to pay him homage or ask for advice and aid. Since tribal custom demanded the sharing of every slaughter with as many men as possible, the arc of generosity was very wide indeed. Villagers stated that the tray carrying the rice and meat was so large that several men groaned under its weight when they set it down in the middle of the Shaykh's guest house. It was said of Kleb Wazir (the son of the eponymous ancestor of the family) as evidence of his goodness and perfect hospitality that he never sat to partake of the meal until all the guests had retired from the repast and all the women and children had been fed.

At the time of the harvest, the Shaykh would send an agent to each village who would call out from the back of his horse, "Oh ye villagers and tillers of the soil, everyone of you prepare a load of wheat for the Shaykh." The agent would rub a stalk of wheat when it was brought to him and if the seeds of the particular peasant's contribution were small, he would demand that another load be brought to him. A recalcitrant villager would receive a visit from the Shaykh himself and as a result would not only lose the load of wheat but also a sheep in the bargain (as the cost of hospitality). The Shaykh might stop at the house of a man to whom a daughter had been born. He would declare, "She is for my brother, Salih," who would have been then just a child. Eighteen years later, when the Shaykh heard that the girl's father had betrothed her to another man, he would visit him and demand a payment to allow the marriage to go on.[16] Thus, through force and self-interest the villagers of Al Kura came together under the leadership of the Wazir family, whose headquarters were in the remote village of Tibne.

The achievement of social status through the display of generosity is related to the fact that for men such as Wazir and his descendants consumption goods were not available, nor were they needed. Men built their own houses, made their own clothing, and grew their own food. A shaykh with an economic surplus invested it in sheep which were slaughtered and served in his guest house on every suitable occasion. Such slaughterings provided opportunities for the gathering of the whole community. The Shaykh's guest house was the political center of the whole region. The leader of this district network utilized the economic tribute (which was frequently in the form of sheep) to win political adherents and to achieve social status rather than to increase his own or his family's standard of living.

The importance of the Shaykh was accentuated by the absence of any centralized administration in the area. No local police post existed. The Ottoman governor or *wali* of the Ajlun district lived in Deraa in Syria. Considering the conditions of communication and transportation in the late nineteenth century, appeal to him against the rule of the Shaykh was out of the question. Moreover, Ottoman authorities found it easiest to deal with the single authority who could collect taxes and maintain some sort of order. The Shaykh became recognized as the political overlord of the area by his own followers, by the Bedouins who opposed him, and by the Ottoman government who sought his aid. The elders of Kufr al-Ma in speaking about Kleb Wazir, the last of the Tibne shaykhs, were unambiguous about the nature of his overlordship, saying, "he used to loose and bind " (*kan yafiq wa yirbuT*).* And the *mukhtar*

*An idiom used to signify the power and authority of the shaykh.

(present day village mayor) was always compared invidiously with the Shaykh of Tibne. He was only another man "from among the peasants" (*min al fellāHīn*).

Wazir's father, Rabba', had succeeded in expelling a group referred to as the Zaydan from Kufr al-Ma, Deir Abu Said, Juffein, and Jenin (see Map 1, p. 3), thus opening up these villages for settlement from Tibne. This probably occurred shortly after the middle of the nineteenth century. At the time, several groups who referred to themselves as "the clans of Tibne" and who claimed to be descended from a common ancestor, Hammad, resided in Tibne. In addition to the Wazir family were Beni Yasin, Beni Esa, Beni Bakr, Beni Yunis, and Beni Abd al-Rahman.[17] Two other groups—Beni Dumi and Beni 'Amr—settled in Tibne later. Indeed, the Wazir family welcomed settlers who would increase their manpower against the Bedouin and unfriendly villages. In Tibne, too, lived the Shuqayrat who were the original settlers of that village.

According to the village elders, the inhabitants of Tibne used to descend from their hill stronghold during the ploughing season, plant their crops in the surrounding area, and return to Tibne until the harvest period. They descended again to harvest their crops, storing sufficient seed in nearby rock shelters for the next year's planting. Then they returned with their crops to Tibne where they spent the off season. As the population increased, the transportation of crops along the treacherous paths to Tibne became increasingly difficult. The inhabitants of Tibne decided to divide the surrounding territory among themselves permanently. This division was known as the *tayr al Hiswa* and probably occurred around the turn of the century.[18] Each descent group settled in the center of the lands it cultivated. Beni Bakr went to Marhaba (see Map 1), Beni Esa went to Irkheim and Es Samt, Beni 'Amr went to Rehaba and Kufr al-Ma, Beni Dumi went to Rehaba and Kufr al-Ma, Beni Yunis went to Deir Abu Said, and Beni Yasin went to Rehaba and Kufr al-Ma.

The permanent land division among the "clans of Tibne" was not, however, the beginning of the breakup of supravillage cooperation. The inhabitants of the villages of Al Kura subdistrict continued to cooperate politically against Bedouins and other enemies under the leadership of the Wazir family. They phrased their unity in terms of the common historical experience their ancestors enjoyed at Tibne and/or actual claims of patrilineal relationship to a common ancestor, Sa'ad (see Chart 2, p. 39). Tibne ceased to be the center of a district political structure only after modern communications made it accessible to centralized government authority.

Before 1922, when Tibne was a refuge from the depredations of the Bedouins and from the arbitrary taxation and conscription policies of the Ottoman Turks, the need to defend it against these enemies encouraged families to settle there. But with population increase and the establishment of centralized government in 1922 the very advantages which had made Tibne a political center in a period of anarchy—its remoteness from administrative centers and inaccessibility to attack—became disadvantages. By settling in the "daughter" villages of Tibne, peasants were not only able to care for their crops more efficiently, but also were able to attend the markets, dispensaries, courts, and land registry offices which had become so much a part of rural life with the spread of centralized government.

Nevertheless, as late as 1922, Kleb Wazir, the Shaykh of Tibne, refused to attach the subdistrict of Al Kura to Irbid under the new state of Transjordan being organized by Amir Abdullah. Kleb set up an independent administration at Deir Yusuf (see Map 1) which printed its official papers in Damascus, continued to collect taxes, and organized fifty police posts in the area.[19] Kleb refused to travel to Irbid, which had been the headquarters of the detested Turkish authorities, to meet with officials of Amir Abdullah's administration. And when officials of the central government came to levy a tax on sheep in Tibne, they were wounded in an exchange of fire. Another force sent to Al Kura to arrest the culprits and subdue the region was murdered in the ravines below Tibne. It was only with the bombing of Tibne by British aircraft in the service of Amir Abdullah in 1922 that the proud overlords of Al Kura submitted to government control. The district organization which had risen to meet the threat of Bedouin incursion and arbitrary rule had, with the establishment of centralized government, lost its *raison d'être*. But the supravillage network of which Kufr al-Ma was a part continued to have some significance for the daughter villages of Tibne as will be observed in the next chapter.

5. LAND TENURE: THE MUSHA SYSTEM

There are five official classes of land tenure in the Kingdom of Jordan:[20] (1) Privately owned land, *arD mamlūka*, is land which the owners can dispose of as they like, whether to exploit, give as security, sell, or bequeath (nearly all the cultivated land in Kufr al-Ma falls into this category). (2) Land held as a religious endowment, *arD mawqūfa*, is property set aside in perpetuity according to Islamic law and for religious or charitable purposes. In Kufr al-Ma eleven acres of land have been set aside as religious endowment (*waqf*). This land is tilled by various sharecroppers every year, the proceeds of the crop being used for the upkeep of the village mosque. (3) State land, *arD amīriya*, is land registered in the name of the state treasury. Its profit reverts to the government although it may be rented to the inhabitants of the area. It may also be sold to them for a price set by the government. Part of it is woodland which the government oversees and protects. One-third of the land of Kufr al-Ma, being woodland, is held by the government as ard amiriya. (4) Communal land, *arD matrūka*, is land close to settlement left for the inhabitants as pasture or woodland. No single person may own it. It is preserved indefinitely for the general welfare. It includes woodlands close to the area of settlement, pasture, and barren rocky lands suitable for grazing. (5) Wasteland, *arD mewāt*, is deserted land, unexploited, unclaimed, and far from settled areas. In Kufr al-Ma, the percentage of land in the above categories is shown in Table 5.

TABLE 5

OFFICIAL CATEGORIES OF LAND TENURE IN KUFR AL-MA

Type of Land	Approximate Area (acres)	Percentage of Land in Village
Privately Owned Land	2,709	69.4%
Religious Endowment	12	.3%
State Land	1,037	27 %
Communal Land	132	3.3%
Wasteland	0	0 %
TOTAL	3,890	100 %

Until 1939, when the lands of the village were individually registered, Kufr al-Ma held the greater part of its cultivated lands under an
unofficial category of land tenure known as *mushā'*. Even during Ottoman times, however, at least one-fourth of the cultivated lands of the
village were exempted from musha', being individually owned. The
musha' system of tenure has been described as follows:

> Mesha'a is a relic of joint ownership of land. Under it the proper-
> ties are regarded as being owned by the community—which is al-
> ways a village community—but are in the actual possession of
> several owners each of whom has a certain share of the joint
> property, though his ownership of any special area is not fixed.
> Usually the fields are redistributed periodically among the mem-
> bers of the community according to some generally accepted
> plan.[21]

A number of contradictory explanations, none of them wholly satis-
fying, have been offered for the development of this type of land tenure
in certain areas of the Fertile Crescent. Some have claimed that
musha' is associated with a former nomadic way of life which stresses
common rights in property among the agnatic groups. But Grannot has
pointed out that in the area of Palestine most susceptible to Bedouin
influence—the Beersheba district—individual ownership holds sway.
Others have suggested that more valuable lands tend to be developed
for profit and registered individually while less valuable lands have
remained under musha' tenure. Weulersse, noting the geographical
incidence of musha' in the arid inland steppes of the Levant—the Beqqa,
Chab, and Amouk Valleys—has associated it with the semicereal mo-
noculture (wheat, barley, and legumes) of relatively fertile plains.[22]
(Kufr al-Ma is located in relatively infertile foothills.) It is "a system

born of aridity and permanent menace of nomads and requiring a concentration of people while the necessities of rotation required strict
communal discipline."[23]

Kufr al-Ma, though it does not lie in the Jordan Valley itself, was
open to sporadic depredations by Bedouins. Its two-crop cereal-growing
regime required the discipline of communal organization. Grannot's
general statement regarding the agricultural regime associated with
musha' in Palestine is also applicable to Kufr al-Ma:

> Mesha'a tenure must not be regarded as simply a form of land
> ownership; it also necessitates a certain style of agricultural
> work. It demands from every co-owner no small measure of acqui-
> escence in methods of cultivation, and in an order and time-table
> of field operations imposed from without. Every co-owner is
> obliged to follow a rotation of crops from the various fields which
> is fixed and uniform for all the co-owners, that is to say to grow
> the same crops, at the same periods, and by the same methods as
> all the rest of the co-owners.[24]

In addition to the fixed dates of planting and harvesting set by the
council of elders and the biennial or triennial rotation, musha' did not
allow the individual peasant to sell his share in the land of the village
to strangers; he was not able to keep idle pasture or enclose his land;
furthermore, public or private paths or dwellings of any sort could not
be kept on cultivated land, for in the redistribution of land they would
be ploughed over.

In Kufr al-Ma, the musha' system necessitated cooperative and
consecutive harvesting. Villagers or kinsmen banded together to harvest the crops of each individual's plot; they would finish it and then
move on to the adjoining plot. A cultivator was not allowed to anticipate
and harvest his plot before his turn came. This prohibition was en-
forced in order to prevent depredation by plough animals and sheep if
harvesting were individually carried out on a helter-skelter pattern. [25]
After the harvest of the whole area, all the cultivators were permitted
to turn their flocks into the fields of the village. A crop watchman
(nātūr) was hired by the village or the respective descent groups to
protect the unharvested crops from thieves and animals. Depredation
was quite probable, due to the fragmentation of each landholding into a
number of widespread parcels.

The fragmentation of land parcels was a necessary part of the
musha' system. Every villager with a share in the land (for it was
shares and not land that were held by the individual) received a parcel
in every one of the categories into which the village lands were divided.
The division of land into categories was to assure every landowner a
portion in fertile as well as barren land, in level as well as sloping
land, in near as well as distant land, in land accessible to springs as
well as that not accessible, in woodland as well as cultivated land, and
in land suitable for summer as well as winter crops. Each family was
assigned the number of parcels corresponding to the number of its

shares in village land. In Kufr al-Ma a landowner commonly held five or six parcels of land. In this situation no single landowner was in a position to guard his own crops or to ignore the field operations of his neighbor.

Extrafamilial cooperation continued on the threshing ground. Kinsmen and neighbors aided one another, particularly if the season had produced a bumper crop. The owner of the crop often staked a goat on the threshing ground. When the threshing was completed the goat was slaughtered and all who had contributed in helping the owner and his family were invited to the feast which often took place on the threshing ground itself.

As mentioned, not all of the cultivated land in Kufr al-Ma was held under musha' tenure. At least a fourth of it had been exempted from periodical redistribution during Ottoman times. The express purpose of the Ottoman Land Law of 1858 had been to fix individual rights of ownership on all lands to which the state had residual title (this included most agricultural land). Although this law was never fully carried out due to corruption on the part of the officials who administered it and evasion on the part of the peasants to whom it was supposed to apply, a number of families in Kufr al-Ma had been able to gain government recognition for their claims to certain areas in the village. The land so exempted seemed to be no better and no worse in quality than the other lands of the village. The Turks, then, albeit inefficiently, had attempted to break down the musha' system as early as the middle of the nineteenth century.

Within the broad category of land tenure known as musha' several variations existed. Under one type (*zukūr*) every male living in the community at the time of the biennial redistribution of land, including infants, received equal shares in the communal land. Under another, land was distributed according to ability to work it. That is, distribution was according to the number of draught animals held by each household. Families without draught animals did not receive shares in the land. Kufr al-Ma represented neither of these types; rather, distribution of land was in proportion to the number of shares in land held by the head of each household. Since the ownership of shares differed widely, the resulting distribution of land between households was relatively unequal.

Whatever the consequences of these variations in the musha' system for economic and social status, in every case, including Kufr al-Ma, the village was regarded as the corporate owner of the land, and a villager could not alienate a share of land to strangers. In Kufr al-Ma, however, it was the clan within which the actual redistribution of land took place.[26] The village lands were divided into three equal parts corresponding to the three clans of the village. (The three clans were of unequal size, however, and often families from the larger clans or independent families would join the smaller clans to even up the division). Each clan was assigned one of the three areas by lot. Then, each clan would redivide the stretch allotted it among its component families. Thus "every humula [clan] or family received an area corresponding to the share which was originally assigned to it in the landed property in the village."[27]

Unlike the zukur system which was basically equalitarian, stressing the right of every living male as a member of the village community and thereby entitled to land, the system of musha' practiced in Kufr al-Ma was basically inequalitarian in permitting the holding of unequal shares in village land based on an initial historic division that was not responsive to population growth. The last historic settlement of shares in land in Kufr al-Ma had probably been imposed by the Turks in the nineteenth century when they had registered a share (*zalame*) of land for every able bodied male (zalame) who volunteered for military service. Thus land rights and military obligations were closely connected, so much so as to be covered by the same term.

In 1928 registration of cultivated land was begun in Palestine and Transjordan. By 1943, 968,500 acres had been settled — eighty-four percent of all cultivated land and nearly all land held under musha'.[28] Land settlement officers reached Kufr al-Ma in 1939. It was not they, however, who carried out the actual partition of land. This task was left to the cultivators who were in a better position to assess the quality of the soil and the numerous factors that affected its fertility. After the initial cadastral survey (which had never been carried out by the Turks whose registration was by personal ownership and not cadastral) and the partition of lands formerly held in common, came the investigation of claims to land ownership and the registration of title. All lands of the village were registered in the names of individuals and a land map (see Map 3, p. 24) was drawn up which demarcated individual boundaries and on which all subsequent sales were recorded. Each villager who possessed shares under musha' now received two plots, one of cultivable land and another of woodland, instead of the five or six held before. Many plots of land were registered jointly in the names of brothers or patrilateral first cousins and still continue to be held in such manner today. With population increase and the division of households, however, such undivided plots may gradually be reduced.

Although state land (*amiri*) devolves on the death of a possessor "in equal shares, gratuitously and without payment of any price, upon his children of both sexes whether residing on the spot or in another country,"[29] and although this rule has been extended to cover privately owned land, numerous local customs have operated to avoid the partition of the inheritance. Land is commonly registered in the name of a son or sons during the life of a father or it may be given as a gift to a single individual. Women are, in this manner, commonly excluded from inheritance. This is particularly true of women who marry out of their community or patrilineal group. The registration of land, then, has not had as revolutionary an effect in terms of land division and, conversely, land agglomeration, as one might have expected from formal considerations. Frequently, "the courts have held that such customs are valid when shown to be ancient and invariable in spite of the fact that they run counter to statute law."[30]

The significance of the abolition of musha' tenure for village and

clan cooperation should not, however, be underestimated. The necessity of the scattering of the land parcels of a single cultivator to equalize
the quality of his land prevented land agglomeration or cooperation
among big landowners. A rich farmer, under mushaʻ, could not purchase land from his less fortunate fellows. He could only purchase
shares in land — land whose quality would change at every distribution.
With the registration of land in individual ownership, purchase of land
became not only possible but potentially profitable. A plot of land of
known quality might now be bought, held over a number of years, and
developed by its owner.

Under mushaʻ, village-wide cooperation in the coordination of
planting, in the protection of crops, and in the consecutive harvesting
of crops and pasturing of animals was necessary. With the registration
of land each peasant determined the crops to be grown and the time of
planting and harvesting. This is not to say that under the present
system — out of his own self-interest — he can completely ignore the
agricultural regime followed by his neighbors on the land. Under mushaʻ, however, punishment for violations of the agricultural calendar
or for crop destruction by livestock was handled by informal village or
kin group consultations. Although minor cases of crop depredation are
still brought before the mukhtar and clan elders in the guest house,
most such cases are now handled by the subdistrict officer or the civil
court in the next town.

Today, Kufr al-Ma cannot be regarded in any sense as a corporate
village with control over economic resources. Land sales occur and
may be to nonvillagers. However, the village has not yet passed from
under the shadow of its corporate history despite the formal revolution
in land tenure (the registration of lands in individual ownership in
1939). Over the course of the last twenty years very little land has been
alienated to nonvillagers (see Map 3, p. 24). Owners of adjacent land
plots are usually granted the privilege of prior purchase before a sale
is made. (Villagers have sometimes failed to exercise this privilege,
however.) Most sales are to neighbors on the land or to lineage mates
and clansmen (often the two are synonymous). A comparison of the distribution of land plots in terms of lineage and clan affiliation in 1939
and in 1960 shows very little change. Owners of abutting land plots tend
to be affiliated with the same clans and lineages (though they may not
be the same individuals) as in the earlier period.

To summarize, this chapter has outlined the various ecological
factors that establish the limiting conditions for the agricultural regime in Kufr al-Ma. Its subsistence agriculture based on a two-crop
rotation is a direct result of these factors. The chance variation in
soil, topography, and rainfall, and the low incidence of the latter, prevents great economic differentiation within the agricultural sector of
the village economy. This fact will be demonstrated more clearly in the
examination of incomes in the next chapter (pp. 26–36). On the basis of
the meager information available, I have attempted to sketch certain
historical events which are important for an understanding of life in the
village today. The two most important events were the breakdown of
the district political structure with the bombing of Tibne in 1922 and

the termination of the communal system of land tenure and cultivation in 1939. The registration of land destroyed the corporate nature of the village, at least in its economic aspect and, in a sense, freed individual households for enterprise within and mobility outside it. The remarkable fact is that despite the revolution in land tenure and despite the increase of occupational mobility, so little change has occurred in the village whether in the actual alienation of land outside it or the agglomeration of land within it. Its religious life remains strongly Islamic and its process of social control equalitarian and traditional. Despite considerable economic differentiation (see Chapter 2) social status differences are minimal. The existence of social stability against a background of economic change poses a fascinating problem with which I have dealt elsewhere.[31] What is important in the present context is that the heritage ·of common political action and common economic control has had positive consequences for village and clan solidarity. Despite basic economic, political, and social changes, the village and clan continue to function as a framework for political rivalry, social status, and social control, and as the loci of kinship ties and land ownership. The following chapters will examine the basis of this solidarity and the factors working toward its dissolution.

CHAPTER TWO

The Social Structure of Kufr al-Ma

1. THE OCCUPATIONAL STRUCTURE

The changes in the land tenure system described in the last chapter must be viewed in their total demographic and ecological setting. Otherwise, the discussion of Kufr al-Ma's occupational structure that follows will not be appreciated. Up until the end of World War I the land of Kufr al-Ma, like that of its sister villages, was given away to men who would settle on it, till it, and defend it (see Chapter 1, p. 16). In 1960, forty years later, the land of Kufr al-Ma was in such short supply that one-half of the families in the village were landless (see Table 6, p. 27) and the remainder (with the exception of nineteen) had to seek alternative part-time employment to eke out a living.

Reduction in the size of land holdings per household has been accompanied by a decline in stock raising. This decline was caused by the creation of a government woodland reserve out of one thousand acres of land on which the peasants of Kufr al-Ma had formerly grazed their flocks; by consecutive years of drought which forced peasants to sell their flocks; and by particular historical incidents such as the confiscation of the sheep of several lineages (in 1922 as compensation after the unsuccessful rebellion of the Al Kura subdistrict against Amir Abdullah and again in 1925 after the murder of local government officials).[1]

The reduction of land holdings, on the other hand, has occurred as a result of the pressure of increasing population on a fixed amount of cultivable land. In the absence of irrigation and with the creation of the woodland preserve, all possible land in the village has been brought under cultivation. The population of Kufr al-Ma has increased considerably since 1940 while the amount of cultivable land has actually decreased. With the registration of village lands in 1939, 1,037 acres were withdrawn from use either as pasture or crop land. This land (about one-third of the total possible cultivable land in Kufr al-Ma) was claimed by the government as woodland preserve (see Map 1, p. 3). At the same time, the population has been expanding steadily. Although no previous population figures are available for the village, a glance at Map 2A (p. 74) will verify the reality of the population explosion. Eighty-seven new houses have been built outside the boundaries of the village settlement since 1940. All of the old houses, in the meanwhile, have remained occupied. It is this relationship of expanding population to shrinking land resources that explains why Kufr al-Ma, in appearance a typical peasant village, counts only thirty-nine percent of its employed men as cultivators of the soil.

TABLE 6

OCCUPATIONAL STRUCTURE OF KUFR AL-MA—1960*

Occupation	Number of Men so Employed
AGRICULTURAL	
Peasant (Owner of Land)[2]	57
Peasant (Owner and Sharecropper for one-half of crop)	36
Peasant (Sharecropper for one-half of crop)[3]	27
Plowman (Sharecropper for one-fourth of crop)	4
Daily Agricultural Laborer	1
Yearly Agricultural Pieceworker	5
Shepherd[4]	17
Total: Agricultural Occupations	147
Percentage: Agricultural Occupations	39%
MILITARY	
Soldier	108
Percentage: Military Occupations[5]	29%
RETIRED	9
Percentage: Retired	2%
NONAGRICULTURAL	
Laborer (Local)	23
Laborer (Distant)[6]	17
Stonecutter	16
Peddler	6
Mason[7]	10
Carpenter	1
Blacksmith[8]	2
Tailor[9]	1
Shopkeeper	14
Magician	1
Imam[10]	2
Mukhtar[11]	2
Watchman[12]	2
Government Employee[13]	16
Muezzin[14]	1
Total: Nonagricultural Occupations	114
Percentage: Nonagricultural Occupations	30%
TOTAL NUMBER OF MEN EMPLOYED OR RETIRED[15]	378

*Notes to this table appear at the back of the book, pp. 158–59.

Typical of the contraction of land holdings in successive generations is the case of the mukhtar of Kufr al-Ma, Muflih al-Hakim.
Muflih possesses four acres in Kufr al-Ma. He owns one plough horse,
two geese, and a few chickens. His father with his two brothers possessed twenty-two acres in Kufr al-Ma, Rehaba, and the Jordan Valley
as well as 250 sheep, seventy goats, one team of oxen, three donkeys,
two milch cows, and one purebred horse. The division of land of these
three brothers among their ten sons has reduced the share of each to
such an extent that seven of the ten have left the village to seek employment elsewhere.

The consequences of such land shortage are seen in the occupational structure of Kufr al-Ma (see Table 6). Less than forty percent
of the employed men covered by my census are engaged in subsistence
agriculture. Of 369 men, thirty-nine percent or 147 are engaged in
agricultural occupations; thirty percent or 114 are engaged in nonagricultural occupations; and twenty-nine percent or 108 are engaged in
military occupations. Beni Yasin, the descent group with the most
land, has only forty-six percent of its employed men engaged in agriculture while the independent families (not associated with the three
main descent groups) have only twenty-seven percent so engaged.
Of 200 household heads censused, 92 possessed no land whatsoever.

The consequences of such an occupational structure for mobility
are plain. A certain number of men find employment in the village as
shopkeepers, artisans, and stonecutters (thirty-four all told); many
others work out of the village but in the locality as builders, peddlers,
and local laborers (thirty-nine); the remainder find employment as
soldiers, government clerks, and laborers in distant towns, in army
camps, and in the capital, Amman (141 fall into this category). In addition, many peasants, particularly sharecroppers, are forced to hire
out their labor in surrounding villages or in the Jordan Valley due to
the shortage of land in Kufr al-Ma.

The occupational mobility characteristic of Kufr al-Ma, while perhaps more pronounced, is not unusual for the villages of the area. Of
the twenty-five villages in Al Kura subdistrict, only five have more
than the 2,700 acres of privately owned cultivable land which Kufr al-
Ma claims as its own. Land shortage, population growth, and occupational mobility characterize all the villages of the subdistrict.

In addition to the ties created by the movement of sharecroppers,
builders, and peddlers into the surrounding villages (where they may
reside for part of the season), numerous kinship and marriage ties link
Kufr al-Ma with other villages in the area (see Diagram 1). These extravillage local ties are related not only to shortage of land and population pressure but also to the district political organization which once
linked the villages of Tibne.

The village of Kufr al-Ma was characterized by long-distance mobility even before the establishment of the British Mandate in Palestine. Nineteen heads of households interviewed by me had resided outside Jordan for a year or more even before 1920. Sixteen of the nineteen had served in the Turkish army for periods varying from four

months to eight years. They had traveled as far as Egypt in the south and Yugoslavia in the north. The mobility which characterized the village after the establishment of the Mandate was primarily for economic purposes. Whereas service in the Turkish army had been mainly by conscription, travel to Palestine after 1920 was entirely voluntary. Moreover, the degree of mobility after World War I was far greater. Of 194 heads of households from whom information was solicited,

DIAGRAM 1

EXTRA-VILLAGE TIES

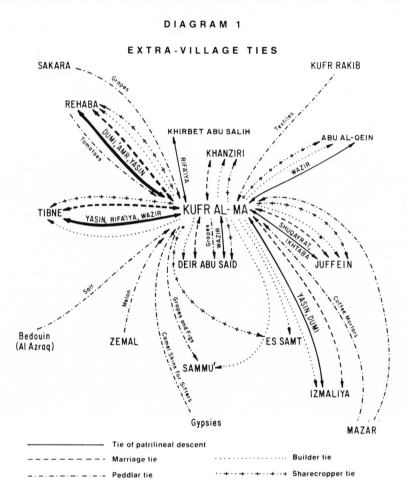

————————	Tie of patrilineal descent		
– – – – – – –	Marriage tie	················	Builder tie
–·–·–·–·–·–	Peddlar tie	··+··+··+··+··+··	Sharecropper tie

ninety-six, or forty-nine percent, had made at least one trip to Palestine to seek employment. The great majority had worked in Palestine on three or more separate occasions. Many would leave after the harvest or during drought seasons to spend three or more months in Haifa or Tel Aviv where they worked as fishermen, construction workers, factory hands, gardeners, and harvesters. In general, the men who made the most trips and stayed the longest periods were men with very little or no land. Of the six landed heads of households of the Shujur lineage, only one worked in Palestine while of the six heads of households of the Diyaka—four of whom were landless—five worked in Palestine.

Some men would continue to work in Palestine until they had earned enough money to hand over the marriage payment; others were attracted by the "high life" of the towns; but most simply made the trip to tide themselves over lean agricultural years or to supplement their income in the off season. Some men stayed in Palestine for several consecutive years; others went off and on for a period of two or three months, while some villagers went only in years of agricultural dearth.

A small number of men have spent much of their lives in Palestine. Such a man was Muflih al-Hakim, one of the two village mukhtars during my stay in Kufr al-Ma.[16] A man of about fifty, Muflih had first gone to Palestine in 1926 at about the age of sixteen. He ran away at harvest time with a friend from the village and secured a job in Tiberias where he helped build the house of a wealthy Jew. Two months later he returned to Kufr al-Ma in time to attend the opening of the school term. A year later, he walked to Haifa, a distance of fifty miles, and worked as a watchman in the garden of a Palestinian Arab. He received three dollars a month in addition to room and board. He returned once again to Kufr al-Ma to finish his third and last year of formal schooling. For the three years following he worked as a ploughman on his father's land. In 1930, after a poor agricultural year, he returned to Haifa where he worked as a fisherman and plasterer. From 1931 to 1933 he worked in Beisan, a small market town overlooking the Jordan Valley from the west bank. He had brought his mother and two brothers to live with him after his father had married a second wife. While in Beisan, an Arab town, he worked in the banana orchards for eight piastres (twenty cents) a day and later, for a year, as helper to a blacksmith. He left his mother and brothers in Beisan and for the next three years, 1934–36, he worked in Jaffa and Tel Aviv under Jews as foreman of an Arab construction gang. During that period he learned Hebrew and, in fact, courted a Jewish girl, all the while posing as an Iraqi Jew. The courtship broke up when his father threatened to disown him. In 1936 he returned to Beisan to enlist as a recruit in the first Arab rebellion against the British. He was placed in an ordnance unit whose duty was to supply rifles, horses, ammunition, and money for the Arab guerillas. Carrying out his duties involved some degree of smuggling, extortion, and thievery. In 1939 he was jailed by the British authorities on the charge of smuggling guns from Damascus and participating in a terrorist organization known as "The Black Hand." On his release in 1941, he worked as a laborer in the construction of the "Eden Line," a defensive line stretching from Umm Qays in Jordan to Haifa, and later he worked in Haifa for the British army, loading ammunition onto ships. Thereafter, he worked for several months in Umm Qays as a mason. He married in 1942 and remained in the village as a *fellah* (cultivator) from 1943 until 1948. With the outbreak of the Palestine War he enlisted in the Arab Legion and saw action in the Jerusalem and Nablus areas. In 1951 he left the Legion and returned to Kufr al-Ma where he worked as fellah until 1957 when he was chosen unanimously by his clan to represent it as mukhtar.[17]

Although a number of other villagers had spent long periods of time in Palestine, had worked under Jews and Englishmen, and had fought in the war, no other person in the village could match the mukhtar's varied experience. He was certainly typical of many of the village men of his own generation in his awareness of the urban culture that existed outside the confines of his village. But he had gone much further than other migrants in associating with and, to some degree, understanding men of another way of life. Having, moreover, some understanding of western standards of education, efficiency, technology, and organization, he was concerned that his village move ahead in the direction towards which the outer world was moving. He threw his firm support behind movements of village reform initiated by the government — movements that were not always accepted enthusiastically   by the elders of the community. He supported the building of a new school, the repairing of roads, and the establishment of a committee for village reform. He was a personal demonstration of the impact which labor migration could have on a native villager. Notwithstanding his wide experience, the mukhtar remained a pious man, a loyal kinsman, and a vigorous husbandman (though he owned only four acres). It was this combination of traditional village values and extravillage experience that resulted in his selection as mukhtar of his clan by acclamation.

Although the immediate cause of seeking extravillage employment may vary with the age of the individual and the crop yield, the underlying cause of labor migration is land shortage. Various attempts have been made to estimate the "lot viable" for an Arab family in Palestine on unirrigated land.[18] This lot represents "the holding necessary   to support its occupants in a reasonable standard of life."[19] To stipulate a certain size lot is extremely difficult in view of the differential precipitation and the varied quality of the soil. After an investigation of the economic conditions of cultivators in Palestine, the Hope-Simpson Report came to the following conclusion:

> Not a single farmer who held less than 120 dunums [30 acres] was able to live on the produce of his farm without outside employment, and of 3,261 holding from 220–240 dunums, 1,657 found it necessary to procure employment in addition to their farming in order to maintain themselves and their families. From this it is quite clear that 120 dunums is not a lot sufficient to support a fellah family with cereal cultivation.[20]

I have already mentioned that ninety-two households in Kufr al-Ma possess no land whatsoever. Of the remaining 109 households eighty-eight possess less than twenty-five acres (see Table 7). Thus only nineteen households in Kufr al-Ma hold plots of such a size as to constitute a "lot viable" in terms of the Hope-Simpson Report. Sixty percent of those holding land hold thirteen acres or less. (Jordan's richer soil, compared to Palestine, is offset by its meager rainfall so as to make the Hope-Simpson estimate for Palestine generally applicable to Jordan.)

Historically, then, Kufr al-Ma has passed from a situation in which land was in such abundance that it was given away provided men would settle on it, till it, and defend it, to a situation in which land is

TABLE 7

SIZE OF LAND HOLDINGS* IN KUFR AL-MA BY DESCENT GROUPS

Name of Descent Group	0–2.5 Acres	2.5–5 Acres	5–12.5 Acres	12.5–25 Acres	25–50 Acres	50–100 Acres	100–125 Acres	Landless
Beni Yasin	0	7†	15	11	5	2	1	34
Beni Dumi	5	7	9	4	3	0	0	23
Beni 'Amr	2	1	11	3	1	2	0	12
Independent Lineages	0	1	7	5	5	0	0	23
Village Total	7	16	42	23	14	4	1	92
Percentage of Village Total	7% of landholders	15% of landholders	39% of landholders	21% of landholders	13% of landholders	4% of landholders	1% of landholders	46% of all households surveyed

*All figures refer to cultivated landholdings only.
†All figures refer to households.

so short that half the families in the village are landless and the remainder (with the exception of nineteen) must seek alternative employment to eke out a living. Indeed, members of lineages which are generally considered to be landed have often to seek nonagricultural employment. Thus, for instance, Mustafa Yusuf of Shujur who owns thirteen acres of good land in Kufr al-Ma has, since 1933, been building houses in the village to supplement his agricultural income.

Occupational mobility, then, largely due to population pressure on fixed land resources, has characterized Kufr al-Ma since the establishment of the British Mandate in Palestine in 1920. But with the end of the Palestine War in 1949 and the sealing off of the western border, the towns that had provided an outlet for such migration—Haifa, Jaffa, Akka, and Tel Aviv—were suddenly cut off. Long-distance migration was now, to some degree at least, directed toward the north (Damascus and Beirut) and east (Amman). But migratory labor toward these cities remained a trickle as compared with the former pattern of migration to Palestine.

It was the expansion of the Jordanian army at the time of and following the Arab-Israeli War (1948–49) that provided the economic opportunities lost by the partition of Palestine.[21] Indeed, the new economic rewards were far better than the old once enlistment occurred. Competition for entrance into the Jordanian army became so intense that bribery was often the only sure means of securing enlistment. It was only forty years before that men had given away their lands in order to avoid service in the Turkish army!

The labor migration to Palestine had been sporadic. Men would leave after the harvest, only to return two or three months later. They might not go again for several years if agricultural production proved sufficient. The monetary returns varied, but they were, in general, small. After three months a man might return to the village with twelve dollars saved, at most twenty-one or twenty-four. Moreover, the daily returns in the fishing industry were unpredictable and it was in fishing that the great majority of migrants were engaged. A day's wage would depend on the catch and would vary from nothing to three dollars. As political disturbances increased, the better paid laboring jobs within the Jewish sector of the economy disappeared, particularly after the decision of the Jewish Agency in Zurich in 1929 to exclude Arab labor from all Jewish enterprises.[22]

Employment with the Jordanian army, on the other hand, guaranteed a young villager a monthly salary. With each additional child, the recruit received an additional stipend. Of nineteen lineages examined in Kufr al-Ma, a soldier was the highest salaried man in seven, while a government employee (working outside the village) was the highest salaried in four. The seven soldiers and the men deriving their income from army earnings who led their respective groups had annual incomes in dollars as follows (see Table 8): 476, 537, 571, 868, 873, 1,024, 1,198, 1,243, and 1,624. The four government employees who led their groups had incomes of 1,176, 1,344, 1,680 and 1,946 dollars (three of these four men lived outside the village in the towns where they worked, but all of them have either land, houses, or wives and children in Kufr

TABLE 8

HIGHEST SALARIED MEN IN NINETEEN LINEAGES
ACCORDING TO OCCUPATION

Government	Army	Agriculture	Other
1,946*	1,624	630	1,024 (A builder receiving two-thirds of his income from army sons)
1,680	1,243	532	571 (A retired farmer receiving two-thirds of income from army sons)
1,344	1,198	520	560 (An unauthorized medic)
1,176	873		470 (A shopkeeper)
	868		246 (A tinker)
	537		
	476		

*All figures are in dollars.

al-Ma). In only three of the nineteen lineages did a cultivator receive the highest income. Their incomes in 1960 were 630, 532, and 520 dollars respectively.[23] The richest farmers in Kufr al-Ma are not, therefore, able to match the income of the salaried employees. In general, a gap of 300 dollars or more separates them. The same gap exists between prosperous village grocers and salaried employees.

Whatever the effect of labor migration on income, social status, and world view of those who participated in it, a solid core of villagers (147 men) continue to look to the land as the primary source of their livelihood. Indeed, the fact of landlessness does not necessarily mean absorption into the nonagricultural sector of the economy. In one lineage, Aqayli, eight of the ten households derive some part of their incomes from agriculture even though six of the ten are landless. By sharecropping a man may claim a share in the yearly agricultural production.

For the villagers who till the soil, economic status remains largely determined by land tenure relationships. Whether the sharecropper tills a piece of land for a fifth, a fourth, a half, or three-fifths of the crop depends partly on ecological factors such as the fertility of the soil, its state of readiness for planting, its situation, and the amount of rainfall likely to fall on it, and on economic factors such as the labor input of the owner, the conditions of land shortage in a particular village, and the amount of capital contributed to the enterprise by the sharecropper. A sharecropper working land for half a share in the crop (see Table 6, p. 27) contributes his labor, the plough animals, and half of the seeds. A sharecropper working land in return for a fourth contributes only his labor, the animals and seeds being contributed by the owner. Exceptionally good land will be worked by the sharecropper for a two-fifths share even though he is supplying the plough animals and one-half of the seeds. A sharecropper will often work land in the foothills overlooking the Jordan Valley for two-thirds of the crop since the land is at some distance from the village and will probably involve the sharecropper's sleeping in the caves of that area during the ploughing and planting period. Of the 130 men censused as tilling land, only fifty-seven, or forty-four percent, worked their own land exclusively, the majority entering into some form of sharecropping relationship (see Table 6).

These land tenure relationships are reflected in terminology and to a considerable extent determine the social status of the individual. The term fellah refers to a man who owns land and derives his main income from it whether he tills it or not and provided he lives in the village; it also refers to a sharecropper who works land as an equal partner contributing capital along with the owner, i.e., his plough animals and one-half the seeds for a one-half share in the harvest. The sharecropper for a one-fourth share, however, is termed *Harrāth* (ploughman). He has no plough animals to contribute and offers only his labor; moreover, he often lives in a room in his employer's house if he comes from another village, and eats with his employer's family; he has such additional duties as feeding and watering the animals and running errands for his employer's household. The daily agricultural laborer or *āmil* works for a daily wage and his employment may be summarily ended by his employer. Finally, there is the agricultural pieceworker or *qatrūz* . He is usually a young man who is hired as a sort of apprentice ploughman. The owner contracts to give him a certain number of sacks of grain at the end of the season in return for his labor on the land. A man without land and who has no other permanent nonagricultural employment (army, shopkeeping, government position) is rather invidiously termed "landless one" (*fellawti*). Each of the terms mentioned refers to one category of land tenure relationship with the exception of the term fellah which includes men who own and till their own land and also sharecroppers working for one-half the crop. This discrepancy may be explained by the fact that the important factor involved from the peasant's point of view is not simply the ownership of land or the lack of it. Kufr al-Ma is, after all, a village of very small landholdings with sixty-one percent of all landowners holding twelve acres or less. The largest landowner owns only one hundred acres. The important factor is the investment of capital in land and the sharing of profits and losses. The sharecropper for half the crops shares these risks. He contributes animals and seeds and shares with the owner the costs of payment of wages to the blacksmith and other agricultural laborers hired in the course of the season.

Among these land-tilling villagers, land tenure relationships not only determine their economic status but also, to a large degree, their social status. The leaders of the village, the elders who assemble in the guest houses of the village to decide upon policy of kin or village affairs belong, in the main, to the category fellah. One landless villager, a stonecutter, was nominated by his descent group to serve on a planning committee for village improvement. He refused to serve, saying, "I have no time for such things. Besides, you know that we are landless ones [fellawti]." And the mukhtar of one of the landed descent groups belittled the claim of another descent group to equal membership on a village committee. "Who are the Beni Dumi?" he asked. "They are nothing but landless ones." He then proceeded to tick off on his fingers the names of the few landowning families of that particular descent group.

There are, then, two economic sectors within the village. The first, the agricultural, is strongly affected by contingent ecological conditions. These conditions have placed a ceiling on economic differentiation and supported an equalitarian ethic rooted in religious belief. Within this sector land is the key to economic and social status. The second and larger sector, the nonagricultural, seeks its income, for the most part, outside the village. Within this sector economic differentiation is considerable. A poor peasant may find his closest kinsman, a brother or first cousin, earning a salary four times his own. Despite this fact, social status differences remain minimal. The mobility of this sector has not affected its religious ethic or its process of social control.

The key to an understanding of such an anomaly lies in the culture and social structure of the village. Indeed, the following sections will demonstrate that the village is far more than a nucleated settlement for men who till the land. Rather, it is the cultural (ideology, values, style of life) and social (marriage and social control) and not the economic (occupation and income) aspects of peasant life that are critical for the understanding of the social stability of the village.

2. DESCRIPTION AND ANALYSIS OF SOCIAL UNITS

A. The Subdistrict: The Heritage of propinquity

Before 1922 Kufr al-Ma was involved in a district organization with political and military functions.[24] This organization was led by the Wazir family whose head lived in Tibne. The head of this family posted many of his close relatives in the surrounding villages as mukhtars or shaykhs.[25] Tribute was collected from these villages at harvest time in return for military support against Bedouin raids and against villages of other districts. It can hardly be assumed, however, on the basis of the sketchy information available that such organization as existed was regular or formal.[26] Bedouin raids into the Ajlun District of Jordan were, after all, sporadic due to the difficulty of the terrain and the remoteness and inaccessibility of the villages. Moreover, aside from the villages immediately surrounding Tibne—Kufr al-Ma, Rehaba, Deir Abu Said, Es Samt, Marhaba, Jenin, and Inbe (see Map 1) over which the Wazir family exercised their control—it is impossible to tell what constituted the geographical limits of that family's influence. It has never been known to extend outside of the Al Kura subdistrict and within that subdistrict its influence may have contracted and expanded with circumstances. After the defeat of Amir Abdullah's forces in 1921, Kleb Wazir's influence spread into the whole of the Ajlun District. But at the time of the crucial encounter with government forces a year later only seven of the twenty-five villages of Al Kura subdistrict remained loyal to the Wazir lineage which was itself marked by dissension.[27] After 1922, with the defeat of Tibne by the forces of the central government, Kufr al-Ma ceased to be a member of any district political organization other than the administrative units imposed by the authority of the Amirate of Jordan.

Of the twenty-five villages of Al Kura subdistrict, a majority of the inhabitants of the eight mentioned above together with the inhabitants of the village of Abu al-Qein claim to be descended from a common ancestor variously named Ahmed, Sa'ad, or Hammad. Peake's account of the origin of Al Hammad corresponds fairly well with the account given to me by the villagers of Tibne:[28]

> The tribe claims descent from Khalid ibn al Welid, but have nothing to support such a claim. It is said that they are descended from a man called Hammad, who with two brothers, Shafi and Nafi, came to Tibna some 500 years ago from the Wadi Hammad of Kerak District. Nafi went to Jerusalem and his descendants are said to be the Khalidi family. Shafi went to Safed and his descendants are said to be the Shahin family of Nablus and the Qaddura family of Safed.[29]

The genealogical relations between the peoples who claim descent from Hammad or Ahmed or Sa'ad together with their appropriate villages of residence are presented in Charts 1 and 2. Of the three large local descent groups in Kufr al-Ma only one, Beni Yasin, claims direct descent from Hammad. Beni Yasin is, however, the largest of the local descent groups in the village, comprising about forty percent of the population and owning over sixty percent of the land. Moreover, the other two local descent groups—Beni Dumi and Beni 'Amr—claim to be "of the peoples of Tibne," having resided there before the division of land at the turn of the century. This division scattered the residents to daughter villages such as Kufr al-Ma. The term, "the peoples of Tibne," then, refers to people who identify themselves by a common historical experience in a certain locale and (for the great majority, e.g., Bakr, Esa, Wazir, Yasin, Yunis) by a claimed common descent from a named patrilineal ancestor.

The people who claim descent from Hammad are scattered over nine villages in the same general area (see Map 1, p. 3, and Charts 1, p. 38, and 2, p. 39) and, to the best of my knowledge, have not combined for political actions, with one exception, since 1922. They do not constitute a localized group. They do not interact regularly on a face-

CHART 1

DIVISIONS OF HAMMAD (after Peake)

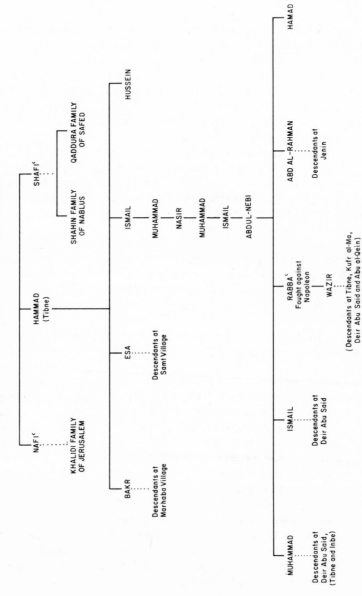

——— Indicates patrilineal descent

············· Indicates patrilineal descent with connecting ancestors unrecorded or unknown

to-face basis. Rather, they constitute an "aggregate", a category of individuals classified together by fact of sharing some common cultural
trait—in this case, descent.[30]

Although the great majority of inhabitants of the nine villages mentioned traced their descent to Sa'ad or Hammad, I have never heard
them refer to this aggregate as Beni Hammad ("sons of Hammad") or
Beni Sa'ad ("sons of Sa'ad"). Rather, they refer to themselves as
ahāli tibnah ("the peoples of Tibne") or *'ashā' ir tibnah* ("the clans of
Tibne").[31] Moreover, the members of this aggregate do not occupy or
claim exclusive rights to a particular territory. In Kufr al-Ma, for instance, live not only Beni Yasin, but also Beni Dumi and Beni 'Amr. No
one of these clans is considered the "owner" of the village lands in the
sense of having residual rights or higher status by fact of original settlement. Although Beni Yasin is the only one of the three clans that can

CHART 2

DIVISIONS OF HAMMAD
(from informants in Kufr al-Ma)

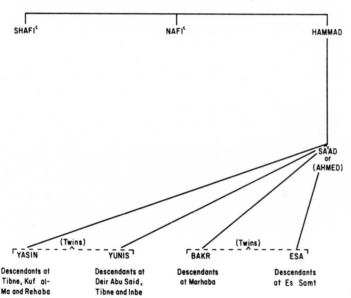

actually trace a genealogical relation to Hammad, it has not converted
this claimed consanguineal relationship into economic privileges or
superiority of status. Actually, the members of Beni 'Amr claim to
have come with Hammad from the Belqa district of Jordan—though they
are never cited as his descendants.[32] Beni Dumi, on the other hand,
trace their origins to the oasis of Jauf—formerly called Dumat al-Jandal—in the Arabian Peninsula.[33]

Although the common ideology of propinquity *cum* descent has not
provided economic privileges or advantages of status for certain clans
it has been associated historically with political cooperation at the subdistrict level. In 1921 the seven villages which remained loyal to Kleb

Wazir were mainly populated by the peoples of Tibne. Moreover, the peoples of Tibne still held certain norms of political action.[34] Among these norms is the one stated outright in the following case, namely— the peoples of Tibne must cooperate in cases of honor involving violations of their women by men of other groups.

CASE ONE

This case represents the only instance of subdistrict political co-operation that I witnessed. The case began when the police apprehended three young men in a taxi with the daughter of a prominent member of a local family, a man who had once served as mukhtar of Kufr al-Ma. The father of the girl was also the first patrilateral parallel cousin (father's brother's son) of the leading notable of the area. In 1927 this notable had been appointed by the Amir of Transjordan as a member of the Jordanian Senate. Previously he had lived in Tibne, the ancestral home, and then in Kufr al-Ma, where he had also served as mukhtar for fifteen years. At the time of the case he still possessed a house in Kufr al-Ma although he had long since moved to Deir Abu Said, the administrative center of the Al Kura subdistrict. One of his wives, a Yasin woman from Kufr al-Ma, was the mother of his favorite son. His ties to the village, then, were of long standing. They were not only consanguineal ties (by the fact that his first cousins lived there) but also economic (he had land in Kufr al-Ma that was sharecropped by peasants), political, and sentimental. The Pasha, as he was called in recognition of his position, possessed ties of a similar nature in nearly all the villages occupied by "the peoples of Tibne."

The three young men who were apprehended with the Pasha's close kinswoman had intended to take her off to a resort in the Jordan Valley where they had once before plied her with liquor and proceeded in turn to have sexual relations with her.

Two of the young men were members of the Zaydan clan. In fact, they were first patrilateral cousins. They lived in Deir Abu Said where the father of one had opened a very successful grocery shop. The people of the Zaydan were not regarded with favor by many of the villagers in Kufr al-Ma. They had occupied Kufr al-Ma in the nineteenth century only to be driven out by the descendants of Hammad under the leadership of the Wazir family. According to the villagers, they had been involved in other cases of immorality that had been shamefully settled through bribery.

One of the young men had become familiar with the girl at her father's farm in the Jordan Valley, a farm which he had often ploughed with his tractor. The other had been seen loitering near the girl's house in Kufr al-Ma. She kept house for her brother who was attending school in the next town while the rest of the family resided in their home in the Jordan Valley. The loiterer had been acting as liaison between the girl and his cousin, arranging the time and place of their rendezvous. One of the shopkeepers in the village had become suspicious when he saw the boy loitering in the vicinity of the girl's house. He asked him what his business was and when the boy gave an unsatisfactory answer told him to leave the village and to stay away from it. This incident occurred about two weeks before the apprehension of the men in the taxi.

After the arrest, the three men were jailed and the girl was released in the custody of her father. It was quite clear from the beginning that the girl had not shown any objection to the escapade. She never gave any cries of alarm nor did she inform any member of her family of attempted molestation.

Several weeks passed during which there were informal negotiations for a money settlement and a quashing of the case. All the while, the four families that constituted the Zaydan continued living in Deir Abu Said, assuming that some settlement could be reached. Yet during this period they neither proposed elopement nor marriage for the girl and one of her paramours, a customary solution that might have saved her life. Meanwhile, the testimony of the culprits became public knowledge. They had unabashedly confessed in detail their actions. This confession increased the pressure on the girl's father to take action.

In this intervening period, a member of the Zaydan approached one of the prominent elders of Tibne asking about the possibility of "sanctuary" or *dakhl* (literally translated as "entrance"), meaning entrance into the protection of another clan who would protect the property of the offenders and their patrilineal relatives and make arrangements for an eventual peacemaking or *SulHa*. (The offenders and their immediate relatives are banished from the area after the truce agreement and so the security of their property is obviously in jeopardy. But other more distant relatives also must officially seek the protection of "sanctuary" even though they remain in their houses and on their lands for their property is also open to the depredation of the victim's group.)

When the Pasha heard of this approach, he called in the leading men of the surrounding villages—men whose ancestors had claimed historical coresidence in the village of Tibne—for consultation. Representatives of Beni Yunis, Beni Bakr, Beni Esa, and the three clans of Kufr al-Ma, Beni Yasin, Beni Dumi and Beni 'Amr (see Charts 1, p. 38, and 2, p. 39) met in the Pasha's house. The Pasha urged them to refuse the Zaydan's plea for sanctuary. All of these men pledged to refuse such a request should it be made.

Meanwhile, the girl's father had gone with her and the Pasha to the town of Irbid where a medical examination was made. The medical report concluded that she was no longer a virgin. (It was reported that the autopsy after her death discovered her to be three months pregnant.) After the examination, the girl's father returned with his daughter to his home in the Jordan Valley.

Early the next day on the morning of the great Muslim "Festival of Sacrifice," the father took his daughter to Deir Abu Said where he went with her to the doorstep of the guardian of the young men (father of one and uncle of the other) who had perpetrated the deed and stabbed her with his dagger. This act of killing on the doorstep of the culprit's guardian was to show the latter that he was responsible for the shame brought upon the girl, the loss of her kinsman's honor, and her subsequent death.

The news of the girl's death reached Kufr al-Ma shortly after the men of the village had left the mosque after the dawn prayers celebrating the Festival of Sacrifice. Immediately, the men and boys of the village set out in a body for Deir Abu Said in a demonstration of feeling against the Zaydan. They forced all the shopkeepers to shut their doors and, proceeding to the culprits' houses, found them guarded by police. Several informants told me they would have burned them down had it not been for the presence of armed force. They then went to the police post where the girl's father was imprisoned. He had voluntarily surrendered himself after the murder. (He later told me that he would have fled to the forest and hidden there had it not been for the fact that his cousin, the Pasha, would have been taken into custody had he done so.) The crowd stood below the police post and demanded to see the prisoner, whereupon he was brought out to the balcony briefly. The crowd cheered him.

Shortly after the murder, the family of the third culprit, who lived not in Deir Abu Said but in Kufr Awan (see Map 1, p. 3), sought sanctuary with a clan in a nearby village, the Rabab'a of Kufr Rakib. The Zaydan, refused sanctuary by "the peoples of Tibne," then went to the Rabab'a seeking protection from them.

The leader of the Rabab'a then came to the Pasha, notifying him of the request for protection by the Zaydan. The Pasha had no objection to the Rabab'a undertaking this obligation. But he insisted that the leader of the Rabab'a return and furnish him with a genealogical tree that would show which of the Zaydan were linked through the third patrilineal ancestor—that is, the culprits' brothers, descendants through their paternal grandfathers and their paternal grandfather's brothers. All of the men so linked had to evacuate the village within three days and seek residence in another area outside of the district. Those linked to the culprits through the fourth or paternal great-grandfather would have to pay "the sleeping camel" (*jamal nawm*), a certain sum which gave them the right to continue living in the area. The descendants linked through the paternal great-great-grandfather had merely to seek formal sanctuary (protection without true payment or flight). Otherwise, they were unaffected.

After the flight had been carried out, a number of incidents occurred which strained the relations between the government authorities and the villagers of Kufr al-Ma. Shots were fired in the night near the house of a member of the Zaydan. A Zaydan orchard was plundered by young men from Kufr al-Ma.

Shortly after these incidents, the mukhtar of Beni Yasin and a large landowner of the same clan, Yusuf al-Tuluq, whose son had been mishandled by the police, went to the house of an employee of the municipality of Deir Abu Said. This employee was a member of Beni Yunis. Both the mukhtar and Yusuf urged the employee to resign along with his fellow employees unless the municipality offices were moved from the building of a Zaydan member (the guardian of the culprits) where they were then situated. Yusuf al-Tulq appealed to the employee on the basis of the solidarity of "the peoples of Tibne":

> We are of Tibne and you are of Tibne. Our honor is one. Where is your manliness? If you don't pull with us this time we will never again come to your aid in an emergency.

When the news of these machinations reached the head of the municipality, a political opponent of the Pasha, he went straight to the district officer in Irbid and charged Yusuf al-Tuluq with sowing discord. Yusuf was picked up by the police by order of the district officer and exiled from the area for a period of several months. It was also believed that Yusuf's exile was due to his threat to charge the police with maltreatment of the young men of the village. The Pasha intervened directly with the district officer and was able to soften the terms of Yusuf's exile. He spent the two months of his banishment in the woodlands living in a tent and caring for his sheep, as was his usual summer habit.

When I left the village, the men charged with the crime were still in jail; the father of the girl had been released on bail awaiting trial. Yusuf had returned to Kufr al-Ma, perhaps chastened for his folly. The father of the girl told me that there could never be a peacemaking with the criminals and that one of them would have to be killed when they were released from jail. The mukhtar representing Beni Yasin told me that there could never be a peacemaking unless the closest agnate of the culprits (father of one, uncle of the other) killed them. But the mukhtar of Beni Dumi who was not so involved in political intrigue and who, in any case, was not of the descendants of Hammad, although his clan was identified with "the peoples of Tibne," thought that a peacemaking was probable. He said that eventually the government would force the father of the girl to make a settlement.

Two important facts are illustrated by this case.[35] First, political cooperation does take place on a supravillage level. The Pasha called in the notables from the several villages that were settled by "the peoples of Tibne." He capitalized on the numerous ties that linked him with the inhabitants of these villages and persuaded them to reject the plea of sanctuary made by the Zaydan.

Second, this action, to a large extent, was based on certain norms of political behavior that are still appealed to among the inhabitants of the villages who trace their origin to Tibne. Yusuf al-Tuluq appealed to these norms. The Pasha's appeal was answered while Yusuf's was not responded to, and only ended in his banishment. Even today, this concept of ideological unity based on place of origin and descent has significance for political interaction on the subdistrict level.

B. The Definition of Social Units: Sib, Clan,
Lineage, Luzum, and Household

I have referred rather loosely, thus far, to the three large named groups of patrilineal kinsmen who inhabit Kufr al-Ma—Beni Yasin, Beni Dumi, and Beni 'Amr—as clans. I have also stated that of the three only Beni Yasin traces its descent to Hammad although the other clans are counted as among "the peoples of Tibne." There are in addition, four smaller independent descent groups living in the village. Three of them (Wazir, Shuqayrat, and Rifa'iya) are counted among "the peoples of Tibne." Moreover, of the three, one (Wazir) traces its descent to Hammad and another (Shuqayrat) is connected to him by a critical marriage to one of his descendants. Each of the three clans has members scattered in three villages—Kufr al-Ma, Rehaba, and Tibne. (I am not considering here labor migrants who live in other towns for temporary periods.) The great majority of those who bear the name Yasin, Dumi, or 'Amr live in Kufr al-Ma. Henceforth these local groups (of Yasin, Dumi, or 'Amr) will be referred to as "clans" while the term "sib" will be used to refer to the aggregate Beni Yasin (or Dumi or 'Amr) wherever its members may be living. Similarly, I have termed the subunits of the sib, "subsibs," and the local resident groups of the subsib, "lineages." I have chosen this terminology in order to distinguish the local group of patrilineal kinsmen whose significance is primarily economic, political, and arbitral from the dispersed group of patrilineal kinsmen whose significance is mainly ideological. It is the clans and lineages that will be analyzed in this monograph rather than the sibs and subsibs, since the former perform the most important functions in the village. The clans and lineages and not the sibs and subsibs are the important units of political representation. It is the clan and not the sib that is represented by a mukhtar.

Table 9 records the number of people in each of the clans and lineages in the village. Each clan or lineage includes the resident men of the group, their wives, whatever their patrilineal affiliation or village of origin, and their children. The totals below, then, are essentially the households living in the village. The figures in the right-hand column are based on the mukhtar's official census compiled for the government wheat distribution.[36] These figures were submitted to the government and formed the basis for the subsequent distribution of wheat in the village. Thus the clan and the lineage and their constituent households are the units of practical administration. In all relations with the government it is not the sib and subsib which is important, for these members are scattered among several villages, but the local descent group—the clan and the lineage.

Table 10 shows the sibs and subsibs of the village and their degree of dispersion. The four independent lineages (Wazir, Shuqayrat, Rifa'iya, and Ikhtaba) are included under the heading of subsib since all four have families of their named unit living in other villages.

While most of the members of the subsibs are living in the three villages of Kufr al-Ma, Rehaba, and Tibne, certain subsibs (e.g., 'Ibadi,

TABLE 9

COMPOSITION OF LOCAL DESCENT GROUPS IN KUFR AL-MA

Type of Descent Group	Name of Descent Group	Number of Households Censused By the Author	Total Number of Persons in the Group Based on the Author's Census	Total Number of Persons in the Group Based on Mukhtar's Census
Clan	Beni Yasin	76	493	786
Clan	Beni Dumi	50	338	548
Clan	Beni 'Amr	31	205	359
Lineage	Wazīr	9	46	46
Lineage	Shuqayrāt	10	71	124
Lineage	Rifā'iya	8	52	55
Lineage	Ikhtaba	7	42	51
Palestinian Refugee Families		4	28	28
Other Families		4	30	30
Village Totals		199	1305*	2027
Lineages of Yasin:	Massā'di	27	178	304
	Qar'oosh	15	101	151
	'Aqayli	10	59	143
	Shujūr	6	48	
	Sabbāh	10	55	94
	As'eed	8	52	94
Lineages of Dumi:	Basbūs	10	60	
	Diyāka	6	43	
	Khalaf	6	32	
	Husayn	5	35	
	Hasan	5	27	
	Qarāqzi	8	69	
	Al Hilu	4	29	
	Shehem	3	18	
	Kamal	3	25	
Lineages of 'Amr:	Sālim	7	45	
	Ghānim	5	40	
	'Ibādi	4	20	
	Jabāli	3	21	
	Al 'Asali	2	11	
	Daknoosh	3	19	
	'Udūl	2	12	
	Berek	2	13	
	Dhiyyabāt	3	24	

*Although my census covers only sixty-five percent of the total population, it includes more than seventy-five percent of the permanent residents of the village, since a large number of men who work outside the village claim Kufr al-Ma as their home.

As'eed, Shuqayrat) have branches in other villages (see Table 10). Thus, while descent creates a profusion of ties between three particular villages—Kufr al-Ma, Tibne, and Rehaba—it also links certain families in Kufr al-Ma with other villages of "the peoples of Tibne" such as Inbe and Jenin and even with villages not so linked by a common historical experience such as Samad, Juffein, and Izmaliya (see Map 1, p. 3, for locations of these villages). Economic and marriage ties, of course, create an even wider network of intervillage links (see Diagram 1, p. 29).

A second important aspect of the sib, besides dispersion, is the depth and authenticity of its genealogy. The depth of the patrilineal genealogy furnished me by Beni Yasin varied from nine to eleven generations depending on the particular branch assessed. The genealogies of Beni 'Amr and Beni Dumi varied in depth from seven to nine generations.[37]

The patrilineal genealogies furnished by clans and sibs[38] are not always an accurate statement of their consanguineal relationships Many lineages have settled in the village permanently and identified themselves with one or another of the clans. In addition, individual families who have settled in the middle of a clan area, supported its mukhtar financially, and married the patrilineally related women of the clan over several generations have come to regard themselves as bona fide members of the clan. It was only after some time that I discovered that Khalid al-Majdub, a man who had identified himself as of the Massa'di lineage of Beni Yasin, had a paternal grandfather who was a Christian. Conversion to Islam, marriage to women of the clan, and residence in the Yasin quarter had, over several generations, been almost enough to erase the distinctive origin of his ancestors. Likewise, many members of the Dumi clan classified the Shuqayrat as being "of Dumi" because they lived in the Dumi quarter and supported the Dumi mukhtar, who had married one of their women.

Not only is the veracity of the patrilineal genealogies questionable, but also the native terms for these descent groups are applied somewhat indiscriminately. Villagers from Kufr al-Ma tracing their locality and/or descent to Tibne and its founders refer to themselves as "the peoples of Tibne" and occasionally as "the clans of Tibne" (*'ashā'ir tibnah**).[39] I have never heard the whole aggregate descended from Hammad referred to as an *'ashīra* or the peoples who historically lived in Tibne and defended its surrounding area referred to as an 'ashira. (Neither have I heard them referred to as a "tribe"—*qabīla*.) The aggregates classified as sibs are also referred to by the term 'ashira. While the term may refer to all members of Beni Yasin wherever they might be living (i.e., the sib, Beni Yasin), in many contexts the term was used to refer only to the patrilineal relatives living in Kufr al-Ma along with their wives and children (i.e., the clan, Beni Yasin).

In the same way, the aggregates classified as subsibs (e.g., Qar'oosh, Basbus) are referred to by the term *fandi* (defined by the dictionary as species, sort, branch, bough, numerous company).[40] But, again, in many contexts the term was used to refer only to the patrilineal relatives living in the village along with their wives and children,

***

*The term 'ashira which I have translated as "clan" also has the following dictionary meanings: kindred, cognation, tribe, kinsfolk on the father's side.

TABLE 10

SIBS AND SUBSIBS OF KUFR AL-MA

Type of Social Unit	Name of Social Unit	Villages in Which Members Are Located
Sib	Beni Yasin	
Subsib of Yasin	Massā'di	Rehaba, Tibne, Izmaliya, Kufr al-Ma, Deir Abu Said
Subsib of Yasin	Qar'oosh	Kufr al-Ma, Tibne, Izmaliya, Khanziri
Subsib of Yasin	'Aqayli	Kufr al-Ma, Rehaba, Tibne, Inbe
Subsib of Yasin	Sabbāh	Rehaba, Kufr al-Ma
Subsib of Yasin	Shujūr	Kufr al-Ma
Subsib of Yasin	As'eed	Jenin, Tibne, Kufr al-Ma
Subsib of Yasin	As'ayyad*	Tibne, Kufr al-Ma
Sib	Beni Dumi	
Subsib of Dumi	Basbūs	Kufr al-Ma
Subsib of Dumi	Diyāka	Kufr al-Ma, Rehaba
Subsib of Dumi	Khalaf	Kufr al-Ma, Izmaliya (Jordan Valley)
Subsib of Dumi	Husayn	Kufr al-Ma
Subsib of Dumi	Hasan	Kufr al-Ma
Subsib of Dumi	Qarāqzi	Kufr al-Ma, Rehaba
Subsib of Dumi	Al Hilu	Kufr al-Ma, Izmaliya, Deir Abu Said
Subsib of Dumi	Shehem	Kufr al-Ma
Subsib of Dumi	Shara'*	Kufr al-Ma, Rehaba
Subsib of Dumi	Kamal	Kufr al-Ma
Sib	Beni 'Amr	
Subsib of 'Amr	Sālim	Kufr al-Ma, Rehaba, Tibne
Subsib of 'Amr	Ghānim	Kufr al-Ma
Subsib of 'Amr	'Ibādi	Samad, Rehaba, Kufr al-Ma
Subsib of 'Amr	Jabāli	Kufr al-Ma, Rehaba
Subsib of 'Amr	Al 'Asali	Kufr al-Ma, Tibne
Subsib of 'Amr	Dakhnoosh	Kufr al-Ma
Subsib of 'Amr	'Udūl	Kufr al-Ma, Rehaba, Juffein
Subsib of 'Amr	Berek	Kufr al-Ma, Rehaba
Subsib of 'Amr	Dhiyyabāt	Kufr al-Ma, Izmaliya (Jordan Valley)
Subsib (Independent)	Wazir	Kufr al-Ma, Deir Abu Said, Tibne, Abu al-Qein
Subsib (Independent)	Rifā'iya	Kufr al-Ma, Tibne, Inbe
Subsib (Independent)	Ikhtaba	Kufr al-Ma, Juffein
Subsib (Independent)	Shuqayrāt	Kufr al-Ma, Juffein, Izmaliya

*The single Shara' household in the village always aligns itself with Qaraqzi; the single As'ayyad household always aligns itself with As'eed; therefore, they do not constitute lineages in Kufr al-Ma and are not indicated separately on Table 9.

that is, to the lineage. In other words, the term 'ashira refers to both the clan and the sib and the term fandi refers to the lineage as well as the subsib, depending on the context in which the term is used. Government officials whose vocabulary is heavily influenced by classical Arabic, often use the term to *Hamūla* to refer to the clan and use this term in its plural form to refer to "the clans of Tibne."[41]

Although the lineage may be the smallest unit of descent in the village composed only of its constituent households, many of the larger lineages are subdivided into units sometimes referred to in the singular as *luzum*. I first heard the term luzum not in reference to a group but in relation to marriage. A female first patrilateral cousin was referred to as *bint 'amm luzum*. A literal translation of this colloquial Arabic term would be "must" or "obligatory". It was obligatory that the girl be offered in marriage to her first patrilateral cousin before she could be offered to any other. Second and third patrilateral cousins were also referred to as *bint 'amm* but without the suffix since the obligation was not considered as binding in their case, although strong objections would be raised by her closest patrilateral cousins if she were offered in marriage to someone else (see Case 5, pp. 66–69, and Case 6, pp. 74–77).

The term luzum was also used in reference to a particular group. One man, before signing his name on a paper creating a village committee that would later have the job of collecting money, asked the meaning of his signing the paper. He said, "Am I responsible for collecting money from the whole of Beni 'Amr? I can only be responsible for my luzum." By luzum he meant his brothers, paternal uncles, and paternal cousins who constituted a family in the village that was identified as "Beni Ghanim." The youngest living adult males of this group were descendants of a single great-grandfather. Because the luzum here coincided with a named group of patrilineal kinsmen living in the same quarter (see Map 2A, p. 74) and was large and influential enough to seek representation on village committees, I concluded that Beni Ghanim was a lineage.

In the course of fieldwork, however, I noted a number of groups above the level of the family and below the level of the lineage who seemed to act as a unit politically. They supported one another in quarrels. They contributed to the compensation collected in cases of honor involving any one of their members. They consulted one another during negotiations for marriage. Often, they attended funerals as a group. In many cases they continued to hold undivided land which, though it was a matter of common interest, often caused antagonism among them. These men lived in separate houses and were part of separate households. They continued, however, to live in the same village area and were often next door neighbors.

The luzum, then, is the close consultation group, whether this consultation be economic, political, or strictly social in nature. Although the core of the luzum is a group of patrilineal kinsmen, matrilateral relatives and affines may also be included. Whatever their relationship, they expect to be consulted by each other in local political matters, marriage negotiations, and the sale and division of land.

Each luzum consists of a number of households. The household is the smallest permanent economic unit in the village. A household possesses a common purse to which all members contribute. This contribution may be in the form of farm labor whose end result is a grain crop which is placed in a common bin or money earned in nonagricultural occupations such as building, shopkeeping, manual labor, or service in the army. Whether this purse be monetary or nonmonetary, its disbursement rests solely with the oldest adult male who is the head of the household. In addition to being an independent economic unit, the household is usually a commensal unit and often a work unit. Its members work and eat together. They may not, however, be involved in constant face-to-face relationships. A soldier or laborer, for instance, might spend most of the year away from the village. But the wife of such a man will often remain with her husband's father in the village while the husband continues to contribute a large share of his income to the general upkeep of the single household which includes both father and son.

In the following sections of this chapter each of the social units defined here—the household, the luzum, the lineage, and the clan—will be analyzed in terms of their functions and their general significance in village life.

C. The Household

In Kufr al-Ma the household is defined by the existence of a common purse to which all members contribute. This purse (whether monetary or nonmonetary) is disbursed solely by the oldest adult male who is the head of the household. The household, then, is a consumption unit rather than a production unit in the strict sense. This fact should be noted since many anthropologists working in tribal and peasant societies have stressed the cooperation in productive tasks (agriculture or herding) among the members of a household. The occupational structure of the village indicates that such cooperation is not present in Kufr al-Ma, for only a minority of the working men are engaged in agriculture.

For example, it might be assumed that the forty "extended families" in the village remained together in order to carry out productive tasks, but of these only twelve include fathers and sons or brothers engaged in the same activity.[43] Eleven of these households tilled the land while the twelfth was engaged in stonecutting. Of the remainder, in seven households the father farmed while the son served in the army, in five households the father engaged in shopkeeping while the son served in the army, and in four the father was retired while the son served in the army. Among the fraternal extended families, the first numbered one brother in the army, another in school, and a third in agriculture, the second numbered one farmer, one soldier, and one who was idle; and the third numbered one soldier and one student. Thus, the very families that might be expected to cooperate in productive activity due to the manpower they represent—the extended families—do not do so. They do not operate as work teams under the direction of the head of the household. They do, however, form units of "organic solidarity" in the sense that the development of different occupational specializations contributes to the maintenance of a single social and economic unit—the household. [44] Often, the son who spends eleven months of the year in an army camp leaves his wife in his father's house where she remains under her father-in-law's authority and under her mother-in-law's direction in carrying out agricultural and domestic tasks.

The size of the household (see Table 11) varies from a single person (in the case of two bachelors) to twenty-two in the case of a man living with three wives and their children. Seventy-nine percent of the households censused included five or more persons while sixty-four percent included six or more persons with the modal number of persons in a household being seven (see Table 11). Despite the size of the households, the great majority of them (seventy-nine percent) may be described as "nuclear" rather than "extended" families. Of 195 households censused, thirty-eight percent were simple nuclear families with husband, wife, and unmarried children (see Table 12), twenty-four percent were nuclear families in an advanced stage, with married sons or daughters having left home and living in separate households, and twelve percent were simple nuclear families with the addition of a parent of one of the spouses, usually the husband's. Only nineteen percent constituted "parental" extended families and, as pointed out above, only one-third of these were productive farming units. [45] Finally, only four households were "fraternal" extended families.

Differences in family size and composition are not clearly related to certain occupations or to the possession of land. The army, for instance, is a lucrative occupation since soldiers receive a regular monthly salary. This salary provides for a much higher income than the income gained from agricultural work (see Chapter 2, pp. 33–34) even with a substantial amount of land. Since the opportunities for entrance into the army are often enhanced by giving the appropriate "gifts" to influential individuals, wealthy peasants are in a better position to gain army posts for their sons than poor peasants. A peasant with 325 dunums (eighty-one acres) and the second largest landowner in the village has three sons serving in the army while an indigent fellah from the village has tried without avail for over a year to register his son in the ranks of the Arab Legion. On the other hand, some men with sufficient land do not encourage their sons to enter the army. On the contrary, the traditional ideal of the successful peasant is to devote a bountiful harvest to each son in order to marry him and settle him permanently in the household of his father. Muhammad Husayn al-Hasan, for instance, who owns fifty acres, has married off four sons in this way. Three of them remain in his household as cultivators and a fourth resides in the village. Even Muhammad, however, was not able to retain all his sons, two of whom moved out of his house and founded independent households in the village. There does not, then, seem to be any clear-cut correlation between amount of land owned, occupation, and size and composition of the household.

TABLE 11

RANGE OF HOUSEHOLD SIZE IN KUFR AL-MA*

Number of Persons in Household	Number of Such Households	Percentage of Such Households
One	2	1%
Two	10	5%
Three	11	6%
Four	18	9%
Five	30	15%
Six	25	13%
Seven	41	21%
Eight	19	9%
Nine	19	9%
Ten	13	7%
Eleven	5	2%
Twelve or more	6	3%

*Tables 11 and 12 do not represent all households in the village. They represent only the households covered by my census. This census covered sixty-five percent of the total population and over seventy-five percent of the households actually residing in the village.

TABLE 12

COMPOSITION OF HOUSEHOLDS IN KUFR AL-MA ACCORDING
TO THE DEVELOPMENTAL CYCLE OF THE DOMESTIC GROUP

Type of Household	Number	Percentage
Husband and wife	10	5%
Husband and wife and one unmarried child	3	2%
Husband, wife and two unmarried children	10	5%
Husband, wife and three unmarried children	16	9%
Husband, wife (or wives), and four or more unmarried children	36	18%
Husband, wife (or wives), and one married son with spouse	27	14%
Husband, wife (or wives), and two married sons with spouses	7	4%
Husband, wife (or wives), and three married sons with spouses	2	1%
Husband, wife (or wives), unmarried children with married sons who have left the household	20	10%
Husband, wife (or wives), unmarried children with married daughters who have left the household	28	14%
Husband, wife, unmarried children plus parent of one of the spouses	24	12%
Brothers, their wives, and children	4	2%
Other	8	4%
Monogamous households	175	90%
Polygynous households (two wives)	17	9%
Polygynous households (three wives)	3	1%

There does seem to be some correlation, however, between polygyny and occupation. Fourteen of the twenty polygynous families censused cultivated the land. In four of the remaining six cases of polygyny, the husband's first wife had not borne him male heirs at the time of
his second marriage.

Because of the variety of occupations, it is not possible to trace a
developmental cycle of the family in terms of ecological factors[46] or
the expansion and contraction of productive farming units.[47] Nor is it
possible to explain differences of family size and composition in terms
of differential rules of inheritance and property control since the Islamic and secular ordinances governing these aspects of behavior are,
if applied, uniform for all villages.[48]

In spite of the difficulty of correlating the developmental cycle of
the family with economic, ecological, or social factors, a cycle of development does exist. Each stage in the family cycle does not, however, lead uniformly to the next. At every stage a number of future
possibilities exist depending on the size of the family, its structure
(monogamous, polygynous, fraternal extended, or parental extended),
the ages of its members, economic necessities (the possibility of feeding the growing group), spatial factors (the possibility of housing the
growing group), the sudden removal of one of its members (by death,
for instance), or the possibility of the fulfillment of parental norms
(such as the obligation of the father to provide the mahr for his son).
A few of the possibilities in the cycle of development are suggested in
Diagram 2. The circled numbers represent the number of such families
recorded in the village household census taken in 1960.

A census of household composition, while it may be a valuable indicator of a family cycle of development, is ambiguous.[49] For example,
in Kufr al-Ma ten households censused showed a man and wife living by
themselves. This particular type of household may be a couple who
have not had sufficient time to reproduce children, a couple long since
married but which has remained childless, or a couple whose married
children have moved away to set up separate households. In the case of
a single parent living with his or her son it is not clear whether the
group was living as an extended family when one of the parents died or
the young couple had established their own household before the death
and had taken in the surviving parent. In some cases, the widowed parent shuttles back and forth between the houses of his sons and cannot
truly be counted as a member of the household in which he is residing
at the time of the census.

Difficult as the reconstruction of the developmental cycle may be,
"fission," when it occurs, often follows predictable lines.[50] This is
particularly true of the polygynous family. On the death of the father
the uterine sons together with their mother establish a separate household. Often the fission of the polygynous family occurs during the life
of the father soon after he marries the second wife. With the marriage
of each new wife, the previous spouse moves into the house of her eldest son, who provides for her from then on. Thus many polygynous
families in the village are merely legal units since the husband lives
with and supports only one of his wives.

The importance of the matricentral unit (the mother and her children) is reflected, more particularly, in the strength of the mother-son tie. Of the twenty-two nuclear families which included a mother in addition to the spouses and their children, in twenty she was the husband's mother. While twenty-two mothers lived as dependents in their sons' households only two fathers were dependents of their children. This situation may be related to the age discrepancy between husbands and wives which results in a greater incidence of widows than widowers

DIAGRAM 2

POSSIBLE RECONSTRUCTION OF THE DEVELOPMENTAL CYCLE OF THE FAMILY IN KUFR AL-MA
(based on the census of households — 1960)

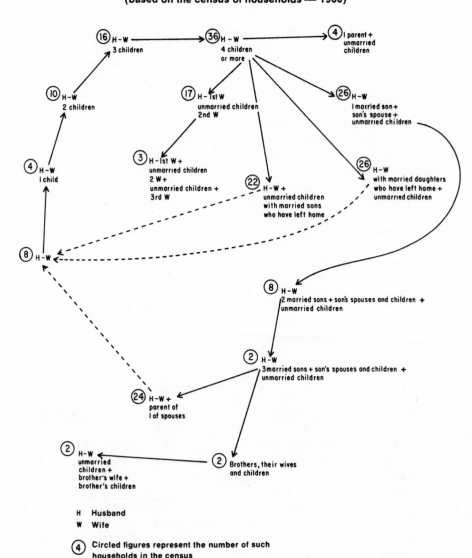

and to the man's unilateral right of divorce and the institution of polygyny which allows men to slough off wives rather than the opposite.

Just as the lines of the fission of the household can sometimes be foreseen in advance so can the causes of the fission. Population increase often taxes the nutritional and spatial capacities of the household. After a succession of poor agricultural years, a father may tell his married son to move out and provide for his own family. This is particularly understandable in the light of the subsistence nature of agriculture in Jordan. The shortage of space may contribute to pressure for fission. In the crowded center of the village there may be no room for a married son. Islamic law and local custom prescribe that each married pair shall have a separate room. Crowding often results in tensions between cowives or mother-in-law and daughter-in-law and adds to the mounting pressure for fission.

Disagreements among women are often cited as the causes for fission. Mothers-in-law often lock food provisions in a chest to assert their authority over their daughters-in-law who can only have access to the chest by formally asking for the use of the key. Mistreatment of one another's children is another cause of disagreement. These quarrels, however, are more often the occasion and the excuse for fission rather than the cause.

Occupational differentiation with resulting differences in "styles of life" exacerbate tensions already existing in an extended family and often result in fission. [51] The women marrying into an extended family insist on equality of treatment from their husbands. This insistence on equality is supported by Islamic law and local norms. However, when their husbands receive different incomes as a result of following different occupations, equality of treatment is not possible. For instance, two brothers who entered the army left their wives with their third and youngest brother who continued to farm the land which was their joint possession. After a few months the soldiers came home on furlough bringing their wives new outfits. The wife of the youngest brother demanded a new outfit too. The soldiers refused the request of their younger brother. Shortly thereafter, the older brothers took their wives to the army camp where they set up separate households while still maintaining their claim to the joint property over which the youngest brother had de facto control.

The household has no necessary relation to any particular type of dwelling unit. Moreover, there are no ready indices of its existence such as separate entrances or granaries or ritual shrines. Indeed, the demarcation of a household by dwelling unit may be quite erroneous as the following case illustrates.

CASE TWO

This case began with my arrival in Kufr al-Ma. I was lodged in one room of a two-room dwelling located in the center of the village and belonging to one of its independent families, the Wazirs. My neighbors in the adjoining room (which was separate from my own although there was a small connecting door) consisted of a man, Hasan (B7 on Chart 8), fifty years of age, his two elderly sisters (B3 and B5), his wife (B8), and his infant child (C4). At various times, his wife's son by a previous marriage (C5) and his sister's daughter and son (C2 and C3) and his sister's nephew (C1) visited the room and often spent the night there. I assumed that Hasan was the head of this household and from time to time disbursed gifts through him to the whole family. I was especially dependent on one of his sisters (B5), who regularly washed my clothes, baked my bread, and cleaned my room. She was a "forsaken woman," *maHjūra* — not divorced but no longer cohabiting or residing with her husband (B6) — living separately with her sister as, I assumed, a member of her brother's household. Hasan himself was my first real informant, and I often accompanied him to the fields where he ploughed, seeking information about the agricultural regime. My assumption that these individuals constituted a household rested on three observations: first, three of the five were siblings; second, they were living at close quarters in a single room; and third, they often ate together around a common bowl. This notion was corrected early one morning when I was awakened by the din of a violent argument between Hasan and his sisters. The immediate cause of the argument was a straw mat which I had given to Hasan but which was intended for the entire household. The sisters accused Hasan of greed and of taking advantage of my generosity. They said that the room was not Hasan's but belonged to their deceased brother (B1) and they declared that they were going to appeal to the mukhtar of Beni Yasin to eject Hasan from the room. Hasan replied that it was his room as much as theirs and that he would not budge from it. Shortly after the argument, the sisters moved the few household utensils they possessed, their own food supplies, and my sack of flour (from which the sister drew to bake my bread and their own, and from which Hasan had been filching) to one side of the room while Hasan and his wife moved their belongings (including the straw mat) to the other. An imaginary line was drawn across the room which neither side crossed for several days except to exit by the common door.

This disturbance directed my attention more closely to the nature of the ties between my next door neighbors. On checking the genealogies of Hasan and his sisters I found that they were only half siblings (see Chart 3, p. 57). The deceased brother (B1) who had owned the room was the sisters' full brother and only Hasan's seminal halfbrother. Hasan had come with his new wife and their child and "squatted" in the room in which his sisters had been residing alone. Payment of the mahr for his wife had exhausted Hasan's financial resources and he was unable to provide a home for her, other than that which he claimed by a tie of half siblingship. The meal around the common bowl had been more of a formality than an indication of a common consumption unit. Whenever Hasan's wife cooked, she invited his sisters to sit with them and share the meal and vice versa. The sisters would eat a few bites, as a matter of courtesy, and retire. My indiscriminate apportionment of gifts, and provision of a sack of flour from which both

drew, precipitated a crisis that made the separateness of the households crystal clear. In spite of their close blood relationship and their
residence in a single room, Hasan and his sisters with their respective
kinsmen formed two separate households. Thereafter, I meticulously
divided my gifts and supplies to my neighbors on the basis of equality
between households in line with the structural realities.

The coresidence of fathers and sons, like the coresidence of
brothers and sisters, is not indicative of the presence of a single
household. Fathers and sons often live with their respective spouses
and children in the separate rooms of a two-room house. They may or
may not constitute a household. Often the son's wife cooks separately
for her husband and this usually indicates separate households. But the
critical factor in defining a household, as mentioned, is the existence
of a separate purse. In the case of a son serving in the army and housing his wife in his father's house, albeit in a separate room, it is difficult to establish the existence of such a purse. Often sons hand over a
large proportion of their salary to their father but whether this sum is
merely in payment for keeping his wife, a donation out of filial piety,
or a genuine contribution to a common purse is difficult to establish.

CHART 3

THE HOUSEHOLD OF HASAN AL-WAZIR (Case 2)

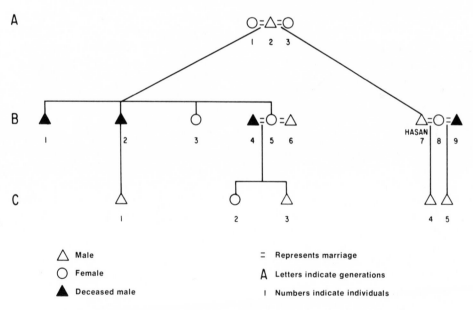

△ Male	= Represents marriage
○ Female	A Letters indicate generations
▲ Deceased male	I Numbers indicate individuals

Often sons return to their father's home after long absences and take
their meals jointly with their father and brothers during their stay. Yet
father and sons have long since ceased to be members of a single
household. On the other hand, father and son may live in different villages and till different plots of land, while still constituting a single
household. Again, a son who works in town may leave one of his wives

in his father's house under his father's authority while continuing to provide all of her necessities.

The size and form of a dwelling does, however, offer some indication of the general type of household housed within it. A one-room house is almost invariably occupied by a nuclear family. A three-room house is often occupied by an extended family. A house of five or six rooms with an inner courtyard for livestock, a formal gateway, and several inner rooms for the women of the household is often occupied by a polygynous family.

In former times, the correlation between dwelling type and household was probably much closer. Houses consisted of a single huge room with a raised platform. At night, the family's livestock was kept below the platform in the front part of the house. The families living inside these houses were usually parental or fraternal extended families or polygynous families who cooperated in productive tasks such as farming or herding. With the differentiation of the occupational structure, the changes in family structure, and the decrease in the number of families acting as large productive units, most such houses have become obsolete and have been torn down or abandoned.

In summary, the household is essentially an economic unit defined by the contributions of its members to a common purse which is in turn disbursed by its head. It may or may not be a productive unit. It may or may not be a commensal unit. It is not a ritual unit. It has no fixed relation to size or form of dwelling. It can be composed of any of a number of family types—nuclear, paternal extended, fraternal extended, and polygynous. The developmental cycle of the families that compose it is complicated by a differentiated occupational structure which makes analysis of the cycle in terms of ecology or the expansion and contraction of productive units impossible. The lines of its fission at various stages can, however, be predicted in many cases as well as the causes for the split.

D. The Luzum: Close Kinsmen in Cooperation and Conflict[52]

In section B the luzum was defined in functional terms as the close consultation group. It is the unit larger than the household and smaller than the lineage whose members expect to be consulted by each other in local political matters, marriage negotiations, and the sale or division of land. These men live in separate houses and constitute separate households, but live in the same village area and are often next door neighbors.

The luzum also performs critical functions for social control. It is this group that is immediately implicated in cases of honor (e.g., murder, homicide, mayhem, assault, elopement, fornication, adultery, rape) to which its members are party. The members of the luzum related by patrilineal descent are obliged to contribute to the "truce money" (*uTwa*) demanded by the victim's group as the price of postponing retaliation pending a permanent settlement. Those obliged to contribute to the truce money include the culprit and his brothers and their descendants, his father and his brothers and their descendants, and his paternal grandfather and his brothers and their descendants. His paternal great-grandfather and his brothers and their descendants are obliged to make a separate payment named "the sleeping camel" (jamal nawm). In return for this payment they are allowed to remain in their homes and are given official protection of person and property. The descendants of the first three agnatic generations, however, must abandon their homes and seek refuge in another area pending final reconciliation (SulHa). Here, then, is the reality behind the "must" conveyed by the term, luzum. Patrilineality is not merely an ideology of descent, but rather the structural principle that underlies tribal law. It is just the individuals mentioned above who constitute the core of the close consultation group if not its total membership.

The membership of the luzum varies considerably. Often the luzum is composed of a group of first or second patrilateral cousins (*banu 'amm*), but it may consist of a group of half-brothers or full brothers. Although its core is a number of patrilineally related men, it may, in exceptional cases, include affines and matrilateral relatives. Often the group is not referred to by the term luzum or by any other distinctive appellation. In other cases it is a named subgroup of a lineage. Such a group of first patrilateral cousins are the Sibba'i (see Chart 4). The fathers of this group of first cousins lived in the same house as one household. This is often the case of the previous generation of men whose sons now constitute the senior generation of the luzum.

Distinguishing the close consultation group from the lineage is not always easy. The difficulty is one that characterizes the structure of Arab descent groups in general, particularly those found in rural and tribal areas. The difficulty is that ideologically, structurally, and functionally, Arab descent groups form a continuum or an overlapping series rather than a set of discrete and inclusive units.[53] I have already referred to the ambiguity of the terms of reference for descent groups e.g., 'ashira, fandi, humula (see pp. 46–48). Likewise, it is difficult to establish how large a descent group must be or how great its genealogical depth or how many collateral segments it must comprehend before it becomes a lineage.

Similarly, functional criteria are also ambiguous. Members of the luzum must consult one another when arranging the marriages of their daughters, but such consultation is also expected of lineage mates. In disposing of land a man should consult both his luzum and his lineage mates before selling it to outsiders. In cases of honor patrilineally related members of the luzum must contribute to the blood money, but members of the lineage are also expected to contribute. Indeed, all members of the village are expected to contribute though in diminishing amounts. Even strictly ethical obligations such as reconciling kinsmen or showing respect for elders, although they fall more heavily on the members of the luzum, are clan-wide and village-wide obligations (see Cases 7, and 8 below, pp. 78–87, pp. 97–102).

Making distinctions between different order descent groups is not impossible but such classification necessarily entails incongruence of descent in much the same way that the sociologist's attempt to separate and rank classes in American society entails incongruence of status:

individuals and groups that rank high by one set of criteria rank low by another. When most formal structural attributes are present but one or two are missing, what classification is to be made? For example, a lineage, as indicated above, must contain significant subdivisions but it must also, itself, be a significant subdivision of a larger group. A lineage (as the Arabic term fandi literally suggests) is a "branch." The independent families (Shuqayrat, Rifa'iya, Ikhtaba) as well as a number of other families of known separate historical origins (e.g., Basbus, Qaraqzi, 'Ibadi—see Table 9, p. 45) cannot trace genealogical links to

CHART 4

THE SIBBA'I LUZUM (Cases 3 and 4)

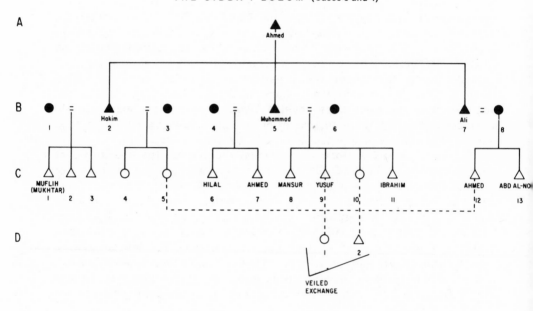

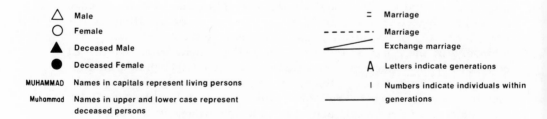

△	Male	=	Marriage
○	Female	- - - - - -	Marriage
▲	Deceased Male		Exchange marriage
●	Deceased Female	A	Letters indicate generations
MUHAMMAD	Names in capitals represent living persons	I	Numbers indicate individuals within
Muhammad	Names in upper and lower case represent deceased persons		generations

collateral kinsmen in the vicinity in order to establish genuine consanguineal affiliation with an inclusive higher order unit, the clan. And yet, they are groups of five generations in genealogical depth, with distinctive proper names, and of such a size as to qualify as lineages. The last three groups mentioned have to a large extent overcome this formal impediment by claiming to be members of a clan (i.e., by claiming to be "of Dumi" or "of 'Amr") and their claims are not rejected although their separate historical origins are known. (See section B, pp. 44–49, and J, pp. 109–13, for the process by which "stranger" groups are incorporated into the clan structure.) Other groups such as the independent families can never be lineages in the fullest formal sense of the term since they insist on maintaining their identity as "independent" families of separate origin and descent refusing to associate with any higher order group, i.e., with any clan. And yet the very groups that are disqualified structurally from assuming full lineage status by fact of their separate historical origins are the most aggressive about claiming full lineage status functionally. That is, they press their claim for political representation on village committees. The comparative social solidarity of the clans may be another important factor in determining whether a close consultation group claims lineage status. Beni Yasin is quite clearly the most unified of the clans while Beni 'Amr is the least unified (see pp. 88–90 and pp. 102–103). Very few of the luzums of Yasin seek lineage status, for they are represented politically by a mukhtar and by the influential elders of their large and comparatively wealthy lineages. The close consultation groups of 'Amr, however (e.g., Jabali, 'Ibadi, Dakhnoosh, Berek, 'Udul, Al 'Asali) are not represented by a mukhtar nor are there any large and influential lineages within their own clan (see Table 9, p. 45). There is a strong tendency, therefore, for each luzum to act as a lineage in the political arena of the village. Each one usually seeks representation on village committees and, if excluded (a frequent occurence due to the large number of lineages in the village), works to obstruct their operation.

Notwithstanding the structural and functional complexity and resulting ambiguity discussed above, it is clear that the luzum represents a point in the developmental cycle beyond the joint fraternal or parental extended family and before the expansion of the group to such a size and genealogical depth that it comprises several collateral segments. In nearly every case a group that has a distinctive proper name attached to it (e.g., Khalaf, Al Hilu, Shujur) has bifurcated at least five generations back from the nearest other named group within the clan. What I am saying, then, is that a luzum develops in the grand-parental generation after the split of the single "house" (dar) into separate households. The lineage develops with the achievement of the necessary structural (size, genealogical depth, bifurcation, and the development of collateral segments with genealogical depth) and functional (economic and political power) attributes. The intermediate stage in the development of the lineage is usually marked by the use of a proper name to describe the group and the final stage in its development (when each lineage is recognized as one segment among other like segments in the clan) is marked when the term fandi is applied to the group.

In like manner, although functions are ranged in a continuum as one proceeds from the luzum to the lineage to the clan, the sanctions and other social consequences for nonperformance differ for the different order groups. The consequences of the refusal to give a daughter in marriage to a brother's son are not the same as the consequences of the refusal to give a daughter to a lineage mate (see Case 5, pp. 66–69, as opposed to Case 6, pp. 74–77). Likewise, the pressure brought to bear upon the members of the luzum to contribute truce money in a case of honor is great enough to prevent defaulting on the payment. On the other hand, lineage members, though they are subject to strong social pressures, are not legally bound to make a contribution. The legal obligation of the patrilineally related members of the luzum to pay is unequivocal and has been reinforced by the official support the Jordanian government gives to tribal law in cases of honor. The subdistrict officer will often insist that the offender's group produce a patrilineal genealogy in order to implement the tribal penalties precisely.

Although sanctions, point in the developmental cycle, and the attachment of names allow the analyst to distinguish between the close consultation group and the lineage, another discrepancy renders the distinction ambiguous in another sense. Sometimes a luzum which does not meet the structural definition of a lineage functions as a lineage. For instance, certain close consultation groups are lacking in size, genealogical depth, or collateral segmentation, and yet they possess the political influence and economic power that allows them, like lineages, to qualify for representation on village committees. Beni Ghanim and Khalaf, for instance, have considerable land in the village, Qaraqzi and Basbus are both large, and Qaraqzi includes the village schoolmaster and several school teachers among its members. Diyaka includes one of the village mayors among its members, Jabali numbers a former village mayor and a large landowner. Groups that do not fully qualify structurally as lineages act as lineages, politically (for the reasons suggested above) since they exert disproportionate power and influence in the arena of village politics. They are luzums of lineage status and are, therefore, represented according to their functional rather than their formal status. They are classified as lineages on Table 9 and Map 2 and will be treated as such in the text. The decision to give priority to functional over structural criteria is supported by the villagers' own evaluations. Thus many outsiders (nonlineage members) would not know whether the Qaraqzi can actually trace consanguineal relationships with other lineages of Dumi. Only a few insiders would know enough to validate the formal structural inadequacy of their claim. All villagers know, however, that the Qaraqzi are a sizeable group cooperating with the rest of Dumi, living in the Dumi quarter, supporting the Dumi mukhtar, and receiving recognition on village committees. Such evidence is quite sufficient to establish their status as a fandi.

Up to this point the luzum has been defined as a close consultation group enforcing traditional norms of kinship behavior and consulting on economic, social and political matters. However, traditional norms of kinship are often ignored, and the expectation of consultation is often disappointed with the almost inevitable consequence of estrangement between members of the luzum.

When the luzum is made up of brothers, full or half, one of the important obligations of the older married brothers toward the younger is to help them to marry by contributing to their marriage payment (mahr). Often, the deceased father's land is held undivided. But the tacit understanding between the brothers is that the harvests, after providing the needs of the respective households, are to go to the unmarried brothers as a contribution toward their mahr. Often this obligation is regarded as onerous by the older brothers and the group of brothers breaks up as an economic and consultation unit as soon as the younger brothers are married or even before that time.

Indeed, the very factors which tie the members of the luzum together—close patrilineal relationship (involving the obligation of giving one's daughter to one's closest patrilineal kinsman and providing one's younger unmarried brothers with marriage payments), common land ownership, and propinquity of residence and land may cause antagonism and estrangement, as the following case demonstrates. It also shows the exacerbation of tensions among close kinsmen and the new challenges to traditional norms of behavior as a result of occupational mobility and economic differentiation referred to in the first part of this chapter. What happens when the youngest members of a group of closely cooperating kinsmen achieve economic power while the eldest member is invested with traditional authority and formal political office? The case below suggests one possible resolution or, better, nonresolution of the problem.

CASE THREE

This case began when several elders of Beni Yasin accompanied by Ahmed al-Ali (C12 on Chart 4), the mukhtar's first patrilateral cousin, entered the mukhtar's guest house. The elders addressed the mukhtar (C1). They told him that it had come to their attention that he had been neglecting his own sister (C5). (She was the mukhtar's seminal half sister and had married her first patrilateral cousin, Ahmed al-Ali.) Why was it that the mukhtar had not visited her for nearly a year? This was not, they stated, conduct befitting an elder brother. The elders wished to reassure his sister's husband, Ahmed al-Ali (C12), before he returned to his army post that the mukhtar would be reconciled with his sister. The mukhtar replied that he had good reason for his actions. He said that when he had guests sitting in his guest house, he had often sent to his sister for some flour or butter to prepare a meal for them, and she had refused to provide anything. He said, moreover, that Ahmed al-Ali had not paid his yearly contribution of grain in support of his clan's mukhtar. Further exhortation by the elders did not move the mukhtar, and the meeting broke up.

The next day, the mukhtar told me that his sister had persuaded her husband not to register land in his, the mukhtar's name. This land was to be the mukhtar's share in the division of the joint property that

was still held undivided by the nine first patrilateral cousins after the
death of their three fathers. The mukhtar said that Ahmed refused to
register the land in his name unless he—the mukhtar—paid the twenty-
one dollar difference between the value of the land (seventy-five dollars) and the value of the mukhtar's share in the ancestral property
(fifty-four dollars). The mukhtar said that if he should die, his shares
would be lost to his children. He said that his first cousins had taken all
the furnishings of his father's house (this was done in his absence from
the village) and had left him with nothing. He said too that his sister
had sold a piece of land without consulting him. This was an act of in-
gratitude since it had occurred after his father (B2) had given his
daughter (the mukhtar's half sister) her entire mahr to keep, setting a
precedent in the village by so doing. He said that, customarily, the
sister relinquished her right to property in favor of her brother, but
his sisters had demanded and received shares in his father's property.

Later in the year, the mukhtar's hostility toward his first cousin
was expressed in the guest house in the presence of a stranger—a
Palestinian. The Palestinian's sister was married to Ahmed al-Ali's
younger brother (C13). The sister was living in Kufr al-Ma and had
complained to her brother that her husband had not been housing her in
suitable quarters. The brother had come to the village to look into the
matter. The elders of Beni Yasin agreed that Ahmed al-Ali was responsible for his brother's actions, since the brother was irresponsible by nature, and that he must house his sister-in-law in a certain vacant house that was now closed up. Ahmed al-Ali replied that the vacant
house was his house, and he would do with it as he pleased. The mukhtar bellowed, in a voice mixed with anger and indignation, that the
house in question was a joint property belonging to the nine cousins and
that, if necessary, he himself would go the next day, break down the
door, and house the neglected girl in it. Ahmed remained adamant, but
he was subdued by the chorus of elders who considered him to be in
error.

The tension between the mukhtar and his kinsmen was due in part
to a conflict between the traditional norms governing relations among
close patrilateral cousins and the economic situation. As the eldest of
the cousins and as mukhtar, Muflih al-Hakim expected his authority to
be deferred to by his younger kinsmen. At the very least, he expected
to be consulted on important matters such as property sale and to be
supported politically and economically in his office as mukhtar of the
clan. Yet, he, the eldest of a group of first patrilateral cousins (banu
'amm), had been neglected in the division of the inheritance. His sister—supported by his younger cousin, her husband—had disposed of
property without consulting him, had failed to support him economically, and had refused to register land in his name. Traditional norms
had been violated—the norm of equal inheritance among kinsmen of the
same degree of relationship (an Islamic rule as well as a local norm),
the norm of respect for the opinions of elders (particularly if they are
close kinsmen), and the norm of sister's deference to a brother's
wishes in property matters. The mukhtar took the opportunity of asserting his seniority over his first cousin when the Palestinian came

to the village. He roused the elders against Ahmed al-Ali and told him he would break open the door of the house, if need be.

Six of these nine cousins, including the mukhtar's own brother (C2), were soldiers. Their regular monthly salaries had allowed most of them to build new houses in the village. Each of the cousins, with one exception, had established a separate household consisting of his wife and children, whereas in the previous generation the nine cousins had lived with their fathers in one large house. The newly won economic independence of the younger cousins had allowed them to ignore the authority of their impoverished elder kinsman. Common ownership of property, close patrilineal relationship, the possession of important political office by one of their number — factors which should have served as a focus of common interest and cooperation — were, in the new situation, the source of antagonism and estrangement.

The new economic situation is not, however, solely responsible for disputes among the members of the luzum. Common ownership of property, preferential rules of marriage, expectations of consultation in mahr negotiation and of contribution to the marriage payment are traditional sources of conflict among the members of a luzum. The following case is an illustration of structural conflict within a luzum over such traditional issues.

CASE FOUR

This case involves five brothers (C6, C7, C8, C9, C11 on Chart 4). Their sister (C10) had been engaged to marry her third patrilateral parallel cousin (D2) who was also a classificatory cross cousin. The eldest of the brothers (C6) and the legal guardian of the girl, was only a half sibling of his sister and her three younger brothers. As a soldier he spent most of the year in the army camp. Consequently, the installments of his sister's mahr were handed over to her eldest full brother (C8) and not to him. The girl's fiancé (D2) was also a soldier and over the course of almost three years had nearly completed the payment of the mahr. Both sides felt that the betrothal had been unduly prolonged, and the soldier was anxious to complete the wedding arrangements.

It was decided that the wedding celebration should take place on the occasion of the eldest brother's (C6) next furlough. When he came to the village he asked his brothers to give him twenty pounds of the 600-dollar mahr in order that he might contribute it as *naqd* (literally, "cash") — the traditional wedding gift due to a sister from her brothers and other close patrilineal kinsmen. The three full brothers (C8, C9, and C11) refused. They said that they wished to keep the full mahr in order to marry the second youngest full brother (C9). The elder brother (C6) then tried to postpone the marriage until he could collect money to contribute to his sister and pay for the wedding celebration which, according to custom, should be held in the elder brother's house. The younger full brothers of the girl were particularly anxious to couple the two marriages. That is, they wished the sister (D1) of their sister's fiancé (D2) to take their own brother (C9) in marriage. There was some objection to this procedure since the second girl's father said that this would constitute exchange marriage (*badāyil*) which is prohibited by Islam (inasmuch as there was no payment of mahr). [54] The three full brothers denied this saying that both girls were being married with a mahr payment and it was only a coincidence that the marriages were taking place simultaneously. In fact, the brothers deliberately planned this "coincidence" in order to reduce expenses since both marriages could now be celebrated by one wedding celebration and one slaughtering. After several days of postponement and wrangling between the brothers, the eldest brother was finally forced to return to his army camp. The wedding celebration and feast for both marriages were held in his absence in the eldest full brother's house.

This case is another example of a luzum with joint ownership of land and expectation of common consultation acting as a disharmonious group of kinsmen whose differing structural positions (full vs. half siblings) inevitably produce conflicts of interest with regard to a single event—the marriage of their sister.

The last two cases (pp. 63–66) and the following case (pp. 66–69) also illustrate that not all members of the luzum play active roles in any given dispute. The structural range over which kinsmen are mobilized depends on the issues at stake. The marriage of daughters and sisters is primarily a family affair involving fathers and brothers although close cousins, lineage mates, and affines may become involved (see Case 6, pp. 74–77). When, however, the complete severance of brother-sister visiting relations engenders animosity between close patrilineal kinsmen and reduces political support for the clan leader, lineage and clan elders (and not just luzum members) become involved (see Case 3, pp. 63–65).

In the following case the refusal to give a daughter to a brother's son also results in estrangement among the members of a luzum, but only among those members immediately concerned—the two brothers. Yet even within this narrow range of social concern, estrangement may lead to serious economic consequences—interference with the performance of routine agricultural tasks. The following case illustrates the fragility of the concept, "the unity of the sibling group," and demonstrates that the very nature of village life and the necessities of economic and social cooperation set limits upon the level of social disruption that may be permitted within the close consultation group.

CASE FIVE

This case began when Uqla Abu Tabanji, a member of an independent village family, came to the mukhtar of Beni Yasin and the imam of the village (with whom he traced matrilateral relationship) and asked them to intervene on his behalf with his older brother, Muhammad. Muhammad had refused to give his daughter in marriage to Uqla's son. The deputation sent to ask the girl's hand in marriage seemed on the verge of success and in fact the women of the household had begun preparations for the betrothal feast when the negotiations broke down over the elder brother's demand for eight dunums (two acres) of land in addition to the 300-dollar mahr.

Nearly six weeks later the mukhtar, the imam, and an elder of Beni Yasin went to Muhammad Abu Tabanji's homestead on the outskirts of the village. (Muhammad was the only farmer who lived isolated from the rest of the village on his own lands. Uqla lived in Kufr al-Ma although his crop lands adjoined those of his brother.)

When they arrived, the mukhtar addressed the elder brother: "We have come to you over the case of Uqla."

He replied: "The girl is gone," meaning he would not consider her marriage to Uqla's son.

The elder of Yasin replied, "Yes, I know, but the son of the paternal uncle has priority (*ibn al 'amm awla*). The son is your son. The brother is your brother. Is there anyone more deserving?"

Muhammad replied, "I have taken an oath of divorce if I give my daughter to my brother."

The elder replied, "Your relatives have the inclination to take your daughter. People respect you and think highly of you."

Muhammad then said that he would give his daughter to Uqla's son only when Uqla's mind settled. He said he had agreed to give his daughter to Uqla for 300 dollars and eight dunums. Several months had elapsed without payment. He had made a mistake and now had no intention of giving his daughter.

The mukhtar replied, "You are an intelligent man. It is you who advise the people. Your bitterness will pass. We are angry with Uqla and besides, the estrangement will become a lasting thing; it will continue through endless tomorrows. You must get together. You both have sheep." (This was an allusion to the possibility of depredation by animals on the crops of one by the sheep of the other if their mutual hostility continued.)

Then the mukhtar proceeded to tell Muhammad Abu Tabanji the story of a previous arbitration in which he—the mukhtar—had played a prominent role. He told him how a father-in-law had been cursed by his son-in-law, how the son-in-law had pronounced the divorce formula once and insulted his father-in-law and his wife in the public ways, and how the father-in-law had appealed to a local notable to mediate and end the marriage by arranging for an equitable division of the marriage payment. The mukhtar told him how he himself and several elders had been nominated to mediate and how he had turned the committee from one that was to arrange divorce to one that fostered reconciliation and consummation of the marriage. The mukhtar ended by reciting what he considered to be a self-evident truth: "Giving [in marriage] is closer to harmony than divorce." He said that if divorce occurred, estrangement would be perpetuated over several generations with the boy saying to his patrilateral cousins: "Your father did not give me my cousin."

At this point, Muhammad revealed his reason for rejecting a reconciliation. He said that his brother had gone to the local notable—the Pasha—and asked him to intercede. The Pasha refused. He had said to Uqla that Muhammad was irresponsible and needed one of his own kind to deal with him. Uqla then went down to the market place and told everyone that the Pasha had given his older brother a severe rebuke.

Muhammad Abu Tabanji ended his repudiation of his brother, saying with disgust and finality: "Government office I wish not and sustenance is with God."

The mukhtar then asked Muhammad if he intended to give the girl in marriage to another member of his own sib—Beni Bakr—rather than to Uqla. He said that it was this belief that had led Uqla to go to the Pasha. Uqla believed that his brother had broken off the marriage negotiations (that would have ended in the betrothal of Uqla's son to Muhammad's daughter) because of a proposal of marriage from another member of Beni Bakr. Muhammad denied this and said that his brother was foolish and had been deceived.

When the mukhtar and imam heard Muhammad's report of his brother's behavior, they expressed shock and agreed that he had been guilty of gross disrespect to his older brother. They immediately gave up attempting to press Uqla's suit and left without accomplishing their mission.

Six weeks after the unsuccessful mediation attempt, Muhammad Abu Tabanji entered the guest house of Yusuf al-Tuluq, the largest landowner in the village, and requested that Yusuf send his son to Uqla to ask him how he proposed to divide their joint land holding for ploughing. The brothers were still estranged, neither greeting nor visiting each other. This state of affairs had put them in a very difficult position, for the ploughing and planting season had long begun and neither brother had started ploughing. Because of their estrangement, they had not demarcated the area to be ploughed by each of them, as was their habit. Muhammad had come to Yusuf al-Tuluq to ask him to act as intermediary in making a division of land for the ploughing. Yusuf sent for Uqla who came to the guest house, but the whole conversation between the two brothers was conducted through Yusuf. The brothers neither spoke nor looked at each other directly. In this way, they were able to arrange their ploughing division for the year.

This case demonstrated that while norms prescribe "the unity of the sibling group," full brothers may be alienated from one another by disagreement over marriage of their children.[55] I am not belittling the importance of the group of brothers or first patrilateral cousins as a consulting and cooperating group. The luzum in Kufr al-Ma represents just this. However, estrangement rather than cooperation or consultation may prevail. Indeed, the preferential rules of marriage (to the patrilateral first cousin or closest patrilateral parallel cousin) often conflict with economic considerations to make estrangement an expectable (but not normative) state of affairs among brothers and cousins (as illustrated in Case 6, pp. 74–77).

The individual villager still expects his brother to give his daughter in marriage to his own son. The elder stated this norm clearly when he said, "The son of the paternal uncle has priority." When Uqla thought that his brother was about to violate this norm, he went directly to the local notable to appeal for intervention.

The estrangement that occurs after the violation of this norm may have serious practical consequences for men involved in "multiplex" relationships.[56] In this case, though the brothers were not neighbors and had established separate households, they held land jointly and had to cooperate in its cultivation each year. Moreover, as the mukhtar pointed out, they both held livestock which, in view of their estrangement, was bound to precipitate quarrels between them. Disputes over crop damage caused by livestock wandering on to a neighbor's plot are among the most common in the village. While, therefore, estrangement may often occur among the members of a luzum, the very nature of the social and economic ties among them creates pressure for reconciliation.

Finally, the importance of negotiation over the mahr should not be overlooked as a cause of the alienation of close kinsmen. Three hundred dollars and eight dunums of land were not an unreasonable demand for a first cousin. The usual mahr for a girl of the clan is 600 dollars. The mahr involved here was worth about 525 dollars. There is an expectation, however, that the patrilateral first cousin will be given in marriage for less than the more distantly related clan member. This expectation together with the mode of marriage itself (see Chapter 3) may exacerbate relations among kinsmen that are already tense for other reasons.

The luzum, then, is a close consultation group composed of a core of patrilineal kinsmen. This core must work together in cases of honor. It is often characterized by disputes over traditional issues connected with marriage and ownership of property, the same interests that serve as the focus of unity. In certain cases conflict is reinforced by economic differentiation within the group. The closer the blood relationship, the greater the expectation of consultation and the greater the conflict when that expectation is disappointed. In the relationship of full brothers the possibilities of cooperation and conflict are greatest. Such conflict can result in a complete break in relations, but, as the last case illustrates, it is often contained by the necessities of agricultural cooperation. These necessities reflect in part the "multiplexity" of the community and the difficulty of severing relations with close kinsmen (and one might add, affines and covillagers) over any extended period of time.

E. The Lineage: Size, Ideology, Name, Social
Relations, and Political Functions

I have defined the lineage as the members of the subsib who reside in a particular village. [57] It consists of patrilineally related men living in Kufr al-Ma along with their wives and children. The villagers refer to this group as a fandi (see pp. 46–48). There are twenty-eight lineages in Kufr al-Ma varying in size from Massa'di, which numbers 304 individuals, to Al 'Asali, which is composed of two brothers and their families, a total of eleven individuals (see Table 9, p. 45). Each of the twenty-eight lineages has members of their subsib bearing the same name living in other villages.

The ideology of the lineage is phrased in terms of patrilineality. One of the clearest expressions of this fact is the idiom by which rights to the patrilateral parallel cousin are asserted. This right was stated clearly by one of the elders (see Case 5, pp. 66–69) when he said "The son of the father's brother has priority" (*ibn al 'amm awla*). When the elder stated that the son of the father's brother had priority he was not merely claiming a girl for her first cousin. He was stating a general principle. The term *'amm*, father's brother, is extended to any male of the clan of a senior generation. It may also be extended to any male of a senior generation as a form of politeness. In the absence of a first patrilateral parallel cousin a girl can be claimed by her second parallel cousin; if not by him, by her third parallel cousin, and so forth.

In other words, according to the ideology, any marriageable person has a large number of "father's brothers" and priority drops from one to the other to the limits of claimed descent. Of course, actual behavior often departs considerably from the ideology. Although the order of priority may be adhered to in some cases (see Antoun, "Social Organization and the Life Cycle in an Arab Village," *Ethnology* [July 1967]) it may be completely ignored in others (see Cases 6, pp. 74–77, and 5, pp. 66–69). Nevertheless, the desirability of these patrilateral parallel cousin marriages is justified in terms of a physiological concept of the adhesion of the blood. When questioned on the subject an informant said: "Blood begets among itself; the blood is one; after five grandfathers the blood is lost" (*al damm bit nāsil ba'Daha al ba'D; al damm wāHid; ba'd khams ajdād Dā'a l damm*). Though consanguinity is, physiologically, always bilateral, the implicit assumption is made that "blood" relations are confined to the paternal side. This assumption is revealed explicitly in the strictly patrilineal character of lineage genealogies (which mention no women).

The ideology of compensation in cases of honor also reflects the priority of agnation in recognizing degrees of relationship. As mentioned in the previous section, the offspring of the third generation of patrilineal kinsmen are obliged to make truce money payments, and the offspring of the fourth generation are obliged to make a different payment of a lesser amount. I do not mean to suggest that either the luzum or the lineage is a corporate blood-money paying unit. The unit paying compensation is redefined for every individual by calculating generations on the genealogy. Indeed, the blood-money paying unit is not even a "kindred" (see glossary) since it is not bilateral in its makeup. It is a five-generation group (*khums*) only in the sense that the apical ancestor of the genealogy on the basis of which compensation is figured, stands five generations removed from the offender. However, the patrilineal idiom of the villagers, "After five grandfathers [meaning patrilineal ancestors counting from ego] the blood is lost" is accurate as a reflection of legal responsibility in cases of honor. It is not accurate, however, insofar as it suggests that while the core of the lineage must contribute the other members of the lineage are free from responsibility. The more distantly related patrilineal kinsmen outside of the five generation circle are expected to contribute to the truce money in lesser amounts according to their ability to pay; and they must certainly contribute to the final blood money settlement (*diyya*), though, again, in lesser amounts and according to their ability to pay.

The principle of the priority of patrilineal relatives is also recognized in the orthodox Islamic inheritance rules regarding movable property. Nearer agnates exclude farther.[58] Moreover, orthodox Islam recognizes agnatic priority in legal guardianship (*wilāya*) again, with nearer agnates excluding farther. According to the Shafi'i school of law the guardian of minors in marriage (*wali al nikāH*) is after the father and grandfather, respectively, the nearest agnate among the descendants of the father, i.e., a full brother, and then, the nearest agnate among the descendants of the grandfather, i.e., a paternal first cousin (see the article on *nikāH* in the *Shorter Encyclopaedia of Islam*, p. 447). The guardian of the property of minors (*wali al māl*) is, according to the Shafi'i school, the father, the paternal grandfather, and the trustee designated by the paternal grandfather in that order; according to the Hanafi school of law* the guardian of the property of minors is the father, the trustee designated by the father, the trustee designated by the father's trustee, the paternal grandfather, and the trustee designated by the paternal grandfather in that order (see the section on "Transactions" in Abd al-Rahman Khayri's *The Book of Jurisprudence According to the Four Law Schools*, pp. 354–56). The fact that an Islamic court was established in the next village fifteen years ago means that these principles have been applied in Kufr al-Ma.

Local custom resembles Islamic law in recognizing the agnatic line in various social and legal obligations. I have already mentioned that the contributions to compensation in cases of honor vary with the proximity of the contributor to the offender in the agnatic line. I have also mentioned the norms regarding consultation of kinsmen before the marriage of clanswomen. In selling land, settling disputes, and even in giving gifts the same principle is enunciated and usually adhered to. The nearer in patrilineal relationship is considered to have priority over the more distant (see R.T. Antoun, "The Social Significance of Ramadan in an Arab Village," *Muslim World* [January 1968] for a description of the gifts distributed to various patrilineal kinswomen on the occasion of the Festival of Ramadan). This consanguineal relationship, conceptualized in terms of the actual sameness of the blood flowing in the veins, is felt and said to be stronger or weaker as one passes up or down the line of patrilineal kinsmen. The principle of agnatic priority, then, is enunciated not merely for the lineage, but for every level of the social structure, and in law as well as in local custom.

I do not mean to suggest, however, that there are no ideologies of relationship other than that of patrilineal descent. The imam of the village, for instance, once described the core of an individual's relatives by a metaphor, at once organic and bilateral. The father, mother, and grandfather (unspecified) he referred to as the origins or head, the son and daughter as the limbs, and the sister, the paternal uncle, the maternal uncle, the paternal aunt, and the maternal aunt as the hands and the feet. In his sermons the same imam repeated what he considered to be the model of any individual's structural obligations. There was the

---

*For legal and historical differences between the schools of law, see Asaf A. A. Fyzee, *Outlines of Muhammadan Law*, and Joseph Schacht, *Origins of Muhammadan Jurisprudence*.

right of the neighbor, *haqq al jār* , the right of the Muslim, *haqq al muslim,* and the right of the womb, *haqq al raHm,* referring to consanguineal ties in general. Each one of these rights had to be recognized. Again, he did not mention the patrilineal line or agnatic obligations. Rather, kinship obligations were phrased in terms of the maternal bond. It is also important to note in this regard that while Islamic law recognizes the ideology of patrilineality in its inheritance and guardianship rules it recognizes women (and bilaterally) regarding the initial upbringing *(HaDāna)* of the child (see Fyzee, *Outlines of Muhammadan Law,* pp. 172–73).

In addition to social and legal obligations defined by an ideology of patrilineality, each lineage possesses a name. This name is added to the member's surname, e.g., Sulayman Hasan "al-Jabali." The group as a whole is referred to by their distinctive name, e.g., "al-Jabali." Certain of the larger lineages have smaller named subdivisions while others do not. For instance, subgroups of Massaʻdi (the largest lineage of Yasin) are largely undifferentiated by name (although two subsections of that group constituting luzums are irregularly referred to by distinctive names). On the other hand, a small lineage such as Berek (composed of only three families) is distinguished by a patronym. It is not clear why this should be so.

Villagers have offered me several explanations for the selection of names of particular ancestors as the names of certain groups. Some say that the man with many offspring and descendants has his name attached to that group while the man with few offspring or none is not noted (and may not even be included in the genealogy). When I collected genealogies, villagers would often ask me rhetorically, "You don't want the names of the dead [or "the lost"] do you?" In each case I discovered they were referring to ancestors who died without leaving offspring. Others reported that famous men attached their name to their group and its descendants. Thus Wazir's military exploits spread his fame as far as Syria. In fact, it took an expedition sent by the Turkish governor in Damascus to subdue him. That his name should have identified the whole subsib is not, therefore, strange. Not all the names used to identify lineages refer to the actual names of ancestors on the genealogy. Rather, they are nicknames referring to certain peculiar traits of an ancestor or particular events that occurred in his lifetime. The lineage referred to as al-Jabali ("mountaineer") is so named because it is alleged that one of their ancestors one day assumed the dress characteristic of the peddlers who came from the western mountains across the Jordan Valley. Such a peddler was traditionally referred to as *jabāli* The name jokingly applied to this ancestor continued to be applied to his descendants. Another lineage is labeled *shujūr* ("trees") because one of their ancestors is reputed to have planted a large number of fig trees on the outskirts of the village. A subbranch of another lineage is called *sibbāʻi* ("those of the seventh") because the patrilateral great-grandfather of the senior generation of living descendants is said to have been born prematurely in the seventh month. A group of three brothers and their children have the term *Hilū* ("sweet one") attached to their names because one of their ancestors is reported to have had an exceedingly sweet disposition. Other lineages (such as Diyaka,

Shehem, Sabbah, Dakhnoosh, 'Ibadi, Al 'Asali, Berek, and Ghanim) are identified by nicknames that have no certain meaning, nor are they names of ancestors recorded on the genealogy. [59]

While the attachment of distinctive names and nicknames to particular groups of various size and genealogical span and depth seems quite random, it serves a useful purpose in distinguishing individuals and groups in a society where repetition of names often creates ambiguity. The various names of the Arab Prophet (Muhammad, Mahmoud, Ahmed, and Mustafa) and the attributes of God (Karim, Malik, and Rahim) as well as the names of Hebrew kings and prophets (Musa, Ibrahim, Da'ud, and Sulayman) are extremely popular. Since a man's full name is a recitation of his patrilineal pedigree—his own name followed by his father's and grandfather's—duplication of names is quite common. There may be four or five men in the village named Ahmed Mustafa Ibrahim. The attachment of a nickname allows precision of identification.

In addition to having a common name, the members of a lineage generally live in neighboring houses. This pattern has not been followed by all groups building outside the old area of habitation since 1940. The Shuqayrat and Ikhtaba, for instance, have regrouped as neighbors outside the old area of habitation but other lineages such as the Qar'oosh have not (see Map 2A, p. 74). Moreover, the pattern of distribution of agricultural land has remained the same. That is, men holding adjacent land parcels are usually members of the same lineage (see Map 3, p. 24). The stability in the pattern of land distribution has been matched by stability in the pattern of land sales. In the last twenty years sales of land have been, mainly, to lineage members.

Lineage membership is important for certain aspects of social relations such as visiting. In the evening, lineage members generally frequent the guest houses of one another more often than they do those of other lineages. Moreover, invitations to feasts always include close patrilineal kinsmen (although neighbors and affines are also invited). On one occasion I noted a startling exception to this rule. Mahmoud al-Salih, a member of the Qaraqzi lineage of Beni Dumi, invited a number of villagers to a feast celebrating the completion of his new house. I counted fourteen men of other clans, and only four of Dumi. I thought I had prematurely grouped Dumi with Yasin as having patterns of visiting confined to the clan. Five of the men were Mahmoud's new neighbors—he had moved to the outskirts of the village to build his new house (see Map 2A, household no. 268, p. 74) while three were affines Three were abjectly poor elders who were traditionally invited to feasts as an act of charity. Even more upsetting to my conception of visiting patterns was the fact that not a single member of Mahmoud's immediate lineage was present at the feast. I discovered later that Mahmoud had been estranged from the men of his lineage after they had broken a preliminary marriage agreement in which he had acted as go-between (see Case 6, pp. 74–77). His failure to invite any of his close patrilineal kinsmen to the housewarming was a deliberate act to publicize his estrangement from them. It was just because Mahmoud knew that failure to invite his close patrilineal kinsmen constituted a departure from custom and would be commented upon that he so acted.

Another aspect of social relations reflecting the lineage structure is marriage. The *jāha*, the formal deputation sent to ask a girl's hand in marriage, is usually composed of elders from each of the lineages of the bridegroom's clan.

More important, members of the same lineage claim the women of the group for their own sons as classificatory father's brother's daughters (*banāt 'amm*). As stated above, although lineage members expect priority, girls are sometimes married out of their lineage and out of the clan despite the objections of patrilineal kinsmen (see Case 5, pp. 66–69, and Case 6, pp. 74–77). However, only one instance of the marriage of a first patrilateral parallel cousin out of the group against the wishes of her father's brother and his son has come to my attention (though several men have refused to give their daughters to their nephews). The daughter of a poor man may not be sought as a bride by her parallel cousins in which case she may marry any suitor who asks her hand, whether from the lineage or not. But if the girl is physically attractive, the daughter of a man with a considerable amount of land or large income, and if she possesses some degree of education —three or four years of schooling—her patrilateral parallel cousins may raise strong objections to her marriage outside the lineage. But the objections of lineage mates, as the following case demonstrates, do not always constitute sufficient pressure to bring the individuals within the group into conformity with the norms governing marriage. The case shows clearly, however, that consultation among lineage mates regarding marriage remains a desirable and expectable action. The case also demonstrates the impact of economic differentiation, occupational mobility, and the single-family registration and exploitation of land on traditional norms regarding marriage (see pp. 23–25, pp. 31–36 and Case 3, pp. 63–65).

CASE SIX

This case began when an elder of the As'eed lineage, Muhammad Husayn Abd al-Rahim (B3 on Chart 8) entered a guest house of his clan and proceeded to address the mukhtar of Beni Yasin and the elders. He said that a member of the Wazir lineage (who were not of Yasin) intended to ask Anhar al-Ibrahim (A1 on Chart 8), also of As'eed, for the hand of Anhar's niece. Muhammad complained that his son (A2) was her closest eligible patrilateral relative and that he was prepared to register land in his son's name as part of the marriage payment. The clan elders listened sympathetically, but nothing was done by them to press Muhammad's claims of priority on Anhar.

The girl had received a number of requests for marriage from suitors living outside of the village— suitors who were willing to pay as much as 1,500 dollars mahr. This enormous marriage payment (it was more than twice the sum usually offered in the village) was offered because of the girl's beauty, her education, and the necessity of her leaving her own village at marriage. Muhammad Husayn could not hope to match such offers.

Anhar did not give his niece in marriage to any of these suitors because he did not want her to leave the village. Mahmoud Abd al-Qadir, a young school teacher of Dumi, was the son of Anhar's neighbor and good friend. Moreover, with his teacher's salary, he was able to pay a mahr of 750 dollars, 150 dollars more than the customary payment for a girl of the clan. Anhar gave her to Mahmoud with the girl's consent. Neither the sympathy of Muhammad Husayn's clansmen nor his own vociferous objections, as her third patrilateral parallel cousin, was able to prevent the marriage.

Anhar's action was not surprising in view of his relations with his own kinsmen. He had long since been estranged from the mukhtar of Beni Yasin over a case of crop damage by livestock (see Case 8, pp. 97–102). He had not paid the mukhtar the annual dues on the threshing ground for several years. He had also disassociated himself from his own clan socially, visiting the guest houses of his friends and neighbors who were mainly of Beni Dumi. Anhar had, in fact, built a house in the Beni Dumi quarter (see Map 2A, Household no. 188, p. 74). His ignoring of the wishes of his lineage members in regard to the marriage of his niece was merely one more event in his alienation from his patrilineal kinsmen. His disassociation from his clan politically, his move out of the Yasin quarter, and his own relatively strong economic position (he possessed twenty-two acres of land) had made him impervious to the social pressure of his own patrilineal kinsmen on this particular matter.

The marriage also violated norms and alienated a member of the Dumi clan. Mahmoud Abd al-Qadir (who married Anhar's niece) had informally agreed to marry a girl from another village. This informal agreement had been arranged by his third patrilateral cousin, Mahmoud al-Salih, who had acted as go-between. When Mahmoud Abd al-Qadir and his father decided to ignore this agreement and proceed with the other marriage, they angered Mahmoud al-Salih who broke off visiting relations with them (see discussion of the housewarming feast pp. 73–74).

It is quite clear, then, that members of a lineage do not always consult their fellow members in regard to the marriage of their wards and, if consulted, do not feel bound to accept their advice. Lineage members cannot always bring effective pressure on individuals within the group to conform. But it is also clear that such consultation remains a norm—a desirable and expectable action—and, if neglected, may result in estrangement of the kinsmen involved.

In evaluating this case it is important to remember that the actions of Anhar al-Ibrahim and Mahmoud Abd al-Qadir were not violations of fundamental norms (as in Case 8, pp. 97–102). No delegation of clan elders was sent to demand compliance. Muhammad Husayn brought the matter up before clan elders not to instigate clan action (which he knew would not be forthcoming) but to air a grievance and solidify public opinion.

Rather, the violations were indices of the growing independence of separate households as a result of an agricultural regime suited to a single family exploitation and an occupational structure producing increasing economic differentiation. On the one hand, members of the same lineage no longer farmed together under a communal system of land tenure. Though Muhammad Husayn and Anhar al-Ibrahim were both peasants and close kinsmen, they did not cooperate in any way in the cultivation of their land. Men employed in nonagricultural jobs (more than sixty percent of the men in the village), on the other hand, were little bound to one another by the nature of their employment. Indeed, such employment often involved long absences from the village. Many men rarely saw their closest kinsmen in the course of several months. Mahmoud Abd al-Qadir, for instance, taught in Palestine and saw his close kinsman, Mahmoud al-Salih only during the religious festivals, if at all. Moreover, Mahmoud Abd al-Qadir's father and Mahmoud al-Salih were not cooperating in agricultural tasks. Both of them were small village shopkeepers, and, as such, competitors rather than the opposite.

The most important consequence of single-family registration and exploitation of land on the one hand and a differentiated occupational structure on the other, is the widening of the range of incomes among the members of particular lineages, Beni Sabbah, for instance, is generally considered a landed lineage. The largest landowner in the village, Yusuf al-Tuluq, who possesses approximately 100 acres, is a member of Beni Sabbah. And yet of the ten households of this lineage, five have no land whatsoever. With the abolition of the musha' system and the registration of lands in individual ownership, Yusuf was able to purchase large areas of land and his income far exceeds the incomes of any of his lineage's members. In Beni Salim, a lineage composed of seven households, the richest man is a soldier with an income of 1,050 dollars and the poorest man a builder with an income of 150 dollars a year. Beni Ghanim, a lineage composed of five households, includes a peasant with an income of 675 dollars a year and a laborer with an income of seventy-five dollars a year. In Basbus, a lineage composed of ten households, the richest man is, again, a soldier (with an income of 576 dollars a year) and the poorest man a retired imam with an annual income of ninety dollars.

Income differences of such magnitude tax traditional loyalties to patrilineal kinsmen. Many men prefer to give their daughters to members of other lineages and clans rather than to their own poor relatives (see Case 6, pp. 74–77). Economic differentiation among close kinsmen has weakened the traditional norm governing preferential marriage—"the son of the father's brother [and also the sons of other lineage members] has priority" (*ibn al 'amm awla*). (See Case 3 for another illustration of the strain created by economic differentiation among close patrilineal kinsmen; see also the section on "The Household," pp. 49–58).

Although some degree of economic differentiation has always existed in Kufr al-Ma, the range has widened and the focus of differentiation has changed from descent groups such as the lineage and close consultation group to the individual household (see pp. 26–36). This differentiation is at least partly responsible for violations of traditional obligations among close kinsmen. (Many conflicts among close kinsmen, however, have nothing to do with the development of economic differentiation and are related to structural conflicts over traditional issues [see Case 4, pp. 65–66 and Case 5, pp. 66–69]).

Besides its importance in such aspects of social relations as visiting and marriage, the lineage is a significant unit in village politics. As suggested above it is the political function of the lineage rather than its structural attributes that is critical for its identity. It is the minimal social unit seeking political representation within the village. That is, when a village committee is to be formed for any purpose, each of the lineages attempts to nominate one of its adult men as a member. (If the purpose of the committee is not approved by members of the lineage, however, they may refuse to join the committee.) Since there are twenty-eight lineages in the village, it is a practical necessity that many, if not a majority, be excluded from any given committee. Those excluded often oppose the work of the committee.

Although all lineages seek representation, neither government officials nor the villagers themselves consider lineages as structural or political equals in all situations. The smaller lineages are usually ignored when composition of committees or other deliberative bodies is arranged and when invitations to important events are sent out. On the occasion of the visit of the king to the area in the summer of 1960, official invitations were distributed by the head of the Municipality of Deir Abu Said to the villages of the district through the mukhtars. The quota of Kufr al-Ma was fifteen invitations. Thus, thirteen lineages were not represented, including Massa'di, the largest lineage in the village. Their exclusion caused considerable rancor against the mukhtar of Beni Dumi who had received and distributed the invitations. Such dissatisfaction was inevitable in a community in which the units seeking political representation were so many, their sizes so disparate, and their cohesion so unequal. Implicit in the view of lineages just presented is the fact that lineages are not permanent and unchanging entities. Due to the vagaries of fortune, population growth, economic contingency, or personality differences, over time, luzums may attain lineage status. On the other hand, the same factors may reduce lineages to the status of luzums. Table 9 reflects the situation that existed in 1959 and 1960.

F. Principles Governing the Alignment of
Lineage Members in Social Crises

The clearest crystalization of lineages as political units occurs at critical moments when men are forced to define their positions and to take one side or another during the course of disputes. When a dispute occurs between patrilineal kinsmen of different lineages which are (each lineage within itself) matrilaterally related by close patrilateral parallel cousin marriages in contemporary and preceding generations, the structural factors governing the alignment of groups cannot be explained in terms of patrilineal ties alone. The factors governing the alignment of groups are more complex. The following case demonstrates four points: that alignments occur initially on the basis of lineage membership; that the idiom of patrilineality is used to describe actions and ascribe motives; that the final alignment of groups and the process of mediation is determined to a large degree by ties through women; and finally that the multiplexity of relationships and long-standing grudges are as important as other structural factors for interpreting events and guiding the mediation effort.

CASE SEVEN

This case began with a fight between the sons of Yusuf al-Tuluq and the two brothers, Khalid al-Yusuf and Barakat al-Yusuf. Yusuf, a member of the Sabbah lineage of Beni Yasin (D3 on Chart 5), owned the most land and livestock in the village. On this occasion his sheep were on their way home after a day in pasture on the outskirts of the village Yusuf's sons (C2 and C3) had collected the sheep for regrouping on the threshing ground belonging to Khalid and Barakat (A1 and A2), members of Shujur, another lineage of Yasin. Khalid and Barakat had ordered the shepherds to take the sheep off the threshing grounds immediately, They had refused and a scuffle had begun. Ahmed Muhammad (C9), a young peasant and member of a third Yasin lineage, the Qar'oosh, had intervened to separate the combatants, but only ended by getting involved himself. 'Abdu (D2), a shopkeeper and a second patrilateral cousin of Yusuf, hearing of the fracas, had come running from the center of the village to aid his own lineage members, but he was prevented from doing so by a clan elder. Others from the three lineages concerned then joined the melée which had by now become a free-for-all. Finally, Muflih al-Hakim (B2), the mukhtar of Beni Yasin, managed to part the combatants.

Yusuf al-Tuluq ordered his sons to gather the sheep, which had strayed off during the fight, and the members of Sabbah withdrew in anger to their own quarter of the clan area, indicating by defiant stares that this was not to be the last of the matter. And, indeed, Yusuf immediately dispatched his sons to the local police post to file a complaint against Khalid and Barakat and Ahmed Muhammad.

A few minutes later the mukhtar, Ahmed Muhammad, the young peasant who had intervened unsuccessfully, and other members of the Qar'oosh lineage gathered in front of the house of the imam, Shaykh Luqman (C7), who, like the mukhtar, was a member of Qar'oosh. Suddenly two members of Sabbah, 'Abdu (D2) and Ikhleyf al-Muflih (C4), who were closely related to Yusuf al-Tuluq, came walking rapidly toward the gathering. On approaching, 'Abdu asked, "Why is it, by the way, that you Qar'oosh always side against us? Why do you side with Shujur?" Ahmed replied sharply that he had only intervened to part the combatants. Both sides then exchanged insults and 'Abdu and Ikhleyf returned to their quarter.

Later in the evening the Qar'oosh concerned assembled in the guest room of Shaykh Luqman. Those present included Shaykh Luqman's younger brother, Ahmed, his father, the Haj Muhammad Husayn (D4),

CHART 5

PATRILINEAL RELATIONSHIP OF THE INDIVIDUALS
INVOLVED IN CASE 7

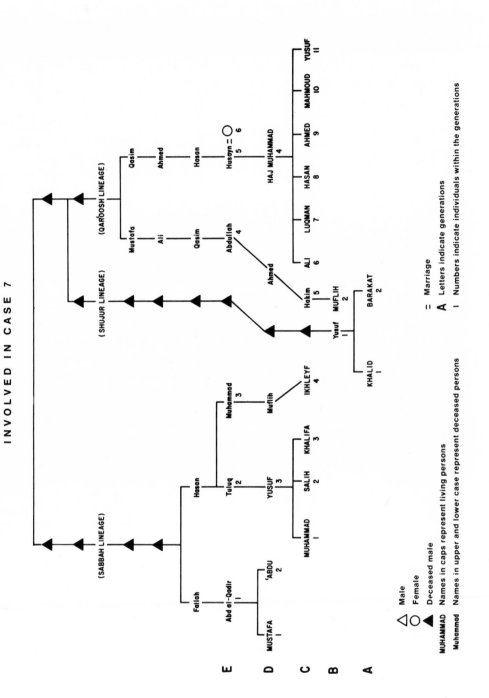

(SABBAH LINEAGE)   (SHUJUR LINEAGE)   (QAROOSH LINEAGE)

E   Fallah

D   Abd al-Qadir   'ABDU
         1   2

C   MUSTAFA
         1

MUHAMMAD   Hasan   Tuluq   Muhammad
     1   2   3

         YUSUF   Muflih
           3

SALIH   KHALIFA   IKHLEYF
  2   3   4

Mustafa   Ali   Qasim
                   Abdullah
                     4

Hakim   Ahmed
  5

Yusuf   MUFLIH
  1   2

KHALID   BARAKAT
  1   2

ALI   LUQMAN   HASAN   HAJ MUHAMMAD   AHMED   MAHMOUD   YUSUF
 6   7   8   4   9   10   11

Qasim   Ahmed   Hasan   Husayn = ○
                              5   6

△ Male
○ Female
▲ Deceased male

MUHAMMAD Names in caps represent living persons
Muhammad Names in upper and lower case represent deceased persons

= Marriage
A Letters indicate generations
I Numbers indicate individuals within the generations

and the mukhtar. Ikhleyf, accompanied by another member of the Sabbah lineage, suddenly entered the guest room. Ikhleyf said that he had
heard the Sabbah side of the story and had come to hear the Qar'oosh's
version even though his kinsmen had tried to dissuade him. He said
that he had intended to come earlier but had been rebuffed by Ahmed's
insults. Ahmed's father asked Ikhleyf why it was that Yusuf al-Tuluq
had left the mosque after mid-afternoon prayers crying (of Ahmed) "Kill
him! Kill him!" Ikhleyf, on his part, wished to know if Ahmed had
yelled (of Yusuf al-Tuluq's sons), "Butcher them! Butcher them! Butcher them!" Ahmed denied this and Ikhleyf seemed satisfied with the denial. Ikhleyf then asked the mukhtar to accompany him to the guest house
of Haj Mustafa Abd al Qadir (D1), the venerable leader of Sabbah and a
close kinsman of Yusuf al-Tuluq in order to explain to the assembled
members of Sabbah the Qar'oosh side of the story. The mukhtar said
there was really nothing to explain, but that he would go. A little later
Shaykh Luqman and other members of the Qar'oosh followed Ikhleyf and
the mukhtar to the house of Haj Mustafa. Shaykh Luqman's father and
his son, Ahmed, refused to go along, however. The Haj said that he and
his son were the injured party, that Sabbah had falsely charged his son,
and that 'Abdu had been heard saying after the fight to one of the combatants, "Why didn't you kill one of them?"

On arriving at Haj Mustafa's guest house, we found these individuals gathered there discussing the past history of the relations between
the families of the three lineages concerned. Yusuf al-Tuluq recalled
that it was the Qar'oosh who had gone to the Pasha (the local political
leader and landowner) with the story that he—Yusuf al-Tuluq—was
pasturing his sheep on the Pasha's land— this, despite the fact that
Ahmed's wife was his own daughter (see Chart 6, A5 and A10). A young
shepherd was brought to the guest house as witness to the fact that
Ahmed had not said of Yusuf al-Tuluq's sons, "Kill them! Kill them!"
during the scuffle. Shaykh Luqman, who, until then, had remained si-
lent, said that it was he—Yusuf al-Tuluq—who had started the business
of forbidding sheep to pass through other men's land. He had done this
to the sheep of Shujur and this was the cause of the Shujur's ill will towards him. Yusuf al-Tuluq was encouraged to withdraw the complaint
filed at the police post. As the hour was late, the elders began drifting
home without having arrived at a definitive settlement.

Next day, Khalid al-Yusuf (A1) of Shujur went to the civil court in
the next town and registered a counter-complaint against Yusuf al-
Tuluq's sons. Khalid said he would withdraw it if they paid him the
twenty-eight piastres cost of the stamps (used to file the complaint) and
if the sons of Yusuf al-Tuluq would stay away from him. Ikhleyf replied
that the twenty-eight piastres were not important but that the second
condition was impossible and defeated the purpose of a reconciliation.
He said, "We must allow one another room in this village."

The following day the mukhtar told me confidentially that the root
of the trouble between Ahmed Muhammad (C9) and the sons of Yusuf al-
Tuluq and the reason Ahmed refused to greet them in the public ways of
the village was that Muhammad al-Yusuf (A2 on Chart 6), Yusuf al-
Tuluq's eldest son, a government employee who worked in a town some

thirty miles distant, had married a second wife (A1 in Chart 6) after he had taken Ahmed's sister (A12 on Chart 6) in marriage. Moreover, he had sent his first wife back to the village to live with his father (Yusuf al-Tuluq) while he remained with his second wife in town. The situation was aggravated by the fact that Ahmed had married Yusuf al-Tuluq's daughter (A5 on Chart 6) in a sister-exchange marriage.

Next evening a number of the Qar'oosh including the mukhtar, Shaykh Luqman, his brother Ahmed, and their father Haj Muhammad Husayn were assembled in their guest house when Muhammad al-Yusuf, Yusuf al-Tuluq's eldest son, 'Abdu, Ikhleyf, and other members of Beni Sabbah entered. Muhammad al-Yusuf (A2 on Chart 6), a law court clerk who worked in the town of Irbid, hearing of the dispute, had come to the village on the weekend. The children and younger men were told to go to bed. Shaykh Luqman left soon after the men of Beni Sabbah entered. Ikhleyf said that they had come on an errand of friendship. Muhammad al-Yusuf then stated that everyone knew how he respected the Hajii (Shaykh Luqman's father), that he would never think of addressing him by his name, that he always addressed him as 'amm (father's brother, a term of respect used in addressing clan elders), and he would never raise a finger in protest if he were whipped by him. He expected the same treatment toward his own father. Yet, his father was being addressed as "Yusuf al-Tuluq" by certain people and these people were encouraging others of their generation to refer to him in the same way.

Then Ikhleyf recapitulated the events of the last four days—his original mediation attempt that was rebuffed by Ahmed's insults, the second attempt which brought the mukhtar to Yusuf al-Tuluq who was persuaded to drop charges against Khalid and Barakat, and his visit to Khalid who had prepared coffee and treated them with utmost propriety. How on that visit after coffee had been drunk and good fellowship prevailed he (Ikhleyf) had joked with Ahmed. And how Ahmed had retorted in anger and insulted him after which he (Ikhleyf) had left. As a result of all this, he felt that there was some underlying cause for the Qar'oosh's antagonism towards Beni Sabbah, and if there was, he wanted to know about it.

The members of Sabbah then proceeded to review the mukhtar's neglect of their lineage at the last fodder distribution and the Qar'-oosh's unjust report to the Pasha regarding Yusuf al-Tuluq's sheep. The Qar'oosh denied any underlying cause for antagonism toward Sabbah and disputed the other charges. The meeting broke up around midnight.

Early the next morning, Yusuf al-Tuluq was asked to the Hajji's guest house for a round of Bedouin coffee and visiting relations were resumed between the two families.

Two days later all of the respected heads of families in the clan of Beni Yasin assembled in the guest house of the Haj Muhammad Husayn to receive the news that they had been issued invitations to attend the wedding celebration of a clansman living in Irbid, the nearest market town. The invitations were passed out and the next day the men of Beni Yasin went to Irbid where they congratulated the bridegroom and presented him, lineage by lineage, with money gifts. The occasion provided

a suitable moment for a show of solidarity among clan members after
the ruffled tempers and hurt feelings aroused by the events of the last
few days.

This case began with a quarrel involving the young men of three
lineages and was immediately followed by a break off of visiting relations with the members of each group withdrawing to their own quarters. Attempts were made almost immediately by members of one of
the groups to reestablish relationships by getting representatives of
both sides to sit down together for a hashing out of difficulties. The
formal resumption of visiting relations was marked by the drinking of
coffee by the heads of the families most concerned.

In analyzing this case, four factors emerge as influencing the
course of mediation and the alignment of individuals. They are as follows: the "multiplex" character of the relationships, the ideology of
patrilineality, the critical nature of matrilateral and affinal ties, and
the existence of long-standing grudges. I shall treat them in order.

Multiplex relationships are those which "serve many interests."[60]
The men involved were not only clan members but also neighbors.
They lived in the same quarter of the village and were thrown together
in a number of daily economic, social, and recreational activities. The
immediacy with which mediation attempts were made after the breach
reflects the character of social relationships in the village. Multiplexity particularly characterized the families headed by Yusuf al-
Tuluq and Haj Muhammad Husayn whose houses were on opposite sides
of the street and whose daughters had been exchanged in marriage for
their sons. With one exception, the Shujur group had no affinal ties with
Beni Sabbah. It was not unusual, therefore, that the mediation attempts
centered on reconciling Yusuf al-Tuluq with Haj Muhammad Husayn
and not with Khalid and Barakat who had actually begun the assault on
Yusuf al-Tuluq's sons.

The second factor affecting the cause of the dispute was the existence of a patrilineal ideology. In describing the quarrel I deliberately
identified the actors in terms of their lineage affiliation. This was not
my own conceptualization of the event after the fact. In the fight the
young men sided with the members of their own lineage and after the
fight the members of each group returned to its own quarter to parley.
Visiting relations were broken off. Moreover, the interpretation of
events was in terms of the action of lineages. It was 'Abdu who asked,
"Why is it that you Qar'oosh always side against us? Why do you side
with Shujur?" The breach was described in a patrilineal idiom referring
to opposing lineages in the clan and not the individuals or families actually involved. More than that, the dispute—which had initially involved only three families—soon spread to involve many other members of the lineages concerned. The mukhtar for instance, despite the
official nonpartisan nature of his office and his mediating action in the
fight, was regarded as siding with his own lineage against Beni Sabbah
(who saw him reluctant to attend the peace meeting). Again, during the
period of strain and for some days after, Barakat and Khalid made a
point of not entering Ikhleyf's grocery shop where they were accus-
tomed to pass the time. Ikhleyf was not involved in the fight but he was

CHART 6

SISTER-EXCHANGE MARRIAGES LINKING
THE PARTIES TO THE DISPUTE (Case 7)

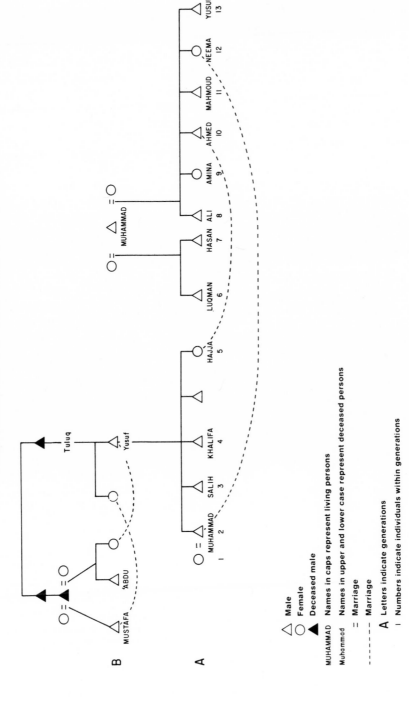

△ **Male**

O **Female**

▲ **Deceased male**

MUHAMMAD **Names in caps represent living persons**

Muhammad **Names in upper and lower case represent deceased persons**

= **Marriage**

----- **Marriage**

A **Letters indicate generations**

1 **Numbers indicate individuals within generations**

a member of Yusuf al-Tuluq's lineage. Thus disputes between families within a given clan quickly assume the nature of disputes between the lineages of the clan. This is in accord with a general principle of social conflict stated by Victor Turner in his book, *Schism and Continuity in an African Society:*

> ... unless the conflict can be sealed off quickly within a limited area of social interaction there is a tendency for the breach to widen and extend until it becomes co-extensive with some dominant cleavage in the widest set of relevant social relations to which the conflicting parties belong. [61]

While the dispute was carried on throughout in a patrilineal idiom and the alignment of parties was influenced by membership in patrilineal groups, the critical ties were through women. In two instances these ties involved sister-exchange marriages. Yusuf al-Tuluq and Mustafa Abd al-Qadir had taken one another's sisters as wives (see B5 and B1 on Chart 6). Mustafa and his brother, 'Abdu, were, therefore, tied to Yusuf al-Tuluq not only as members of the same lineage—they were second patrilateral cousins—but through their sisters. One of the reconciliation sessions took place in Mustafa's guest house and 'Abdu, with Ikhleyf, acted as self-appointed mediators between Beni Sabbah and the Qar'oosh. More importantly, in the younger generation Ahmed al-Muhammad and Muhammad al-Yusuf were linked in sister-exchange marriages (see A2 and A10 on Chart 6). In such a marriage both wives are or should be accorded equal treatment. The slightest discrepancy is immediately noted and commented upon. Ill treatment of the wife in one pair is followed by ill treatment of the wife in the other. A break off of relations between one pair is followed by a break off of relations between the other. Muhammad al-Yusuf had contracted a second marriage (A1 on Chart 6) and had sent his first wife, who had borne him three children, back to the village to live with her father-in-law (B5 on Chart 6) while he remained with his second wife in town. Muhammad al-Yusuf's treatment of his first wife in the context of the structural interdependency of the families linked in sister-exchange marriage had already created serious strain before the incident involving Yusuf al-Tuluq's sheep. The affinal ties here were of equal if not greater importance than the bonds of patrilineality in assessing the causes of the dispute and the alignment of parties, as the mukhtar was quick to point out in his own analysis of the situation.

In addition to these sister-exchange marriages, a number of affinal ties linked the mukhtar, Muflih al-Hakim (B2 on Chart 5), with the Shujur group. His half sister's mother was married to a man of Shujur as was his father's sister in the previous generation. Muhammad Husayn's mother (E6 on Chart 5) was of the Shujur group and he himself had taken as his first wife (B6 on Chart 6) a woman from Shujur. Thus when Beni Sabbah accused the Qar'oosh of siding against them there were good structural reasons for their suspicions.

Matrilateral ties proved even more significant for the course of the mediation process. Aside from the mukhtar whose official position impelled him to act as mediator regardless of his personal feelings or structural position, it was Ikhleyf al-Muflih (C4 on Chart 5) who played the dominant role in conciliation. Ikhleyf was a second patrilateral cousin to Yusuf al-Tuluq (a few months later his daughter became engaged to Yusuf al-Tuluq's son). But Ikhleyf's mother was a member of Shujur. He was, therefore, in excellent structural position to act as arbitrator.

What I am saying, then, is that the men who banded together in a moment of social crisis were men doubly and triply linked through women. In societies characterized by a considerable percentage of endogamy such links may become crucial in the alignment of groups.[62] The case discussed above demonstrated the critical importance of matrilateral and affinal ties for any analysis of Arab descent groups. It supports a view long ago advocated (but generally unheeded by social scientists and area specialists) by Emrys Peters in his brilliant analyses of tribal and peasant communities in the Arab world. [63]

It may still be asked, may not the links in this case be a matter of coincidence? Or, was not the alignment of individuals in terms of membership in particular patrilineages? May it not be that some other underlying factor such as land tenure explains the alignment of groups?[64]

Two points must be considered in reply. First, other members of the lineage, Beni Sabbah, were closely related to Yusuf al-Tuluq patrilineally, as closely related as either Mustafa Abd al-Qadir or 'Abdu (B10 and B11 on Chart 7). They were Khalil Ramadan, Ahmed Khalil, and Abdullah Imhawish (B13, B8, and B4 on Chart 7). These men played little or no part in the mediation effort. They were not linked to Yusuf by either affinal or matrilateral ties. Second, I do not wish to claim that in every quarrel the alignment of men will be regulated by their ties through women or that the mediators in the quarrel will always occupy the structurally appropriate positions. A structural analysis only aims to outline the significant ties in any community—those ties that are POTENTIALLY operative in every situation.[65]

The final factor affecting the course of the dispute was the historical pattern of grudges. A number of grudges were brought out into the open during the reconciliation sessions. Shaykh Luqman pointed out that Yusuf al-Tuluq had acted against the Shujur group in a previous sheep grazing incident. The mukhtar was accused of discriminating against Beni Sabbah in the fodder distribution. Ahmed's intervention in the fight (for the purpose of mediation) was regarded as an indication of the grudge he bore against Beni Sabbah for the way in which his sister had been treated by Muhammad al-Yusuf. Each man's action was interpreted in terms of past family disputes, rarely in terms of an objective assessment of the man's character or motivation in the light of the actual situation and its requirements. Ahmed Muhammad was, in fact, known to be highly strung, sensitive to the innuendoes of others, and prone to rashness in word and deed. But his temperament, the mediating role he played in the particular situation, and the structural factors that actually tied him closely to Yusuf al-Tuluq (he was Yusuf's son-in-law) were discounted in favor of an analysis based on the existing pattern of grudges. The historical pattern of grudges, then, is as

CHART 7

THE BENI SABBAH PATRILINEAL GENEALOGY (Case 7)

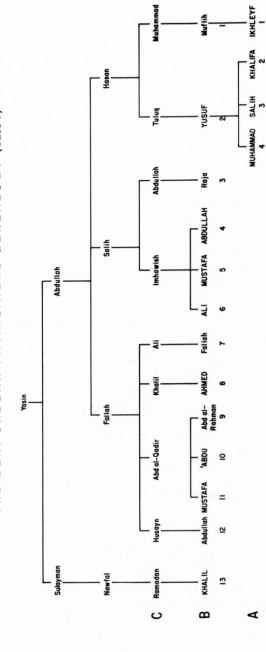

MUHAMMAD Names in caps represent living persons

Muhammad Names in small letters represent deceased persons

A Letters indicate generations

I Numbers indicate individuals within generations

important in the determination of the alignment of individuals as other purely structural ties such as patrilineal descent, affinity, or matri-laterality. They may reinforce the existing structural ties, stress some at the expense of others, or crosscut them.

To review the argument of the last five sections, local descent groups (households, luzums, and lineages) have been described essentially as political, arbitral, and consultative units. While their ideology is patrilineal and the metaphors which refer to it are couched in terms of blood kinship, the descent groups themselves are not rigidly defined well-integrated corporate groups. Individuals and whole lineages who are not able to trace blood relationship to a common patrilineal ancestor have attached themselves to particular descent groups and, in varying degrees, identified themselves with them (see pp. 46, 109–10, and 161–62 for an elaboration of this point). On the other hand, individual members of clans and lineages have been able to disassociate themselves in varying degrees from their patrilineal kinsmen while formally remaining members of the group.

Clans and lineages, however, are not merely "social organizational" groupings.[66] That is, they are not recruited on an ad hoc basis to carry out certain social enterprises. Membership in the group is based on clear-cut principles of descent, and the behavior of their members is defined by a certain set of norms. At moments of crisis when men must choose sides between contending parties, the element of choice is reduced to a minimum. The alignments are social structural rather than social organizational.

But it is not a choice between two structural principles—patrilineality and matrilaterality—which faced the individuals involved in the case. Rather the villagers formally recognized one general principle, patrilineal descent, and explained their actions on its basis, while operating on the basis of another—matrilaterality. The second (matrilaterality) did not contradict the first (patrilineal descent) but rather acted within it as a principle of greater discrimination. That is, the men in the case invariably sided with members of their own lineage. Within that group, however, they were tied more closely to some than to others. It was these matrilateral and affinal ties that generated the highest degree of cooperation and support within the group of patrilineal kinsmen.

However, I regard it as an error to go to the extent of giving preeminence to matrilateral and affinal ties in explaining the behavior of Arab peasants while treating patrilineal descent as an idiom and an ideology constructed and manipulated by the actors in given situations for their own purposes.[67] Patrilineal descent is more than an ideology. It is the main principle for the recruitment of permanent structural groups. It is the basis of political representation within the village. Visiting patterns and day-to-day activities reflect its importance. Social control may be exercised in the name of a group composed on its basis. Finally, it is one of the factors governing the alliances and alignments of individuals at moments of crisis.

As the case above shows, these alignments do not take place strictly according to patrilineal principles, but, on the other hand, they do not deny these principles. Rather, alignments depend on the particular social ties—be they patrilineal, matrilateral, or affinal—and the particular pattern of estrangement that marks the relationship of the individuals at any given moment.

G. The Clan: Its Ideology, Social Relations, and Economic Activities

Patrilineality serves not only as an overall ideology for the lineage and the close consultation group but also as an ideology for the clan. Patrilineality is the idiom in which everyday relationships are expressed and actions explained. The patrilineal descent line is likened to a staff of cane which, being dipped in water is not soaked (*ramH qusayb yinghaT la yinbal*). When this staff is dipped in water and taken out there is no sign on it of its surface having been immersed. For the peasants of Kufr al-Ma this metaphor suggests the solidarity of the patrilineal descent group, whatever its order, and its imperviousness to outside influences.

The principal vehicle for asserting the ideology of the clan is its patrilineal genealogy. In this connection it is significant that the three clans do not adhere to this ideology with equal affirmation. It was stated (see p. 161 n37) that both Dumi and 'Amr were composed, in part, of attached groups some of which readily admitted their distinctive origin and did not attempt to relate themselves to the common ancestor from whom their sib is said to have descended. All the lineages of Yasin, on the other hand, were able to trace their·descent to the eponymous ancestor. Moreover, the elders of Yasin showed great interest (while I was collecting their genealogy) in knowing exactly where their particular lineage "tied in." When I produced the finished genealogy of the whole sib, which encompassed all families who claimed to be of Yasin, and related them to the common ancestor, the Yasin elders showed considerable pride in this achievement. For them, the genealogy was a manifestation of their ideological unity. Their behavior was in marked contrast to that of the elders of Dumi who carelessly omitted a subsib from the genealogy and to the elders of 'Amr who readily admitted their separate origins. The members of Yasin often contrasted the claimed purity of their own descent line with that of the other two clans in the village. For them it was a mark of the superiority of their own status within the village. One Yasin elder told me: "All of the others go about collecting [with the connotation of collecting kinsmen as a beggar collects food and clothing]. As for Yasin, it is all brothers and sons of brothers. There is no wrapping around it." (*hadolak byahawshū. yasin, kulu ikhwa wa ibn ikhwa. ma·fiha lafaf.*) Be this as it may, no single Yasin elder was able to recite the entire genealogy. One elder was able to recite nearly half of it, but the rest had be gathered, piecemeal, from the elders of the various lineages.

The differences between the clans are not confined to size and ideology of descent. They extend to their actual social relations, in particular to their visiting patterns. Considering the tendency towards spatial clustering of patrilineal kinsmen (see Map 2A, p. 74), it is not unusual that visiting occurs mainly between clan members. Aside from

the nightly visits which the heads of households pay one another in the
guest houses of the village, visits take place on formal occasions such
as feasts given at the time of circumcision, on religious holidays, and
after the completion of a new house. Among Beni Yasin and Beni Dumi,
invitations to these feasts with few exceptions went to the elders of the
various lineages within the clan. The exception might be an affine (perhaps the maternal grandfather of the child to be circumcized) or a good
friend.

Invitations to feasts were not confined to patrilineal kinsmen
among Beni 'Amr, however. At one feast given by a member of Beni
'Amr, of thirteen men present, seven were from Beni Yasin and only
six from Beni 'Amr. Three of the latter probably came in their capacity as neighbors rather than patrilineal kinsmen. At another feast given
by a member of Beni 'Amr, patrilineal kinsmen were outnumbered by
members of other clans by a count of fifteen to four. Eight of the men
present were neighbors and not patrilineal kinsmen.

Two factors—size, and the distribution of economic and political
power and religious authority—account for the difference in visiting
and feasting patterns as between Yasin and Dumi on the one hand and
'Amr on the other. 'Amr is the smallest clan and, since it is considered appropriate to cram a guest house full on the occasion of a feast
(to show the host's generosity), invitations must inevitably go out to
members of other clans in order to fill the room. Most of the notables
of the village—the large landowners, the mukhtars, the imam, the magician, and the respected elders—come from other clans and some of
them, at least, should be invited on such occasions. A circumcision
feast requires the presence of the imam or of a pious man, a pilgrim,
to chant the story of the prophet Muhammad's life. No such man is
numbered among Beni 'Amr. He must always be recruited from other
groups. Moreover, it is necessary for the members of Beni 'Amr to
cultivate the good will of the mukhtars of Beni Dumi and Beni Yasin
since they are not at present represented by a mukhtar. Therefore, one
or both of the mukhtars is usually present at their feasts. It is this
combination of small size, lack of key specialists, and ideological
weakness that has made Beni 'Amr, politically, the weakest of the
three clans. As stated, many of the lineages that compose it admit to
having separate origins. It was dissension among these lineages that
caused the last mukhtar of Beni 'Amr to resign from his position. The
continuing lack of political cooperation among the lineages of 'Amr was
clearly expressed by their former mukhtar: "Dumi and Yasin are very
happy now," he said. "They can run things as they please. We [meaning
'Amr] have no name in this village any longer." He attributed the weakness of his clan to the dissensions among its members and to the lack
of prominent elders who could be appealed to to settle disputes and
"make peace" between estranged members.

Visiting patterns and invitations to feasts are not the only aspects
of social relations that reflect the clan and lineage structure. The recruitment of the deputation (jaha) that makes a formal request for a
bride on behalf of a given individual (after the negotiations over the
marriage payment have been completed) is almost always confined to

the members of the clan. Usually, each of the lineages in the clan is represented in the deputation. Marriage and residence, however, may cause departure from the principle of representation according to patrilineal groups. In the case of Beni Yasin, Raji Wazir, a member of an independent lineage, was included in the deputation. Raji lived in the Yasin quarter and had married a Yasin woman.

Although the clan is characterized by a patrilineal ideology (strong and explicit for Yasin, less so for Dumi, and weakest for 'Amr) and social relations which take account of that principle, it does not exercise corporate control over resources. Even under the musha' system of tenure (see Chapter 1) it is doubtful whether the clan exercised such control. Village elders state outrightly that the clan was the effective group within which redistribution of land took place. Because of the inequalities of population between clans, however, families from one clan often joined a smaller clan in the division of land. Independent lineages not affiliated with one of the three clans (see Table 9) and residing in the village also joined with the smaller clans, Dumi and 'Amr, in the division of land. Thus it would be more accurate to describe the units of partition as cores of clansmen with attached families of other lineages in the village.

When the central government registered land in individual ownership in 1939, the village was divided into three equal areas (equal in value rather than size) following the procedure under musha'. At that time, the leaders of the three partitioning groups were prominent landowners rather than the leaders of the clans. Two of them were from Beni Yasin and the third was a notable, the Pasha, who was neither a member of a clan nor a resident of the village, although he possessed a house and a large bloc of land there. It is doubtful, then, whether the clans, as such, excercised corporate control or even corporate functions under the musha' system. They certainly do not do so today.

Be this as it may, the pattern of land distribution in 1939 at the time of registration and in 1960 after the elapse of over twenty years remains largely on the basis of clans and lineages (see Map 3, p. 24). That is, peasants with adjacent land parcels are, with few exceptions, members of the same clan and lineage. Beni Yasin occupies the largest bloc of land towards the northwestern side of the village, Beni Dumi occupies a much smaller bloc of land directly south of the village, and Beni 'Amr occupies a small bloc of land to the northwest of the village. (Exceptions to this pattern of distribution are Basins 10, 11, and 14. In Basins 10 and 11 several large landowners from various lineages and clans joined together, with governmental encouragement, to divide the land in large blocs. Basin 14 was set aside for the planting of trees and distributed among all the families in the village with a share in land.) Although there have been a number of sales of land in the twenty-year interval, the pattern remains largely the same. Sales have generally been to patrilineally related kinsmen and not to members of other clans. With the exception of the alienation of some forest land which is located at a considerable distance from Kufr al-Ma, there has been very little alienation of the village's lands to other villages.

The spatial distribution of houses in the village is, likewise, on the basis of lineages and clans, although houses built after 1940 outside the original area of habitation show some departure from this pattern. Beni Yasin occupies a large densely settled area on the higher eastern side of the village, Beni Dumi occupies a less crowded area on the lower western side of the village while Beni 'Amr occupies the houses on the northern side of the village (see Map 2B, p. 90). The independent lineages tend to be located on the outskirts of the settled area particularly on the northern and western sides. Considering the tendency of patrilineal kinsmen towards spatial clustering, it is not unusual that the visiting patterns mentioned above are confined, mainly, to clan members.

The significance of the clan is not, however, to be gathered from an examination of its social (visiting patterns), ideological (claims of common descent), or economic (control over resources) aspects. Its significance lies in its political and arbitral activities. Its political activities are carried out by its political representative, the mukhtar, and its arbitral functions are carried out by its elders in the settlement of disputes. In the next two sections each of these aspects of the clan will be discussed in turn.

H. The Mukhtar

The mukhtar (mayor) is at one and the same time the representative of his clan, his village, and the central government. It is the peculiar combination and interpretation of these three political roles that makes the mayorship a pivotal position within the village.

The mayor is, first of all, a functionary of the central government. He bears the official seal of his office granted to him by that government and he affixes it to all the documents he has occasion to draw up or witness. He serves the government by keeping records of births and deaths and by testifying to the veracity of statements made by villagers on official documents. In this capacity, the mukhtar is necessarily a literate man though seldom a learned one, even by village standards. He is charged with meeting and entertaining government officials such as the tax collector, the health inspector, the local agricultural agent, and the forest ranger when they come to the village. He is charged with reporting criminal acts and preserving order within the village. He organizes special activities initiated by the local subdistrict officer such as government wheat and water distributions (in time of drought). In short, he is the liaison man between the lowest level administrative officials of the central government and his native villagers.

The members of the respective clans, however, consider the mukhtar (literally, "the one selected") to be a representative of their own clan and not the village or the government. In speaking about the role of mukhtar one informant told me: "Why do they call him mukhtar? Because the people of his clan have selected him." The clan, in fact, is the largest political unit within the village possessing a single representative vis-a-vis the outside world. The village itself is not so rep-

resented, since there are two (in Kufr al-Ma) and sometimes three (in other villages) mukhtars who claim to speak for it.

The mukhtar is supported financially by the clan which selects him. Every landowner in the clan is obliged to give him ten pounds (two rotls) of wheat or barley annually for every kirat of land. Or he may be given seventy cents instead.[68] The mukhtar usually collects this grain in kind on the threshing ground after the harvest. However, in 1960 the mukhtar of Beni Yasin received only about half of the grain that was due him. Three successive poor harvests had made the members of his clan recalcitrant in payment. A number of the members of Beni Yasin have refused to pay anything to support the present mukhtar due to old grudges. Some of them blame him for being fined by the government for the crop damage done by their livestock. On the other hand, the large landowners among the independent lineages and a few of the landowners of Benr 'Amr (who are not represented by a mukhtar) support either the mukhtar of Dumi or Yasin by paying him in kind at harvest time. In return the mukhtar will counsel them when they wish advice, verify their applications and petitions to various government agencies and witness such transactions as marriage, divorce, inheritance and sales. Officially, of course, each mukhtar is bound to perform these services for all villagers, but, actually, he performs them for his own supporters. At any moment in time, then, the political support of the mukhtar is not composed of his own clansmen and only them. Rather, it will include most of them as well as families from other lineages and clans.

In return for the services he performs for them, the mukhtar expects his clansmen to fulfill certain obligations toward him. When collecting funds to provide entertainment for some government official, he looks to the wealthier members of his clan for support and does not canvass other villagers. He can call upon their labor at certain times. When the king visited the area in the summer of 1960 and the subdistrict officer ordered the mukhtar to organize parties to fetch wood for the celebration, the mukhtar of Beni Yasin led a party from his own clan to the forest to collect it.

Although the mukhtar represents his own clan, organizes its activity in relation to governmental decisions (e.g., by allocating water delivered to the village among his own clansmen), and receives his support, in the main, from it, the weakness of the political bonds between clansmen is quite apparent. If members of the clan refuse to pay their dues to the mukhtar, he is powerless to force them to do so. Often, members of Dumi bearing a grudge against their own mukhtar come to the mukhtar of Yasin (and vice versa) asking for advice or for some service. At present, the two mukhtars have a gentleman's agreement by which they agree to refuse to serve dissident members of each other's clans. (I have, in fact, seen the mukhtar of Beni Yasin refuse to sign a document given to him for signature by a member of Dumi). But the very need for such an agreement signifies the loose bonds among clan members. Individuals who have refused to pay their dues or have consulted the mukhtar of another clan—who have, in a sense, opted out of their own clan, if only for a temporary period, are not ex-

pelled from the group even though they may be subject to the social control of malicious gossip.

The opposition of a clan member to his own mukhtar may be quite open. In 1960, a petition was passed around the village condemning the mukhtar of Beni Yasin for drawing up the government grain distribution list in favor of rich families in the village and to the detriment of poor families. Several members of Beni Yasin signed this petition (albeit a small minority of the total signatures). Many of these men were abused publicly and threatened with social boycott, but none of them withdrew their signatures or apologized for publicly opposing their own mukhtar.

An index of the weakness of the mukhtar in relation to his own clan is his reluctance to use the governmental authority vested in him against recalcitrant clansmen or even other villagers. By virtue of his office he can call on the support of such government officials as the forest ranger, religious judge, civil judge, subdistrict officer, and police chief in any crisis. And yet he seldom does so. Even when government intervention is requested, it is done in such a way as to minimize its effect and assure its quick withdrawal (see Case 8, pp. 97-102). In a twelve-month period the mukhtar of Beni Yasin requested the intervention of governmental authority only twice. Once, he genuinely feared that unless mounted police were sent to the village serious violence might occur. When the mounted police arrived several hours later the mukhtar apologized and told them that the dispute had been settled amicably by the villagers themselves. The police were entertained and sent back to their post. The other dispute concerned the violation by numerous villagers of two clans of the right of public way. A path that had been demarcated as a public way over thirty years before had been encroached upon. Some men had taken parts of it as garden land while others had extended their stone fences to enclose sections of it. The mukhtar complained on behalf of the village (although all of the individuals concerned except one were members of his clan) and the civil judge came to Kufr al-Ma to investigate. Ten villagers were fined amounts ranging from six to fifteen dollars for their encroachment. The action of the mukhtar in this case seems to contradict the assumption made above that the mukhtar avoids initiating government action which might injure his clansmen, the very source of his authority and financial support. It was not the mukhtar however, who originally raised the issue of encroachment on public ways. It was raised as a result of a previous dispute between two villagers over land boundaries near the public way. The mukhtar was following as much as leading public opinion when he raised the charge of land encroachment on behalf of the village.

The reluctance of the mukhtar to seek government support cannot be explained, however, solely in relation to the threat of alienation of clan members by such action. Such behavior is related to the conception that the village is the proper locus of social control (see p. 107ff). Justice is rendered within the village and according to certain traditional processes that take place in its guest houses rather than by government officials in courts and offices (see Case 9, pp. 134-39). Moreover, one of the most important functions the mukhtar performs for his clan involves the warding off of government action or, at least, its manipulation to serve the purposes of clan members. In other words, he acts as "fixer."[69] He is expected to utilize his knowledge of government officials and their ways to "fix" what might otherwise be the unpleasant consequences of their action. Villagers express their belief in the influence the mukhtar wields in government offices by saying, "he has a word [say] with the government" (*'endu kilma ma'a al Hukūma*).

The role of fixer involves more than warding off the consequences of government action. The mukhtar is expected to manipulate his government contracts to secure the largest share of any government distributions for his own clan. Indeed, the mukhtar is criticized by members of his own clan if he fails to serve its interests, even when serving such interests is at the expense of the general welfare of the village. For instance, the mukhtar of Beni Yasin, was criticized for being outsmarted by the mukhtar of Beni Dumi, who had managed to get a larger share of fodder for his own clan at the government fodder distribution. A failure at fixing may affect the interests of the whole village and involve general village and not merely clan dissatisfaction. The mukhtar of Beni Yasin was criticized for not being present to greet the subdistrict officer when he came during the harvest period to estimate the degree of dearth in the village. The villagers alleged that the officer had underestimated the degree of crop failure due to the mukhtar's absence and that as a result the village would not receive its rightful tax rebate. The former mukhtar of Beni 'Amr was widely criticized for not persuading the local notable, the Pasha, to annul a fine levied on the whole village. Shepherds from Kufr al-Ma had trespassed on the Pasha's land with their flocks. At the time, the mukhtar of Beni 'Amr was sharecropping the Pasha's land and was expected to have some influence over him.

That the villagers of Kufr al-Ma, regardless of clan membership, condemned the mukhtar for the fine that was levied upon them, that they, regardless of clan membership, submitted a petition to the government against him shows that the mukhtar is far more than a servant of his clan. He is a representative of the village. More than that, he is legally responsible for the village in the case of offenses against government property (such as woodlands) in the area of the village by unknown offenders. The fine is levied in the name of the mukhtars against the entire village; it is the mukhtars who are responsible for the collection of the fine from every household.

Local administrative policy favors one mukhtar for every thousand persons. Kufr al-Ma is a village with a population of approximately two thousand. Therefore, it has two mukhtars who may speak for it. Since there are three clans in the village, at any particular moment one must be denied representation. At present, Yasin and Dumi, the larger clans, are represented by mukhtars while 'Amr is not. This causes considerable chagrin to some of the members of 'Amr, as witnessed by the statement of the former mukhtar of Beni 'Amr when he stated that his clan no longer had any name in the village, an indication that the mukhtarship, regardless of its inherent weaknesses as a political office, carries considerable prestige within the village. Many of the poorer members of 'Amr, however, are quite contented to do without a mukhtar representing their particular clan, for they need not then contribute to his financial support; when forced to call upon the services of a mukhtar, they patronize the mukhtar of Dumi or Yasin on an ad hoc basis, usually without payment.

The mukhtar, then, is not the linchpin of the political, economic, and ritual structure of a corporate village. He has no ritual functions and does not act as village priest. He cannot grant rights in land (which are individually registered), and he does not supervise its cultivation. He cannot use his official position to force his own clansmen to pay their dues or to contribute to fund collections. The fact remains, however, that the clan that selects the mukhtar, regards him as its exclusive representative, and provides most of his economic support. He, in turn, works for their interest as mediator in their disputes (see Case 6, pp. 74–77, and Case 7, pp. 78–87), as counselor, and most importantly, as fixer. He is also the representative of the village and is legally responsible for certain acts of its members. He counsels the villagers in their relations with government, mediates in their disputes (see Case 9 pp. 134–39), and cushions them from the effects of government action. Finally, the mukhtar is a functionary of the local government hierarchy, transmitting its directives, interpreting them at the local level, informing government officials of village sentiment, and entertaining official guests in his guest house.

I. The Clan in Social Control

In all that has been written above, the clan has been pictured as a rather weak social unit. It exercises no corporate control over resources. Although it is usually represented by a mukhtar, his position is vulnerable and his support often comes from outside the clan. Even the ideology of clanship is weak with each of the clans differing considerably in their affirmation of patrilineal descent. It does, however, exercise one very important corporate function—the application of social control against its own members.[71] Social control is the process by which an individual is led to subordinate his own desires to the interests of the group or community of which he is a member. The leading elders of the clan acting as self-appointed representatives can act in the name of the clan against an individual or individuals who have violated basic norms. (The mukhtar usually acts with these elders, but he does not necessarily do so and if he does, he may not be the most prominent among them.) While the elders cannot expel an individual from the group for noncompliance, they can resort to social and economic boycotts and insidious gossip to make noncompliance well nigh impossible.

The pressure exerted by the elders of the clan—pressure initiated by them—against their own members cannot be exerted effectively against members of their sib living in other villages or against members of other clans living in the same village. The following case illustrates the effective application of social control by elders of the clan against members of the clan.

Mukhtar (left) and elders investigating a dispute over land boundaries

CASE EIGHT

This case began with a quarrel between Haj (so titled for having made the pilgrimage to Mecca) Yusuf Dhiyyab, a bearded patriarch above the age of eighty, and Muhammad Ali, a ploughman in his middle thirties. Yusuf and Muhammad were both members of Beni Yasin and lived in the clan area, but they were members of different lineages, As'eed and Massa'di respectively.

Muhammad Ali went to the mukhtar of Beni Yasin and told him that Yusuf Dhiyyab had claimed that his, Muhammad Ali's, cow had eaten his crops. Muhammad asked the mukhtar to come and examine the damage.

The next day, Yusuf (C1 on Chart 8) entered Muhammad Ali's courtyard and complained again about the cow and demanded compensation for damage done to his crops. Muhammad Ali denied the charge and, in a fit of temper, struck Yusuf several times with his walking stick, driving him out of the courtyard into the street.

That afternoon Yusuf went to the guest house of a respected man of Beni Yasin and showed him and the other elders present the bruises he had received at the hands of Muhammad Ali.

Later in the afternoon, a group of elders representing most of the lineages of Beni Yasin marched to Muhammad Ali's house. They told him that if he were not willing to send an official deputation (jaha) to Haj Yusuf to ask for forgiveness and to kiss his hand in obeisance and if he were not willing to accept a decision of impartial judges on the cost of the damage to Yusuf's crops and to slaughter a sheep, the men of Beni Yasin would have nothing more to do with him.

The reconciliation ceremony (sulha) was arranged for the afternoon of the following day, a Friday. It took place after the Friday congregational prayer. The elders of Yasin, as planned, went to the house of Haj Yusuf. They said that they had come to beg forgiveness for Muhammad Ali and after some reluctance Yusuf accepted their good offices. Muhammad Ali was brought in, bent low, and kissed the back of Yusuf's hand and his beard. Then Muhammad Ali kissed the cheeks of the other members of Yusuf's lineage and they reciprocated in kind. Coffee was served and drunk. Apparently, a properly made peace had been achieved.

One of the members of Yusuf's lineage, however, refused to attend the reconciliation meeting. He was Ahmed Mandil (B1 on Chart 8), a young soldier who had returned to the village for a few days on furlough. Muhammad Ali had been formally reconciled with everyone except him, and the mukhtar went to bring the soldier to the guest house. When Ahmed entered the guest house, Muhammad Ali rose to greet him and stretched out his hand in welcome. Ahmed countered by slapping him sharply across the face. Muhammad was too stunned to do anything, but the other members of Beni Yasin seized hold of Ahmed and proceeded to pummel him. Then the elders left the guest house in a body. Muhammad Ali's sheep which had been staked outside awaiting slaughter was returned to its owner's house and the rice that was brought along was taken back.

CHART 8

THE AS'EED PATRILINEAL GENEALOGY (Cases 6 and 8)

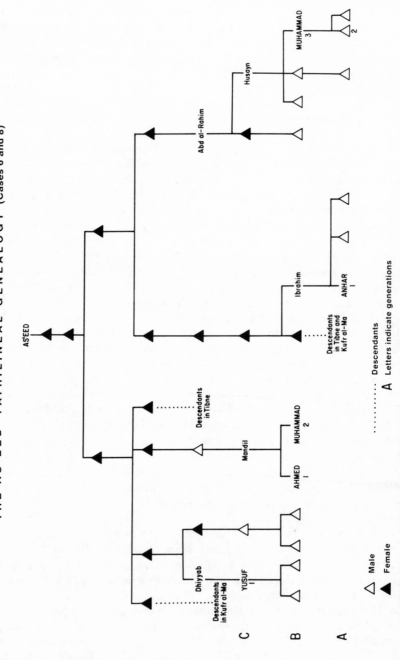

△ Male

▲ Female

MUHAMMAD Names in capitals represent living persons

Muhammad Names in small letters represent
deceased persons

········· Descendants

A Letters indicate generations

I Numbers indicate individuals within generations

The elders reassembled in the house of one of their number to discuss the sudden turn of events and the next move. Ahmed's behavior constituted an insult to the whole deputation. It was a "tearing of its face" (*taqtī' al wijh*) and a violation of the sanctity of the reconciliation. Many thought that a complaint against Ahmed Mandil should be filed at the police post. The mukhtar counseled restraint. He said that such a complaint might result in the soldier's losing his army position. The mukhtar then sent a message to the police post asking for the dispatch of a policeman in order to prevent further incidents. Then Muhammad Husayn Abd al-Rahim (B3), a leading elder of Haj Yusuf's lineage, came to the mukhtar and asked him what could be done. The mukhtar told him to go to the Beni Dumi quarter and recruit a deputation of respected men from that clan who would come to Muhammad Ali and ask for his forgiveness on behalf of Ahmed Mandil. Muhammad Husayn acted on the mukhtar's advice and recruited a deputation from Beni Dumi which then proceeded with him to Muhammad Ali's house. A sheep was slaughtered and a common meal was shared by all the elders who had participated in the deputation and had been affronted by Ahmed Mandil's action.

Muhammad Husayn, however, was not satisfied that the deputation of Beni Dumi had effectively dealt with the ill feeling that was harbored by the elders of the Yasin clan against his own lineage. Muhammad Husayn still feared that Muhammad Ali might file a complaint with the police against his kinsman, and so he went to the next town to urge the local notable, the Pasha, to intervene and effect a reconciliation. The Pasha deputed his brother who came to the village and was entertained in Muhammad Husayn's guest house. But the Pasha's brother was not able to effect a further reconciliation between the elders of Yasin and the leading man of the As'eed lineage. Before the Pasha's brother left the village, however, Muhammad Husayn entertained him in high style by slaughtering a sheep in his honor.

Meanwhile, the mounted policeman sent for by the mukhtar had arrived in the village. By then, the deputation of Beni Dumi had finished its work. Although the final reconciliation between Muhammad Ali and Yusuf Dhiyyab had yet to be achieved, the conciliation process had been set in motion. The mukhtar told the policeman that there was no longer any need for him. The policeman told the mukhtar that his superior would be displeased when he discovered that a mounted policeman had been sent without cause. The mukhtar told him not to worry, for he would speak to his chief in person and that he need only tell his chief that the mukhtar of Kufr al-Ma invited him to share in the reconciliation feast that was soon to be held.

Thus Haj Yusuf Dhiyyab's lineage lost two sheep in one day and received none, while at the beginning of the afternoon they had stood to gain one and lose none.

Several days later, a number of elders of As'eed met in the house of Anhar al-Ibrahim (A1), one of their leading men. They agreed that Muhammad Ali should pay the cost of the sheep slaughtered for the Pasha's brother. In addition, they expected Muhammad Ali to slaughter a sheep in honor of Yusuf Dhiyyab—the same sheep that had been earmarked several days earlier.

The elders of Beni Yasin assembled that same afternoon and discussed the situation. One elder said that he could not understand why
As'eed was now asking for money compensation when Beni Dumi had
decided several days earlier that there would be a return slaughter and
that would end the matter. Why had the elders of As'eed now changed
their minds?

The mukhtar said that Anhar al-Ibrahim simply wished to sow the
seeds of discord, that it was Anhar who was at the root of all the trouble. He said that if Anhar wished to foment discord, that he should come
and stand in front of men and state his case and not gossip next to
women. The mukhtar said that Anhar had caused trouble on three separate occasions. Anhar's sheep had eaten his (the mukhtar's) sesame
seed the year before. Then he had uprooted it all and hidden it to prove
to the investigating group of elders that the mukhtar was a liar. And
Anhar had written him a threatening note. This was in contrast to the
mukhtar's own behavior. How at the time when a member of another
clan had knocked his paternal nephew unconscious with a rock, he had
calmed his kinsmen and opposed his own lineage members in arranging
for a peacemaking. The mukhtar said that As'eed were at fault for the
slaughter of the extra sheep—that he had been against calling in the
Pasha and had told Muhammad Husayn that the villagers could fix the
matter among themselves. It was only necessary for him to persuade
Beni Dumi to come as intercessors. The first slaughter, the mukhtar
said, was for the honored guest and the second was to honor the clan's
deputation to make up for the "tearing of its face."

A clan elder said: "Ahmed Mandil's error was erased by the
slaughter in the house of Muhammad al-Ali and Muhammad Ali's error
must be wiped out in the house of Yusuf Dhiyyab." Another clan elder
was sent to the house of Muhammad al-Husayn to sound him out on the
possibility of a final reconciliation the following day.

The mukhtar said of As'eed: "They must know the worth of face—
the worth of people." The mukhtar said that after he saw the bruises of
Yusuf Dhiyyab, he had told him to go to the police post and file a
charge against Muhammad Ali, and that he (the mukhtar) would accompany him and act as witness. But Yusuf decided not to go. The mukhtar
said that the Qar'oosh (his own lineage) were more upset by the incident
than Yusuf's lineage.

On the afternoon of the next day, a Friday and a week after the
original breach, the Pasha came to the house of Muhammad Husayn and
said to him: "We want to end the acrimony by Muhammad Ali's coming
over and slaughtering his sheep." Muhammad Husayn told the Pasha
that he was upset because the sheep should have been slaughtered at
the house of the elder who had headed the deputation, for it was the
deputation which had been insulted. Instead, it was slaughtered at the
house of Muhammad Ali.

Later in the day Muhammad Ali entered Yusuf Dhiyyab's guest
house and kissed the elder's hand—for the second time in a week. And
the sheep that had been marked for killing a week earlier was slaughtered.

The first fact to note about this case is the importance attached to
the slaughtering of sheep. For Transjordanian peasants the slaughter
of a sheep constitutes a considerable loss of capital or, for the great

majority of peasants who own no livestock, the incurring of debt. It is the symbolic meaning of slaughter, however, that is of prime importance here. This meaning was involved in the number and order in which the sheep were slaughtered, the identity of the slaughterer, and the act of slaughtering itself. All of these matters were subjects of conversation and dispute. This was so because each slaughtering was interpreted as restoring the previous balance of right and wrong that was brought about by the preceding breach. If the numerical loss of sheep was to be construed strictly in terms of the slaughterer's lineage identity, then, clearly, one lineage was more in the wrong than the other. The mukhtar's interpretation placed another meaning on the second act of slaughtering which explained and justified the numerical imbalance. The general point here is that honor, an abstract concept, is symbolized by material goods whose exchange serves as some sort of balance sheet for calculating the relative quantity of intangible resources (honor) held by each side in the dispute.

The second fact to note about this case is that the initial breach was a violation of a fundamental tenet of kinship and village morality—namely, respect for the aged. The breach was, therefore, a matter that concerned the whole clan and the whole community and not merely the lineages immediately involved—As'eed and Massa'di. Moreover, the men who acted to check the initial breach did so in their capacity as heads of families and pious men as well as clan elders.

Yet only the clan elders of Yasin acted against Muhammad Ali. They acted on their own initiative shortly after seeing Yusuf Dhiyyab's bruises. Only they were in a position to threaten him with a social boycott. It is true that not all of the lineages of Yasin were represented in the deputation. The important point is that they spoke for Yasin. The absence of representatives of one or two lineages would not alter this fact.

The elders threatened Muhammad Ali with a social boycott rather than repressive, economic, or ritual sanctions. Yet this threat was quite sufficient, and Muhammad Ali proceeded with the elders of Yasin to Yusuf's house where he asked for, and was granted, pardon.

When Ahmed Mandil slapped Muhammad Ali, it was the whole of Yasin whose honor had been besmirched. The elders got up as a body and left the guest house. The slaughter by Ahmed Mandil was as much for them as for Muhammad Ali, as one of the elders pointed out. Here the clan was regarded as a prestige unit whose "face" had been "torn."

With the alienation of all the Yasin elders, the members of Ahmed Mandil's lineage, As'eed, had to call in another clan, Beni Dumi, to act as mediators. They were called in because of certain formal considerations pertaining to the sending of a deputation and its operation in the guest house. First, the pleader never presents his own case; and second, of those who can present it for him, outsiders (nonkinsmen) have greater "face" than insiders (kinsmen) and are able, in a sense, to apply more pressure for concession—concession in the guest house where the guest must, above all, be honored and granted his wishes. The members of Dumi did not, however (like Yasin), act on their own initiative with the threat of applying social sanctions, nor could they

have done so. They had few common economic, political, or affinal ties
with either Muhammad Ali or Ahmed Mandil. Both Ahmed and Muhammad lived in the midst of their Yasin clansmen and not in the Dumi
quarter. They were susceptible to a social boycott by Yasin but not by
Dumi. It was the prestige of Beni Dumi as a leading clan with prominent elders that was sought rather than the weight of their sanctions.
Clans, then, act as units of social control not only in the sense that
their elders can successfully apply pressure against their own members, but also in the sense that their prestige can be invoked in situations involving members of other clans.

After the second breach the conciliation process widened to include mediators out of the clan and even out of the village. The interesting point about this extracommunity intervention was that it was not
effective. The policeman was told to go home and the Pasha's brother,
after chiding the peasants for the excessive show of hospitality, also
returned home without having effected a reconciliation.

Although this case has been presented as an example of social
control by clan elders of clan members, I do not mean to indicate that
elders of the clan can intervene of their own volition against any clan
member at any time. Most of the disputes that arose in the village in
the year of my residence involved differences over the interpretation
of facts (over land boundaries or crop damage, for instance). Such disputes are settled by the investigation of the mukhtar or by a local government official. A number of disputes involved families locked together in "multiplex" relationships. [72] That is, they were tied to one another
simultaneously as agnates, cognates, and neighbors and they interacted
in relationships serving many interests—political, economic, recreational, etc. Such disputes (usually related to matters of marriage,
divorce, or inheritance) are most frequently settled by the families
themselves (see Case 4, pp. 65–66, and Case 7, pp. 78–87), or, exceptionally, by the intervention of a leading personality of the community at
their behest (see Case 9, pp. 134–39). Spontaneous action by clan elders
occurs only when the norms violated are of such a fundamental character as to have resulted in moral condemnation of the act by the whole
community. Muhammad Ali had beaten a respectable elder of the clan,
a pious man, a pilgrim—beaten him in his own (Muhammad's) house.
Such action in a community which reveres the patriarch and honors the
guest was intolerable. It was the gravity of the offense that propelled
the mediation effort and carried it through to a successful conclusion.

The dispute just described, exceptional in the nature of the offense
treated and in the unanimity and spontaneity with which clan elders
rose to resolve it, is but one of many cases of reconciliation in which
the elders of Yasin took part. A number of indices show the superiority
of Beni Yasin over the other clans of the village as an effective unit of
social control. One index is the great number of disputes which Yasin
elders were called on to mediate. The great majority of cases I witnessed involved Yasin elders, this being so even when the dispute did
not involve members of that clan. Members of other clans frequently
called on elders of Yasin to mediate in their disputes.

The superiority of Yasin as a unit of social control is also seen in the number of guest houses in the village. When I asked the village watchman, a member of Beni 'Amr and a frequent attender of guest houses in the course of his daily round, how many men could genuinely be regarded as "serving coffee" in their guest house, he named fifteen men, ten of whom were of Yasin. On any given night a number of their guest houses would be open and serving coffee. It was to them that disputes were most often brought.

A third index is the slaughtering of sheep for funerals. I once asked the imam why slaughtering of animals continued on the fourth day after the death of a Yasin elder. He himself had told me earlier that, according to religious law, all public funeral mourning and its attendant ceremonies should end on the third day after burial. He replied that so many elders of the Yasin sib had come from other villages with sheep to be slaughtered that it was impossible to fit them into the three-day period. Yasin, he pointed out with pride, was not like the others, waving his hand in the direction of the quarters of Dumi and 'Amr.

The members of Yasin regarded themselves as genuine patrilineal kinsmen and as a more cohesive group than the other clans in the village. When a robbery occurred in the lower quarter of the village, an elder of Yasin commented that it was only to be expected. Such a robbery could not have been perpetrated in the Yasin quarter, he said; the thief would have been uncovered almost immediately. On one occasion, on the marriage of one of their patrilineal kinsmen in the town of Irbid some twenty miles away, a delegation of men representing each of the lineages of Yasin went to attend the wedding celebration and to offer money gifts as was the custom. I never witnessed any such symbolic show of unity on the occasion of marriage by any of the other clans.

Various factors account for Beni Yasin's position of superiority as an effective unit of social control. Size is one of them. The clan of Beni Yasin includes almost forty percent of the population of the village. Yasin numbered many more respected elders than the other clans combined. Economic resources is another. Yasin owns more than two-thirds of the landed property in the village. Their elders can afford to brew and serve coffee nightly in the guest houses of the clan. The presence and the strong personalities of two important village specialists—the mukhtar and the imam—is a third. The mukhtar of Yasin was sought far more as mediator than the mukhtar of Dumi, a younger and less knowledgeable person. The imam regarded peacemaking as a religious duty and was often called upon to reconcile estranged kinsmen.

Thus the frequency of Yasin's consultations, the importance of its elders, and the number of its guest houses made the operation of social control more effective among them than among the other clans. Their claim to solidarity was not merely an expression of their patrilineal ideology but reflected their actual social relations.

J. The Village: Criteria for the Identification of "Community"

One of the most difficult tasks facing the anthropologist is the definition of the social unit under study together with a proper demarcation of its boundaries. When the anthropologist undertakes to study a whole people who are not separated from others by clear-cut physical boundaries (such as water for the Pacific islands) or demarcated by administrative boundaries (whether native or European), or distinguished by racial or linguistic peculiarities (such as the Bushman of Southwest Africa), the task becomes formidable. [73]

But the anthropologist who confines his research to a single community has, at first sight, solved his problem by definition. The "community," however, is not such a self-evident unit as one might anticipate. In Central Africa, for instance, the "village" is composed of homesteads scattered far and wide over a considerable expanse of territory. In West Africa settlements merge one into the other so as to be nearly indistinguishable.

In the Middle East, on the other hand, villages are usually crowded nucleated settlements with their surrounding cultivable lands separating them from other like settlements. With the increase in population, building has taken place on the outskirts of the village with the result that villages are gradually expanding towards one another (though they remain fairly distinct social units spatially). In Kufr al-Ma a few men who originally lived within the old area of habitation have built houses at points equidistant from Kufr al-Ma and the neighboring town of Deir Abu Said. Spatially, it is impossible to class them as residents of one or the other. Other criteria must be used to determine their community affiliation.

One of these criteria is the affiliation of the individual to the administrative unit. The village is the administrative unit carrying out government edicts and benefiting from government services. Its mukhtars represent the village in government offices and in the village itself where they must meet and entertain government officials who come there in the course of their work. Each individual must affiliate himself with the mukhtar of one village or another if he wishes to benefit from government services and handouts.

I have already pointed out that the census figures reported to the government are village totals rather than sib totals. The basis of all the government plans and estimates is the village rather than any other social unit.

In addition, although it has no such legal status, the village operates as a municipality in certain respects. It pays the mukhtars who represent it (although, strictly speaking, they are paid by their own clans). It hires and pays village watchmen who protect it and serve its mukhtars. It pays the imam, who is charged with providing ritual services to the villagers congregationally in the mosque and individually on the occasion of various life crises.

Although the village forms a discrete spatial unit, clearly separated from other settlements, and although it constitutes an administrative unit and performs certain municipal functions, no central meeting place exists where community activities can take place. The village has no spatial, cultural, political, or economic center (see Map 2A, p. 74). In this respect it is a typical of the descriptions of Palestinian, Syrian, and Lebanese villages provided by some commentators. [74]

Kufr al-Ma from its center facing north toward the police post (Note sesame seed plants—right of center—set out for drying on roof.)

The mosque is in the Beni Yasin quarter of the village. Aside from its use for daily prayers and the Friday congregational prayer, it is not used as a meeting place for any other community activities. The schools are located on the outskirts of the village and are not loci for extracurricular activities carried on by villagers. One might argue the political center of the village is the mukhtar's house, wherever that happens to be. Since there are two mukhtars, there can be no single locus of activity. Moreover, elders of the clan are often more influential than the mukhtars, and their guest houses, rather than his, will be the centers of political activity. The closest approximation of a central square or village area is the large open space on which front four grocery shops (see Map 2). Many men often gather there to gossip during lulls in daytime activity and in the early evening. This area is, however, in the Dumi quarter and men of Yasin and 'Amr are not generally seen there. They tend to congregate at the shops in their own quarters.

In addition to its administrative status and its municipal functions, the village is a legal corporation in regard to certain criminal actions. When public land (such as state-owned woodland) or large amounts of private land are defaced or destroyed and the culprits are unknown, the inhabitants of the village suspected are held corporately responsible for the deed. A fine is levied by the government on the village, and the mukhtars are held responsible for the collection of the fine in equal amounts from each adult male in the village.

The village is not only an administrative unit, a legal corporation, and the framework of political rivalry, but also the framework for status differentiation among individuals and groups.[75] I have already referred to the statement of the former mukhtar of Beni 'Amr regarding the position of his clan in the village: "We have no name in this village." Beni 'Amr is not represented by a mukhtar who can speak for it in government offices and village councils. Status can be achieved only in some significant structural framework and that framework is in the village. When a member of Beni Yasin refers to his clan as being pure in descent as compared with the others which are characterized by "wrapping," he is comparing Yasin with Dumi and 'Amr and not with descent groups in other villages.

The village also represents a prestige unit vis-a-vis other villages. When asked to list the guest rooms in the village, the village watchman reeled off the names of fifteen men who made coffee in the evening in their guest rooms. He made it a point, however, to note that the maintenance of a guest room was not just significant in terms of a man's status (or the clan's) in the village. The man who maintained a guest room "veiled the village" (*biyistar al qarya*). Any stranger or visitor, whether government official or peasant, could be sent to the owner of the guest room (*maDāfa*) in the assurance that he would be sheltered, fed, and entertained. The owners of guest rooms protected the name of the village, securing its renown for generosity and hospitality at the same time they were adding to their own stature as generous and honorable men.

In addition to its existence as a framework for political rivalry and status differentiation, the village is a locus of kinship (as opposed to descent) ties.[76] There is a decided tendency for men and women to marry within the village. Of 754 marriages of men living and dead, for which I have collected figures, 590 of them were with women from Kufr al-Ma. Of 429 marriages of women, living and dead, recorded by me, 335 of them were with men from within the village. In both cases seventy-eight percent married within the village. The village of Kufr al-Ma, then, resembles a "deme." It is an endogamous local community, the members of which are bilaterally linked through marriage; kinship connections are traditionally accepted as tying together all members although these connections cannot always be traced.[77]

Men are often reluctant to marry their daughters outside the village (see Case 6, p. 74–77). It means that they pass into another social world where effective ties with their families of origin will be considderably weakened, if not severed. This reluctance is often manifested in the demand for a higher marriage payment (at least 840 dollars as opposed to the 560 demanded from a villager) from men of other villages who seek women from Kufr al-Ma as wives. Movement out of the village often jeopardizes the woman's fundamental source of support against her husband and his kinsmen, should she receive mistreatment at their hands. She can always flee to her father's or her brother's house and seek refuge there until her penitent husband seeks her out. Marriage in another village, close though it may be, makes the in-marrying bride a "stranger" (unless she marries a cousin) in her husband's village.[78]

The point I wish to make here is that a village represents a focus of kinship ties that distinguishes it from other villages. Marriage ties men and women together who are already linked by residence, patrilineality, and common political and economic interests. Equally, if not more important than the fact of villagewide linking is the fact that these links are recognized and described in an idiom of kinship. The idiom is that of matrilateral relationship (makhwal). This idiom allows all sons of the village to claim consanguineal relationship (by their own marriages or those of their parents or grandparents) with certain patrilineages and through them, eventually, with all clans and independent families within the village (see pp. 114–16, and 134–40 for a fuller discussion of the significance of matrilateral ties for village unity). Thus the idiom of matrilaterality crosscuts all patrilineal descent groups and makes all villagers, not merely affines, but also kinsmen.

The demarcation of the community in terms of formal characteristics—spatial, administrative, and legal—or in terms of its existence as a framework for political rivalry and status differentiation or even as a locus of kinship ties does not, however, reveal the essential aspect of community life. The village is a common area of living where limits must be placed on the show of hostility and where men can be made to subordinate their own desires for the interests of the larger unit of which they are members. The village is, in short, a unit of social control.

In the past, social control was only one of the corporate functions assumed by the village community.[79] The villages of northern Jordan have, historically, assumed other corporate functions. They were units of defense. In Tibne, for instance, all who would settle in the village and help defend it were given land. They were units of corporate land ownership and division under the musha' system. Many of them may have been corporate taxation units. Until recent times, mukhtars in Palestine were responsible for the collection of taxes from the villagers.[80] In addition, of course, the village was a unit of social control. In Tibne the Shaykh and the elders of the community could compel any villager to appear in the guest house to explain his actions. And, conversely, any villager could demand his rights before the assembled elders in the Shaykh's guest house. In the past, action was often taken by "village" leaders rather than by leaders of descent groups. The leaders of the 1939 permanent division of land, for instance, were not the heads of the clans of Kufr al-Ma but prominent landowners of the village.

These corporate functions have, however, long since disappeared. Land now is individually and permanently owned and not communally owned and divided. Taxes are now fixed on individuals and collected by administrative officials (although cancellation of taxes in drought years is based on an estimate of the total village harvest). Defense is now a national function. The disappearance of corporate functions and the differentiation of the occupational structure have not, however, changed some of the basic conditions of life in a nucleated village. The village remains today what it was in the past—a social unit in which the basic fact of existence is the necessity for residents to live together amicably or, at the very least, tolerantly. The successful pursuit of agriculture and shepherding requires cooperation among villagers (see Cases 5, pp. 66–69, 7, pp. 78–87, and 8, pp. 97–102). Over half the employed men in the village engage in agricultural activity, at least for part of the year. Many of those that do not (army men for instance) have close relatives owning and tilling the land. In a nucleated village close kinsmen will almost inevitably "brush elbows" in the course of carrying out their day-to-day activities. They may be forced to consult one another, even if indirectly, to carry out these activities (see Case 5). They may meet one another by the very proximity of their houses, their orchards, or their croplands (see Case 7). Large numbers of sheep and goats are grazed in the village and their wanderings account for a large proportion of the village's disputes (see Cases 5, 7, and 8). Unless such disputes are resolved fairly and quickly, they may result in serious social and economic disruption for all the parties concerned. The village is regarded as a common area of living and toleration where limits must be placed on the show of overt hostility. Ikhleyf al-Muflih explicitly recognized this principle (see Case 7) when he said, addressing the members of Shujur, "We must allow one another room in this village."

The effectiveness of the community's exercise of social control is enhanced by the sedentary nature of life in a peasant village. Kinsmen may become estranged from one another, but they continue to live in the same village and, in most cases, in the same quarter and the same house. Even if they spend most of the year away from the village working as laborers in towns or serving as professional soldiers in military camps, they maintain their affiliation with the village by regular visits. They do this because the basis of their subsistence—their land—is there and/or because the basis of their social identity—their family, their relatives, their village mates and their coreligionists—remains in the village. Tensions among kinsmen that might be resolved by schism in more labile groups such as slash and burn cultivators or nomads are maintained in being in sedentary village communities. The very persistence of these tensions and their potential for chronic disruption of social relationships mounts pressure for eventual reconciliation of the estranged parties (see Case 5 for an explicit recognition of this fact by the mukhtar of Beni Yasin). The passage of time before the reconciliation effort depends on the seriousness of the original breach and the practical nature of its consequences.

In the past the need to cooperate was given a sense of urgency by the necessity of defending the village and holding its land corporately. Men who were willing to settle down and help defend the village were given land and attached to the dominant descent group by marriage. The Wazir family was so attached in Tibne (see Chapter 1). In Kufr al-Ma, the Jabali lineage was attached to Beni 'Amr by fact of cooperation in land division under the musha' system and marriage over successive generations into that clan.

Attachment to the community did not then and does not now occur as a matter of general right by fact of residence in it. Attachment to the community always takes place through particular families and descent groups. The individual supports the mukhtar of a group and thereby shares in government handouts. He lives in the area of a group; therefore, he offers and receives hospitality from its members. It is through these members, mainly, that he gains access to women who may prove eligible mates for himself or his sons. It is through them that he gains credit in village shops. It is from them that he can request water when his own cistern has run dry.

Thus, each individual, if he remains in the village, must belong to a "social network."[81] The members of this network are kinsmen, affines, and friends with whom he associates on a day-to-day basis—men to whom he regularly offers hospitality and from whom he receives it. However much he may reduce his ties with his patrilineal kinsmen whether as a result of marrying his daughter out of the lineage, refusing to give financial support to his clan's mukhtar, or moving out of the area altogether, he does not cut the bonds which bind him to the village community. To claim the rights of village membership—the rights to its human and natural resources, its fellowship, and its distribution of justice—he establishes a new social network among his new neighbors or adjusts his old network by replacing alienated kinsmen by other relatives. He cannot withdraw from the community short of moving away from it.[82] Wherever he moves inside the village, he must establish new links, political, economic and social, if he has broken the old ones. Having established this network to claim the privileges of village membership, he becomes bound by the obligations which such membership imposes. Membership in a network brings him within the sphere of village social control. As a member of the community, he can be held responsible for his actions.

Perhaps because attachment to the community is always through particular kinship groups, that attachment is described in a kinship idiom. Men either identify with a patrilineal descent group or stress their matrilateral and affinal links with a group, referring to its members as "mother's brother" or "sister's son" or "affine" as the case may be.

But even when attachment is expressed as attachment to a patrilineal descent group, it is attachment to the community that has in fact occurred. By identifying himself with a descent group whether in its political (paying dues to its mukhtar), social (sharing hospitality with its members), economic (cooperating in day-to-day activities), or ideological (claiming membership in the group) aspect, an individual is really at one and the same time establishing and legitimizing his position in a village community. Many villagers recognize that the fundamental fact is living together and not membership in a descent group. As one villager expressed it, referring deprecatingly to the genealogies I was proudly showing him, "it is all putting together" (*kulu tarkīb*). Improvisation of genealogical links and claims of descent group membership were regarded as the traditional procedures for legitimizing village residence.

The involvement of a man in the community, in whatever way it may occur, brings with it the enjoyment of certain rights and privileges, some of which have been briefly mentioned above. The son of the village (*ibn al-balad*) enjoys the privilege of consultation with its municipal officials.[83]   From the imam he may receive advice regarding his spiritual welfare as well as counsel in Islamic Law and from the mukhtar he may receive advice and often mediation in dealing with government officials. He can seek the mediation of the elders of the community when he becomes involved in a dispute with other villagers. In doing so, he can be assured that the case will be treated in the customary way in the guest house where he will have full freedom to present his side in as forceful and histrionic a manner as he wishes. He knows that there, consensus will develop only after the total social and ethical context of the dispute have been taken into account. Credit will be extended to the son of the village by village shopkeepers, extended over several years in some instances while it would not be so extended to nonvillagers. Conversely, villagers are expected to pay itinerant peddlars from the surrounding villages immediately, for they are not sons of the village even though their frequent visits to the village would make short-term deferred payments possible. (But there is a limit to which shopkeepers will allow monetary debt to pile up. In Kufr al-Ma, after three successive bad harvests, shopkeepers, at the risk of alienating their fellow villagers, pressed for the collection of debts in the courts.)

In addition to credit, the son of the village has access to the women of the village as potential mates in marriage. Not only is he given priority over nonvillagers (see Case 6, pp. 74-75), but also the marriage payment expected from him is much less than that expected from an unrelated nonvillager who seeks the hand of a daughter of the village: $560 (1960) and $700 (1966) for the villager as opposed to $840 (1960) and $980 (1966) for the stranger.

In a period of drought the water of the cisterns of the village will be reserved for its inhabitants. In the summer of 1960 after scant winter rains, only a few of the cisterns of the village contained ample water supplies. A number of Bedouin from the Jordan Valley were, at the time, grazing their sheep on the outskirts of the village. They arranged with one of the villagers to water their sheep every day at noon at his cistern. On hearing about this, the mukhtars of the village went directly to the owner of the cistern and remonstrated. They declared that if the water was to be sold to anyone, it must be sold to inhabitants of the village. The Bedouin were forbidden to water in the village from that time forward.

The son of the town has free movement in his home village. But the stranger is subject to keen scrutiny: his movements are followed and his errand questioned. It might be said of the village that it has an "early-warning system" of its own; the villagers police their own neighborhoods. I once observed a shopkeeper from Kufr al-Ma accost a young man who was loitering around the village without apparent cause. The shopkeeper asked the fellow what he was doing in the village. When he gave evasive replies, the shopkeeper told him to leave the village and not return unless for some good reason. The young man did as he was told. On another occasion a magician from another area was practicing his craft furtively in a quarter of the village. One of the mukhtars ran into him accidentally and, noting him for a stranger, proceeded to question him. Upon receiving evasive answers, the mukhtar apprehended him. After investigation of his activities he was condemned as a bogus magician, pummeled when he resisted arrest, and driven out of the village. Of course, Shaykh Basim, the hometown magician, was placed in a different category, and continued to ply his craft undisturbed.[84]

Conversely, in Deir Abu Said (or in any other village in the area, for that matter) the resident of Kufr al-Ma is a stranger. Since Deir Abu Said is the administrative center of the subdistrict, residents of Kufr al-Ma often go there to the courts or government offices. Invariably, the villagers gather in the shop of Jabr Abdullah, who lives in Kufr al-Ma. In a sense, Jabr's shop represents their post in alien territory. Finally, the ibn al-balad can expect the good fellowship of his covillagers. Neglect of customary visits is noticed and commented upon, and estrangement of covillagers is regarded as an unnatural and unethical state of affairs according to both local and Islamic norms (see Case 3, pp. 63–65, and Case 5, pp. 66–69).

The status, son of the village, while it confers many privileges, imposes certain disabilities. The most important of these is the susceptibility to social control. The son of the village can be held responsible for his actions, particularly when these actions involve violation of important norms. In the cases discussed above, pressure was put on elders, rich peasants, soldiers, and young ploughmen. Even the schoolteacher who came from another village and was not a permanent resident was subject to pressure by villagers. Although he was not a son of the village, he had taken on one of the important components of this status by sharing hospitality regularly with the villagers. After several of their sons had failed to pass the examinations, they came to remonstrate, requesting favors on the basis of the bread and salt they had shared. I myself was subject to pressure on the same basis. Extended residence in the village and regular sharing of hospitality had led the residents to treat each of us, in some respects, as a son of the village. In order to extricate himself from these pressures, the schoolteacher refused to accept hospitality from any of the villagers from that time forward. In effect, he sealed himself off from the community, spending his leisure time in Deir Abu Said. I was too much involved in village affairs to assume the same attitude. I continued to offer and receive hospitality; he did not. After the incident, the schoolteacher was often compared invidiously with me. He was "in" the village but not "of it." No peasant could have emulated the schoolteacher's action, for each was bound by many more components of the status, son of the village, than mere residence and sharing of hospitality. Each inhabitant of the village was tied to the community by political affiliation, economic cooperation, and affinal bonds. Defined in this sense, the community may include individuals who are not spatially part of the village and exclude residents within it.

In assessing the importance of social control for community life, the role of Islam must be considered. The village constitutes a ritual unit. There exists within it an agent who considers it his duty to reconcile all villagers. Each Friday the elders assemble at the mosque to hear the imam's sermon. The content of these sermons is not, on the whole, concerned with theology or the performance of religious ritual (obligations of prayer, fasting and pilgrimage), but rather with ethics. Men are told how they should conduct their life as Muslim brothers. Even when ritual is discussed, it is the attitude that underlies it rather than its performance that is stressed. During the course of his sermon the imam makes obvious, if discreet, references to happenings in the village during the previous week that violated Muslim ethics.

The imam does not confine his influence to the mosque. He is often present on peacemaking occasions. In fact, the reconciliation (sulha) is regarded as a religious obligation. He makes this point crystal clear on these occasions and, in his absence, the pious elders are sure to make it for him several times. Estranged "brothers" must be brought together. Pious men should forgive erring "brothers," particularly if they are younger and thereby considered less responsible.

Although the imam of Kufr al-Ma has not had formal training at a school of higher Islamic education, he is regarded as—and indeed by village standards is—a man of learning (see Antoun, 1967). More than this, he is at certain moments, because of the earnestness of his conviction and the piety of his behavior regarded as being able, aided by the rest of the congregation, to draw the attention of God to the plight the believers. The occasion for this appeal is the prayer for rain which the imam leads in the mosque on infrequent occasions in the winter after the regular Friday service. Two of these rain prayers (*istisqā*) occurred during the winter of 1959–60 after prolonged periods of drought in what was supposed to be the rainy season.

The imam, perhaps more than any other individual, represents the unity of the whole village. He is paid a certain amount of grain on the threshing ground for every male resident, regardless of age. His duties—performance of ablutions for the dead and their burial, officiating at divisions of movable wealth according to legal prescriptions after death, and conciliation of estranged individuals—takes him into nearly every house in the village at some time. His sermons are always well attended.

The strengthening of religious norms was not confined to the mosque or the efforts of the imam. During Ramadan, the month of the fast, villagers usually invited their neighbors, their kinsmen, their friends, and destitute individuals to share in the meal just after sunset (see Antoun, 1968, for an analysis of the social significance of the fast of Ramadan in Kufr al-Ma). Ramadan was regarded as the appropriate time for resolving old disputes and reconciling estranged friends and kinsmen. Two of the most important reconciliations I witnessed took place during this month. Both of the reconciliation sessions were preceded by the chanting of a story about the life of Muhammad by the imam. I noticed, generally, that Friday afternoon, after the congregational prayer, was regarded as the appropriate time for sending a deputation with the object of "peacemaking." The activities of the imam, then, more than any other individual, assumed the village to be the locus of social control.

The pressure of Islamic norms, therefore, acting with other ideologies of social relationship, reinforces the pressure generated by the circumstance of living in a crowded sedentary village to bring about the eventual reconciliation of estranged villagers. Social control, then, has its ideological (Islamic beliefs) as well as its sociological (multiplex relationships), economic (two-crop dry cereal farming and grazing livestock in open fields), and ecological (sedentary life in a nucleated settlement) sanctions within the village community.

CHAPTER THREE

Marriage

The previous chapter has been devoted mainly to an analysis of the recruitment, composition, spatial relations, ideology, social relations, and economic, legal and political functions of the patrilineal descent groups in Kufr al-Ma. The study of a community's social structure is not, however, complete unless the ties linking what otherwise might be regarded as discrete segments within the community are described and analyzed. In Kufr al-Ma these are usually ties through marriage.[1] Indeed, in the last section the village community itself was described from one angle as a web of kinship established by the intermarriage of its inhabitants. The next section will examine briefly the significance of matrilaterality for the existence of a single community structure. The sections following will describe the actual mode of marriage and the various patterns of marriage found in the village. Finally, the social consequences of two specific patterns—cousin marriage and sister exchange—will be examined in a detailed case study and a brief functional analysis.[2]

1. THE KHAL: MATRILATERAL TIES AND VILLAGE UNITY

The term *khāl*, or mother's brother, is used in reference and address not only to refer to a person's actual maternal uncle but also to his mother's khal and to his father's khal. The term khal is extended to the whole lineage of which the khal (i.e., ego's mother's brother and the mother's brothers of his parents) is a member. I noted one instance in which only the mother's uterine brother was referred to as khal. In this case the term khal was not used in reference or address to the members of the khal's lineage.

If, on the other hand, ego or his father stand as khal to some group, they address the male members of that group as khali (my mother's brother) and state that there is *makhwal* or "mother's brother-ship" between them. For instance, if ego's father's sister had married into another lineage, her children would refer to her brother as khal, they would address him as khali, and they would extend these terms of reference and address to the other male members of his lineage. Ego (and his father), on the other hand, would address his father's sister's children as khali (*khalti* for the female) and assert that there was makh-wal or "mother's brothership" between them. In other words, whether the individual stands at the mother's brother or sister's son end of the relationship, the terms of address are the same and the relationship is conceptualized as mother's brothership.

When the khal is a mother's brother of ego's grandparents (on either side) or the matrilateral link is so remote as to be unknown, the term khal is not used in address or reference. However, ego recognizes this tie by saying, "There is mother's brothership [makhwal] between us," meaning between ego and the members of the whole group with whom makhwal is claimed. Moreover, ties through women are often assimilated to mother's brothership and described as such. Thus, two men whose mothers are of the same lineage often refer to and address one another as khal. Finally, the term khal is sometimes used in address when no kinship tie whatsoever exists between the speaker and the person addressed. It is used in such a manner when ego wishes to establish some degree of intimacy (at least superficially) with the person addressed as a prelude to asking a favor or for advice, or conversely, the refusing of a request.

The term khal like the term 'amm, covers many relationships. Moreover, the ideology of matrilateral relationship like the ideology of patrilineal descent is correlated with certain expectations of behavior and is manipulated in order to take advantage of these expectations. A khal is appealed to for material aid in various situations. He is often called in as an intercessor in disputes between close patrilineal kinsmen. A man will often till the land of his khal. The wedding celebration may take place in his khal's house if ego's or ego's father's residence is not suitable. The mother's brother-sister's son tie also has some political significance, for a khal is expected to support his sister's son (and vice versa) in cases of honor although there is no legal obligation to do so.

A woman, on the other hand, will often call on her khal to support her against her brothers or her brothers-in-law if they infringe on what she considers to be her rights. A woman, on quarreling with her husband and leaving him "in a state of anger" (za'alāne), will often go to live with her khal if her patrilineal kinsmen are not available. A woman who has lost her husband (by death or divorce) will often seek residence with her matrilateral kinsmen.

The sister's son, on the other hand, is expected to help wash the body of his mother's brother before burial. During the three-day mourning period, matrilateral relatives often assume the various duties of entertaining, serving coffee, and cooking meals in place of the grieving patrilineal kinsmen of the deceased. A sister's son will often call on an actual or classificatory mother's brother to act as go-between during preliminary marriage feelers (the wāsiTa).

Any person who stands as khal to a lineage may be approached by others who wish brides from that group. He is called on to act as go-between on behalf of the suitor because of his makhwal with the bride's family (see Antoun, "Social Organization and the Life Cycle in an Arab Village," *Ethnology*, 6 [July 1967]).

It is important to note that in the case of a patrilateral parallel cousin marriage, actual or classificatory, the term khal is used in reference and address not only for the mother's brother (who is also a classificatory 'amm) but also for all the men of his lineage of the same generation. In other words, matrilateral ties take precedence over patrilineal descent in terminology when the two coincide.

The readiness with which men and women use and extend terms indicating matrilateral linking is partly explained by the particular affective nature with which ties through women are regarded. "Affection comes by way of women," I was told by one man. "You are always closer to your daughter's children," I was told by another. Marrying the daughter of a mother's brother is regarded as a guarantee of harmony in the family just as marrying a woman whose sister is already married to one's brother is regarded as a guarantee that one's own children will be treated with care and affection. Thus, appeals in the idiom of "mother's brothership" are considered more effective than others, for they stress the tie through women and it is these ties that are regarded as having special affective significance. Yet, intensification of kinship ties, even when it comes by way of women, has a double edge. On the one hand, affective ties are built up; on the other, strains are produced. The ideology of matrilateral linking is not a completely false conception of social reality. But it dramatizes the harmonious aspects of such relationships and ignores the structural conflicts implicit in them.

Finally, the fact that the village resembles a deme (an endogamous local community bilaterally linked by marriage) is a result of ramifying matrilateral (or viewed differently, affinal) ties. The fact of linking is, however, less important than the interpretation placed upon it. The individual relates himself to other members of the community by tracing affinal ties laterally across lineage boundaries rather than lineally within them. But, and this is the point to note, these ramifying ties are rarely expressed in an idiom of affinity (*nasab*) but rather, almost invariably, in an idiom of matrilateral relationship (makhwal). This interpretation reinforces and dramatizes the cohesiveness of the community since the village is viewed as a genuine web of kinship rather than a series of discrete patrilineal descent groups on the one hand or a series of marriage alliances on the other. Social integration is not "accomplished vertically, through genealogical reckoning to common ancestors" as Murphy and Kasden argue for nomadic and, by extension, sedentary Arab groups (Murphy and Kasden, "The Structure of Parallel Cousin Marriage," 61:27). It is accomplished laterally by marriage ties interpreted in a symbolism of blood kinship through the idiom of matrilaterality.

2. THE MODE OF MARRIAGE[3]

A marriage in Kufr al-Ma is contracted in several steps whose order may vary. The first event is the sending of the go-between (wasita). This is followed by negotiations over the marriage payment culminating in the betrothal (*khuTba*). Next follows the sending of the formal deputation (jaha) to ask the girl's hand in marriage. The act which makes the marriage legal (according to Islamic law) and gives it religious sanction, the formal marriage contract (*'aqd al-nikāH*), usually takes place sometime between the sending of the deputation and the fifth event—the completion of all marriage payments (mahr) by the bridegroom or his father to the girl or her guardian. Finally, the wedding celebration (*faraH*) and the consummation of the marriage on "the day of entering" (*yawm al dukhūl*) mark the end of the process of contracting marriage and the beginning of the actual marital state.

The original wasita may take place between women, the mothers of the boy and girl to be matched. If this initial sounding out receives a favorable response, the boy's father will dispatch a close patrilineal kinsman or, even more likely, some close friend who can claim matrilateral relationship (makhwal) with the girl's father or guardian, who is her closest patrilineal kinsman. Often a number of different men will be sent as wasita as the situation changes.

The wasita is a critical occurrence in the life of a particular household and may set off a series of unanticipated events. Various norms and loyalties which in the past were taken for granted without precise definition and ordering must suddenly be weighed and given an order of priority. Kinsmen suddenly assert their claims to women on the basis of normative and structural factors and any particular marriage can be viewed as a statement or evaluation of their worth at that particular moment.[4]

In the past, betrothals were sometimes arranged at the birth of a girl, during her childhood, or at the death of her guardian.[5] Today such a child betrothal constitutes an a priori claim to a girl, but is, by no means, a hard and fast obligation.

Child betrothal, moreover, is not considered legal according to Islamic law unless the girl gives her consent to the match on reaching maturity. Shaykh Luqman, the imam, was very much aware of this stipulation. At any rate, even if the child betrothal met with the approval of both sides, a wasita would have to be sent, when the prospective spouses reached maturity, in order to settle the amount of the marriage payment.

If the suitor's family has not seen the girl through informal contacts of the mothers concerned (a village girl would in any case be well known), some attempt is usually made to expose her to view during the wasita. She may offer tea to the guests. Yet this is not always so. One young man of the village complained that he resented marrying a girl he had never seen. He said that when he asked to see the girl before agreeing on the marriage payment, her father replied, "Why do you wish to see her? Is she a cow? One marries the pedigree [nasab] of the man." Pedigree is, indeed, one of the prime considerations in the choice of a bride. Another villager told me, "I have not betrothed her for her good qualities, but for the good qualities of her father." The origin (*aSl*) of the girl and the honor (*sharf*) of her family are also important.

Physically, the girl should meet certain specifications. One villager described a bride who conformed to the ideal (she had just been betrothed) as follows: "Her flesh is full; she is not just skin and bones. Her face is of a good width [meaning that she had a wide, full face rather than a small face and a small nose]. Her fingers are this length [he indicated with gestures that she had long and tapering rather than squared fingers]. Her eyes are wide and large; the whites of her eyes are whiter than a white Bedouin shawl. Her skin is red and tender [and not yellow]. She has a small mouth. Her teeth are white." He went on to say that her wrist bones would be examined to see if they were well covered with flesh. Her ankle bones and her foot would be observed for the same reason. Any bodily defects that impair her work capacity or blemishes that detract from her beauty are carefully noted.

The girl's personality is also appraised. Irritability or quarrel-someness is not regarded with favor. It scarcely needs mention that the spouses of most arranged marriages do not conform to the standards stipulated by the norms.

Thus, entirely apart from the economic and structural considerations concerning the choice of spouse, there exists a certain set of norms relating to aesthetics, personality, pedigree, and honor that govern marriage choice. These norms may conflict with personal preferences or with factors of social and economic status. Such conflict occurs in regard to the observance of the structural norm which stipulates preferential marriage to the patrilateral parallel cousin (see Case 5, pp. 66–69, and Case 6, pp. 74–77). In the instance quoted above, the young man showed acute dissatisfaction with the norm defining marriage primarily as a matter of pedigree, honor, and economic status to be settled by the families concerned and not the respective spouses.

The conflict may not be of kinship norms and personal preference or kinship norms and economic status but of local custom and Islamic law. An example is the prescription regarding marriage payment (mahr) in which Islam stipulates one mode of behavior and local custom another.

The negotiations which settle the size of the mahr take place during the wasita or at some time following it. These negotiations are usually carried on by the father of the boy and the closest patrilineal kinsman of the girl. If the latter is the girl's father, he will usually call in his brothers for consultation—particularly his elder brother. (See Case 5, pp. 66–69, for the consequences of neglecting such consultation.) As the villagers phrase it, "The father's brother has the right of consultation" (*al 'amm 'alay mushāwara*). In addition to the marriage payment, marriage negotiations usually arrange for the number and type of house furnishings (including chests, pillows, quilts, and household utensils), the items in the bride's outfit (*kiswa*), and the number of cloaks to be distributed to the bride's father and uncles. In the case of a poor family, the marriage payment and nothing else might be handed to the girl's guardian. In this circumstance, the marriage payment is stipulated at the time of the negotiations as, for example, "560 dollars complete" (*imchafchara*). Such an agreement avoids haggling over property exchanges at later stages in the contraction of marriage.

According to Quranic injunction, the marriage payment ought to be paid to the woman, be she sister, daughter, or niece of her legal guardian (wali).[6] In Kufr al-Ma, however, disposition of the mahr by the legal guardian shows wide variation. Of 162 marriages of women for which information was collected only fourteen (eight percent) showed the bride receiving the complete mahr.[7] On the other hand, only nine (five percent) showed a complete "eating" (*akl*) of the mahr by the father. In most instances, some portion of the mahr was given to the girl by her father or legal guardian. Seven percent gave her one-tenth, eighteen percent gave her one-quarter, fourteen percent gave her one-third, nineteen percent gave her one-half, and four percent gave her two-thirds.

The amount given to the daughter depends on various factors. A rich man can afford to give his daughter a large share or all of the mahr. He may even refuse an offer of a very large mahr if he feels that the particular marriage is not to his ward's advantage (see Case 6, pp. 74–77). On the other hand, a poor man is in quite another position as the following informant told me:

> The big families, those who are not hungry, consult [the girl]. As for the poor man, he does not consult [the girl]. And she says to her father, "What pleases my father pleases me." The poor man is forced to accept the offers of those who seek him out. Many men come to the rich man. They offer 500 pounds because he [the father] will give her back half of it and perhaps contribute an additional amount. The poor man looks for another poor man of his own status.

Thus consent of the girl, an Islamic requirement for a legitimate marriage, while it may be formally adhered to in the presence of a religious official, may in fact be ignored. Consent of the girl, like apportionment of the mahr is largely dependent on economic circumstance. There are men, however, who, despite their poverty and out of religious conviction consider it necessary to give their daughters the whole mahr.

Apart from the factor of general economic circumstance, the portion given to the girl depends to a large degree on her personality and the temperament of her father. Although she is guaranteed certain rights and the possibility of enforcing them, the woman often surrenders these rights to her father or brother as a matter of local custom. One man summarized the situation by saying: "The important thing is that he [her guardian] please her. He gives her a piastre, ten, a hundred until he pleases her." On the other hand, she may defy her brother or father and claim her legal rights (see Case 3, pp. 63–65).[8]

In considering the effect of Islamic rules on marriage customs in Kufr al-Ma it is important to remember that the Islamic court in the Al Kura subdistrict was only established in 1952. Previously, a woman from the village would have been forced to travel to the religious court in Irbid, a distance of seventeen miles, in order to claim her rights. Given the rudimentary transportation facilities and the dependent economic position of the woman, this journey was virtually impossible.

Of the 162 marriages mentioned above, forty-one or twenty-five percent were exchange marriages (*tabādal*)—a man giving his sister or daughter for another man's sister or daughter. Such an arrangement avoids payment of mahr by either side and also reduces expenses of the wedding celebration since the two marriages may be celebrated simultaneously. Although, for economic and social reasons, this type of marriage remains popular, it is deprecated by the villagers themselves who are aware of its invidious character in terms of religious law (for there is no mahr payment) and marriage stability (see Cases 4, 7, and 9).

The mahr for a girl from the village is usually 560 dollars.[9] If she is a patrilateral parallel cousin, some reduction in the mahr can be expected. But, occasionally, a man will pay more than the usual sum for his parallel cousin, particularly if she possesses exceptional qualities such as beauty or education. He considers such a payment as a token of his esteem for her. If the girl is from the village but from another clan, he might pay a slightly larger mahr or offer a more sumptuous set of house belongings or bridal outfit. A man will usually ask 840 dollars or more for his daughter if the suitor is from another village (see Case 6, pp. 74–77). In an exchange marriage no mahr is paid regardless of the geographical origin or kinship status of the girl.

The mahr is not only a symbol of a man's esteem for his wife and her family but also an indicator of his own prestige. Among close kinsmen, the principle of reciprocity and equality of marriage payment is observed. Thus, when a man is approached by his close patrilineal kinsmen regarding the marriage of his daughter to their son he will say: "We shall give just as we gave to our brother's son." That is, the father expects a marriage payment of the same amount as that given to his older daughter or sister when they married close kinsmen. In turn, when this same father marries his son to a close patrilineal or matrilateral kinswoman, her relatives will demand of him a mahr of the same amount which they paid in the previous marriage transaction.

The mahr is not necessarily a money payment. Frequently, it is figured in terms of sacks of grain, olive trees, land, houses, or livestock (sheep, goats, and cows). In most cases, the mahr consists of some combination of these along with a money payment.

The factors which affect the amount of mahr paid in any single marriage and the portion given by father to daughter apart from the general considerations already mentioned (type of marriage, place of origin of the woman, economic circumstance, religious conviction) are numerous. For instance, a father will generally give a larger portion of the mahr to his daughter if she is leaving her home village. During bad agricultural years, marriage payments tend to decrease. During war years, which bring economic prosperity, marriage payments increase. Widows and divorced women receive considerably lower marriage payments than maidens, perhaps half as much.

In forty-four percent of the marriages mentioned, the girl received a "morsel" (*tu'ma*) from her father. That is, she received one-third or less of the mahr. In the exchange marriages (twenty-five percent of the marriages I surveyed) the girl received nothing. I have recorded one case in which a man abducted another man's wife and then gave his own daughter as compensation (diyya).[10] The mahrs of daughters are used to get brides for sons, to buy land, and to pay off debts. In the case of child betrothals the girl's mahr may be "eaten" (to pay family expenses) even before she reaches maturity.

Such facts raise the question of whether women are, in fact, treated as chattels by their legal guardians—quite apart from their legal status in terms of Islamic law.[11] I once posed this question to a pious village elder. He replied, "A woman is like the land. It is owned." I rejoined that a woman had rights against her husband such as the ownership of property. He replied:

> And the land has rights too. I must plough it and weed it and fertilize it and in return it gives me an increment. If I do not give it its rights and stopped cultivating it, the land would, after a year, be covered with weeds and herbs and be unfit for planting. Also the woman has rights against me. I must clothe her and feed her and do my utmost for her. And she must honor me and be sincere in the performance of her obligations and upbringing of the children and must guard her honor.

Another villager, the husband of two wives, told me: "As for the peasants, as soon as there is money, either we buy a steed or we buy a woman." Fathers often assess the marriage of a son or daughter principally in terms of a gain in labor power (by the addition of a daughter-in-law) or a loss of labor power (by the removal of a daughter— see Antoun, "Social Organization and the Life Cycle in an Arab Village," *Ethnology*, 6 [July, 1967]).

I do not wish here to argue for or against "bride-purchase."[12] I do, however, wish to suggest that in Kufr al-Ma wide divergence exists between the Islamic rule on the one hand (guaranteeing women rights in property), and local norms on the other (denying them these rights). This variation between the two norms is shown in the behavior of fathers with regard to the disposition of their daughters' mahr. Some men keep the whole mahr and deny the pertinence of Islamic norms for their action; others keep the mahr or large portions of it, realizing the unethical nature of their action while excusing it on the grounds of economic necessity; and still others, mainly rich but some poor, hand over the entire mahr to their daughters and take pride in doing so. Thus, while mahr constitutes in Islamic law a "marriage settlement," in Kufr al-Ma it partakes of the nature of bridewealth or marriage settlement depending on the particular marriage examined.[13]

Following the betrothal (khutba), which is marked by the agreement on the marriage payment and ancillary transfers of property, comes the sending of the official deputation (jaha) which makes the betrothal public. The jaha is usually composed of the respected elders of the different lineages comprising the clan of the bridegroom. These men go to the house of the guardian of the bride and formally ask her hand in marriage. The guardian of the bride (her father unless he is deceased) and the members of the deputation then agree on a spurious mahr sum from which various amounts will be cut for the sake of certain distinguished clans or personalities or honored guests present until the amount of the mahr is whittled down to the previously stipulated sum (*rābiTiya*) at the time of the betrothal. It may even be whittled down slightly under the rabitiya (say, by fifteen to thirty dollars). These latter cuttings are referred to as "what flies by" (*Tayyāriyāt*). The metaphor seems to refer to the winnowing process in which the chaff flies away leaving the seeds of grain. In other words, the substantive agreement was the khutba and any cuttings on the occasion of the jaha are regarded as unsubstantial. The jaha, then, besides publicizing the betrothal and providing an opportunity for a symbolic demonstration of unity among the lineages composing a clan, allows the assembled elders to indulge in shows of generosity (in the reduction of the mahr for the sake of various individuals and groups) and hospitality. The members of the deputation are invited by the bride's father to partake in the meal provided by the "slaughter of the asking" (*dhabīḥat al Tulba*). Although the feast takes place in the bride's father's house and the sheep (or goat) is slain by him, the animal is always provided by the bridegroom or his guardian.

While the wasita, the khutba, and the jaha usually take place within a few days of one another, the next phases in the contracting of the marriage—"the knotting of the marriage" (*'aqd al-nikah*)[14] and the completion of the marriage payment—may occur long after the initial steps. The completion of the marriage payment may take place two years after the betrothal (see Case 4, pp. 65, 66) or it may never be completed. On the other hand, a wealthy man may betroth, complete payment, "knot the marriage," and celebrate it within a period of a few days. The religious covenant that makes the marriage legal ('aqd al-nikah) may precede or follow the completion of marriage payment. It must follow the betrothal, however, since the contracting of every orthodox Islamic marriage should include a formal asking (*Tulba*), the consent of the girl and her guardian, and an agreement on a marriage payment.[15] The religious covenant is compulsory for all Muslims, since marriage, like divorce and inheritance, lies within the scope of Islamic law.

The 'aqd al-nikah usually takes place in the presence of a religious official, the *ma'thūn*, who makes the necessary investigations regarding the fitness of the parties of the marriage. A marriage is valid, however, without the presence of such an official. There are no special rites or ceremonies that mark the marriage. The actual contracting of the marriage, however, must follow a certain form. There must be an offer or declaration of intention (*ijāb*) on the one side and an acceptance (*qubūl*) on the other. In addition, at least two witnesses must be present at the ceremony and testify as to the fitness of the parties to the marriage. These witnesses attest that there are no legal impediments to the marriage.[16]

The important impediments to Muslim marriage are as follows: blood relationship (of certain kinsmen and kinswomen), foster relationship, affinal relationship, existence of previous marriage, existence of triple divorce or *li'ān*, social inequality (applicable to Sunni Muslims and not to Shi'a Muslims), differences of religion, and temporary obstacles (such as the waiting period of the woman after a previous marriage). Chapter 4, verse 23, of the Quran stipulates the kinship, affinal, and foster prohibitions as follows:

> Forbidden unto you are your mothers, your daughters, and your sisters, and your father's sisters, and your mother's sisters, and your brother's daughters, and your sister's daughters, and your

foster-mothers, and your foster sisters, and your mothers-in-law, and your stepdaughters who are under your protection [born] of your women unto whom ye have gone in—but if ye have not gone into them, then it is no sin for you [to marry their daughters]—and the wives of your sons who [spring] from your own loins. And [it is forbidden unto you] that ye should have two sisters together, except what hath already happened [of that nature] in the past. Lo! Allah is ever Forgiving, Merciful.[17]

In the actual covenant, the guardian of the bride clasps the hand of the bridegroom. The bride is not present nor, for that matter are very many relatives on either side.[18] The ma'thun asks the bridegroom whether he offers to marry the girl on payment of the specified mahr. The guardian of the girl has already proceeded to the room where the girl is waiting and, in the presence of the ma'thun and two witnesses, received her consent to the marriage for the specified mahr. (In the case of a maiden, silence is construed as consent.) The ma'thun then asks the legal guardian of the girl (who has clasped the right hand of the bridegroom) whether he offers to marry the girl on payment of the specified mahr. As soon as both parties have answered in the affirmative, the ma'thun reads the first verse from the Quran and the marriage ceremony is completed.

Muslim marriage, then, is a contract, albeit a religious covenant, between the bridegroom and the legal guardian (wali) of the bride made according to a certain form and involving certain rights and obligations stipulated by Islamic law. It is not a sacrament.

The marriage payment may be any object of value in the eyes of the law. It is not necessarily paid at once. It can be divided into two categories, immediate and deferred. The deferred payment is not, in fact, paid unless one of the partners dies or divorce ends the marriage In Kufr al-Ma all agreements for payment of mahr that I witnessed in 1960 stipulated only a sum for immediate payment.[19] However, stipulation of deferred payments was customary in the towns of the district. In Kufr al-Ma marriage payments are usually demanded in full before consummation of the marriage and not after, as some commentators have suggested for other Muslim areas.

Following the 'aqd al-nikah and the completion of the marriage payment, in whichever order they occur, is the wedding celebration (farah). The bridegroom's father pays for the expenses of this three-day period of joy-making. Young men assemble at the bridegroom's house in the evening to dance the traditional *dabbki* among themselves until the early hours of the morning while the young unmarried women—in both cases relatives and friends of the parties concerned—sing and beat the kettle drum and tambourine. Adults gather round and watch the festivities or (the men) assemble in the guest house of the bridegroom's father to drink coffee and tea. The noise of the wedding celebration and the light of the kerosene lamps lighting the path of the dancers announces to the whole village (regardless of whether they attend the celebration or not) that so-and-so and so-and-so are to be married.

Sample Document of Marriage*

(The Mukhtar's Statement Affirming the Legal Age of Marriage
and the Absence of Legal Prohibitions)

Husband: Khalid, son of Khalil al-Salih, of Kufr al-Ma, age 21, single,
and free of other wives or wives divorced less than thrice.

Wife: Rasmiya, daughter of Husayn al-Mahmoud, of Kufr al-Ma,
age 16.

Immediate mahr: two hundred dinars only.

To his honor the Religious Judge [Qadi] of Al Kura:

We, the Mukhtar and selected representatives of Kufr al-Ma, testify that the male Muslim, Khalid, son of Khalil al-Salih, having reached
puberty, a Jordanian citizen, and free of wives or divorced women lia-
ble to return, wishes to marry his betrothed, the female, virgin, and
Muslim, Rasmiya, daughter of Husayn al-Mahmoud, age 16 according to
the document of birth, Number 5098, with an immediate payment of two
hundred dinars, Jordanian. Moreover, we testify that there exist no
legal prohibitions (religious or civil) to this marriage and that the legal
guardian of the bride, her father, has agreed to her marriage and that
the bride and bridegroom are of the residents of our village and of its
native-born population and we testify that there exist no prohibitions to
this marriage. We thereby give this document signed according to custom.

Mukhtar   Notable   Notable

I, the legal guardian of the bride, her father, Husayn al-Mahmoud, am
agreeable to the marriage of my daughter to her betrothed, the above-
mentioned, and to this effect I sign as follows.

Signature of the legal guardian
of the betrothed, her father

*This document is forwarded to the religious court or the ma'thun accom-
panied by the bride's birth certificate.

On the fourth day, "the day of the nuptial procession" (*yawm al zifāf*), the father of the bridegroom again slaughters one or more sheep or goats (*dhabīHat al zifāf* or "the slaughtering of the nuptial") and invites his relatives, his friends, and respected elders to partake of the feast. In the afternoon the bridegroom is mounted on a horse and, accompanied by a number of young men, taken to a large open space (*sāHat al 'urs*) where more dancing takes place. At this time various relatives and friends who were invited to the wedding celebration or the feast contribute money gifts (*nuqūd*) to the bridegroom. The girl, meanwhile, is bathed and dressed by her young unmarried relatives who are, all the while, chanting songs bemoaning her departure. After sunset, she is veiled and mounted on a horse, and, accompanied by her female relatives, led to the house of the bridegroom. The "day of consummation" (*yawm al dukhūl*) is ended by the appropriate act that evening. This act at one and the same time ends the series of phases which constitute the contracting of the marriage and begins conjugal life.

3. PATTERNS OF MARRIAGE

Patterns of marriage may be distinguished in any given community by noting the rules of marriage, assuming they are followed, and noting the implications.[20] When these rules stipulate exogamy for certain groups or marriage with certain designated kinsmen and kinswomen such a procedure is useful, provided the investigator actually knows that the rules, to some degree at least, are being followed. By utilizing such a procedure the structural and geographical spread of ties can be plotted and marriage patterns distinguished.[21]

In Kufr al-Ma, however, no rule of exogamy exists to direct marriage outside the descent group. Moreover, there are no rules which "require" marriage to certain kinsmen or kinswomen. Patrilateral parallel cousin marriage, is, however, a preferred form. That is, a male "should" marry his father's brother's daughter and she "should" marry him. Several cases I collected in the field illustrate the difficulties that arise between close kinsmen when this expectation is ignored. These difficulties arise even when the girl is not a first, but a second or third patrilateral parallel cousin. The preference for a close patrilateral parallel cousin is not binding, however, and other marriages such as to the mother's brother's daughter are considered highly desirable. Moreover, the availability of women at any single moment in time restricts the number of possible spouses of the preferred category. Among the lineages of Kufr al-Ma marriages to first patrilateral parallel cousins usually constituted about fifteen percent of all marriages. No lineage for which I have collected marriage data has contracted more than fifty percent of its marriages with extended patrilateral parallel cousins (up to fifth).

There are distinguishable patterns of marriage in Kufr al-Ma, but these patterns are not based on rules of marriage. I have extracted them simply by recording the marriages of the members of different lineages in terms of the social structural (descent group and kinship tie) and geographical (village) origin of spouse and then noting the different implications of such linking for the group concerned.

SAMPLE OF AN OFFICIAL MARRIAGE CONTRACT (Bridegroom's copy)

No. of contract _____   Date of contract _____

Islamic court _____   Place of contract _____

	Home village	Place of Residence	Age	Nationality	Occupation
Name of Husband					
Mahmoud Abd al-Qadir	Kufr al-Ma	Kufr al-Ma	24	Jordanian	Teacher
Name of Wife					
Wudad bint Ahmed Ibrahim Sulayman	Kufr al-Ma	Kufr al-Ma	16	Jordanian	****

Documents proving age and absence of legal prohibitions — Mukhtar's and witnesses' statements, the petition of the bride, and the permission of the Islamic Court.

Mahr and its type

Immediate   250 dinars ($700)

Delayed   30 dinars ($ 84) — given in the event of legal dissolution (death or divorce)

Other stipulations   none

Mode of payment of mahr — The wife Wudad, above-mentioned, affirmed on the occasion of the drawing up of the contract that she had received the sum of 30 dinars only, and the rest remains with the husband (to be paid) on the occasion of nuptial procession.

The parties to the contract — Everyone of the spouses Mahmoud above-mentioned and the agent of the wife in the contracting, her father's brother, Anhar Ibrahim Sulayman.

Witnesses to the contract, the trusteeship, and the identifiers of the spouses

The acknowledgement of the mahr [was by] two legally capable men, Abd al-Rahman Ali Gargaz and Abd al-Kahim Ibrahim al-Ali, both of Kufr al-Ma.

Special stipulations by either spouse

- - - - - - - - - -

Guarantee of the stipulations

- - - - - - - - - -

Consent of the legal guardian or the court

The legal guardian of the betrothed and the nearest in patrilineal relationship, her father's brother, the above-mentioned Anhar, agreed to her marriage and the Islamic court recognized this [agreement].

Form of the contract

The contract occurred [according to the usual form] by the offer from the side of the agent of the betrothed, her father's brother, the above-mentioned Anhar, to the above-mentioned Mahmoud with his words "I have married her Wudad, the daughter of my brother, Ahmed, for an immediate mahr of 150 dinars and a delayed mahr of 30 dinars" and the immediate acceptance of her husband, the above-mentioned, of his own accord, by his words, "I have accepted marrying her to myself, and have agreed to it."

Identity of the Ma'thun

I, Ahmed Dukhlallah, the Ma'thun for the contracting of marriage in Deir Abu Said, have made out this contract according to the above-mentioned details after investigation and affirmation of the stipulations and lack of legal prohibitions.

Signature of the Ma'thun

Signatures of the Witnesses

Signature of the Husband

Signature of the wife or her agent

Signature of the guarantor of the stipulations

Seal of the Court

My selection of the lineage as the social unit of comparison was made out of practical considerations. The clan is too large a unit to be characterized in terms of any single pattern and the close consultation group is in many cases too small to make these patterns manifest.

I have distinguished four patterns of marriage in Kufr al-Ma. I have referred to them, provisionally, as the scatter pattern, the close parallel cousin intralinking pattern, the two-family alliance pattern, and the exchange pattern. These patterns are not mutually exclusive. That is, a lineage characterized by a scatter of marriage ties into a number of different lineages in and out of the village may also be intralinked by close parallel cousin marriages. Yet, a significant number of these marriages may also be exchange marriages.

The terms I have used to describe these marriage patterns are not merely descriptive structurally ("close parallel cousin" and "scatter") but also functionally ("alliance" and "intralinking"). By these functional terms I mean to indicate that certain marriage patterns have certain effects in terms of the social relations of the families linked by the marriages. I shall illustrate this point quite specifically in Case 9, pp. 134–39, and below, and more generally in the explanation of patterns that follows. In the discussion of these patterns I am always concerned primarily with the structural intraweaving (or lack of it) in the particular lineage as a result of the marriages contracted by the members of the group. Secondly, I am concerned to demarcate the direction of these ties, varying from those groups which scatter their ties over a wide structural range to those which confine them largely to the clan or within the clan to close cousins, to those which, while they may scatter their ties in a number of lineages, reinforce particular links by exchange marriage.

I wish to make clear, at the outset, that my marriage figures for each lineage are not complete, as can be observed by referring to any of the charts included below. I cannot, therefore, claim that the patterns represented might not be altered with further information. In most cases, however, the figures include at least seventy percent of the marriages contracted by the group and in several instances over ninety percent. Charts 12, 13 and 14 do not include all marriages recorded since they were not pertinent to the point being illustrated.

The scatter pattern is illustrated by the lineage, Qaraqzi (see Chart 9, p. 147). The thirty-nine marriages contracted by the men and women of this group for which I have records are scattered among seventeen lineages within the village six of which are within the same clan. There seems to be some indication, it is true, of a concentration of ties in the direction of Basbus and Ghanim (see Chart 9), but the concentration is not of a sort to establish a two-family alliance. That is, the marriages, while they are into the same lineage are into different families of that group. For instance, members of three different families of Qaraqzi married into three different families of Basbus.

The scatter of marriages within a lineage may differ in pattern as between its various lines. This is the case of Beni Sabbah (see Chart 10). The Salih line of Sabbah has pitched its ties through three generations into the various clans in villages surrounding Kufr al-Ma. Fallah and Hasan, on the other hand, have concentrated their marriage ties through three generations not only within the village but also within the various lineages of its own clan—Beni Yasin.

While seventy-eight percent (thirty-six marriages) of their marriage ties were scattered among other lineages, the members of Beni Sabbah contracted eleven marriages with their own patrilateral parallel cousins (to fifth). If one examines the four main lines of the group—that is, the descendants of Sulayman, Fallah, Hasan, and Salih (see Chart 10), it can be seen that every branch has at least one intensifying first parallel cousin link and at least one other cousin marriage to one of the other main lines of the lineage. Three of the branches (Fellah, Hasan, and Salih) have marriage links to two other lines of the lineage. Beni Sabbah, then, is not only characterized by a scatter pattern but also by a close parallel cousin intralinking pattern which makes patrilineal kinsmen affines (for those of the same generation as the married pair) and matrilateral relatives (for those of descending generations).

The lineage Shujur (see Chart 11, p. 148) is characterized by an even more intensive close parallel cousin marriage pattern. Thirteen of the thirty-nine marriages recorded by me for that group are cousin marriages. Shujur is composed of three lines—Yasin, Awad, and Khalil. Yasin is linked by two marriages to Khalil and by four marriages to Awad over three generations in addition to one intensifying first parallel cousin marriage. Awad is linked to Khalil by two marriage ties and to Yasin by four marriage ties over three generations in addition to a single intensifying first cousin marriage. Finally, Khalil is linked to Awad twice and to Yasin twice over three generations without an intensifying first cousin link.

In describing a close cousin marriage pattern as "intralinking" or "intensifying" I am not merely saying that a group is characterized by a significant percentage of these marriages but rather that enough marriages have occurred to link the various branches of the lineage with one another. It is the dispersion of marriage ties and their direction that is critical rather than their number. A few close cousin marriages widely dispersed within the lineage may be more significant for group solidarity than a much larger number of such marriages concentrated in a narrower structural range. When marriages begin to be concentrated in this manner it is not the structural unity of the lineage that is being forged, but rather the solidarity of certain of its component parts.

The latter function characterizes the third pattern of marriage— the two-family alliance (see Chart 12). One example is the alliance of the family headed by Haj Muhammad Husayn (A1 on Chart 12) of Qar'oosh with that headed by Mahmoud al-Ali (B10) also of Qar'oosh. Although they are patrilineal kinsmen and these marriages may be regarded as bint 'amm (patrilateral parallel cousin) marriages, seven generations separate the two families. The important point, however, is that repetition of marriages between two families creates a distinct pattern that must be treated apart from close cousin marriages. Four of Muhammad's sons have married three of Mahmoud's daughters and one of his sisters. Mahmoud himself married one of the Hajji's daughters in an exchange marriage. Five marriages have linked the two families in the space of twenty years. In addition to this marriage alliance, Mahmoud al-Ali and his sisters (B11 and B13) had married into Beni Bakr. Mahmoud (B10) had married the sister (B9) of a prominent member of Beni Bakr, Uqla Abu Tabanji. As I have pointed out elsewhere (Antoun, "Social Organization," *Ethnology*, 6 [1967]), Uqla's claim to priority over another member of the village, Ali al-Husayn, in asking for the hand of Mahmoud's daughter in marriage was based upon the affinal ties which already existed between Mahmoud and Uqla. Uqla's attempt to marry his son to Mahmoud's daughter was an attempt to strengthen the Bakr-Mahmoud alliance. The Haj (A1) had, as well, in a sense contracted a secondary alliance when he married his son Ahmed (B5) and his daughter Neema (B6) into Beni Sabbah in sister-exchange marriages. The two families of Haj Muhammad and Mahmoud al-Ali provide a remarkable example of the tendency to concentrate affinal ties in particular families and to strengthen the ties once made by following marriages (see Antoun, "Social Organization," *Ethnology*, 6 [1967], for a detailed analysis of the solidification of the two-family alliance). Out of twenty marriages contracted by the members of these two families only three were not directed into families where previous or accompanying (in the case of sister exchange) ties existed.

The fourth pattern distinguished is that of exchange marriage. The exchange marriage usually pairs a brother and a sister with another brother and sister (see Chart 12, B5 and B6). But a father may be paired with his daughter. He receives another man's sister or daughter and gives his own daughter. The two marriages take place simultaneously and are not accompanied by any marriage payment although a token and and purely formal mahr is stipulated. In more complex exchanges a man, in the case he has no daughters, may, with his brother's permission, give his niece for another man's sister or daughter. As a result of this transaction, some amount of property usually passes between brothers to compensate for the loss of the woman to one of them, or else one brother promises to place his infant daughter at the disposal of the other when she comes of age to replace the one taken. I have recorded one case in which a man exchanged the same daughter twice after the first exchange marriage ended in divorce on both sides. Although the exchange is usually immediate and the marriages take place simultaneously, the young age of one of the parties may necessitate delayed exchange. In this case, the older pair marry without marriage payment and the younger pair marry as soon as they come of legal age. The siblings paired in the exchange may be full siblings or half siblings, uterine or seminal (see Chart 13, B1 and B2, C5 and C6, and C8 and C10).

Granqvist has referred to a type of marriage which she designates as "veiled exchange."[22] That is, a brother or father marries his sister or daughter to a man and receives a marriage payment from him. The brother or father then uses the payment to marry a woman unrelated to his sister's or daughter's spouse. The brother and sister (or father and daughter) are paired in the sense that the marriage payment given for the sister (or daughter) fetches the bride for the brother (or father).

There are several important differences between "veiled exchange" and what I have designated as "genuine exchange." First, the villagers of Kufr al-Ma recognize the latter as exchange and refer to it by a word (tabadal) that means exchange. On the other hand, as stated in the previous section, they deny that "veiled exchange" is exchange marriage. for a marriage payment is paid in the case of both marriages. Moreover, the marriages do not take place and are not celebrated simultaneously. Finally, an important structural difference separates the two types of marriage. Genuine exchange forges a double link between two families. Veiled exchange does not serve this purpose.[23] In genuine exchange the marriages of the sibling pairs are interdependent. Harmony in one marriage may not necessarily breed harmony in the other, but disharmony in one marriage almost inevitably breeds discord in the other. (See Case 7, pp. 78–87, and Case 9, pp. 134–39). Such interdependence does not characterize veiled exchange marriages. I have already discussed the complications which may arise on the occasion of a veiled exchange (see Case 4, pp. 65–66).

Exchange marriages, like close parallel cousin marriages, occur in every lineage. But in certain groups their preponderance is evident. Such is the case with the Mutliq subdivision of the Massadi lineage (see Chart 13). Of thirteen marriages contracted by the descendants of Mutliq, eight involved exchanges. Eight of the thirteen (not the same eight) were with patrilateral parallel cousins. Six of these marriages were with first cousins.

Aside from the preponderance of exchange marriage, two other points must be made about the Mutliq group. First, the contraction of a levirate marriage between B4 and C11 (Chart 13) has introduced structural complication into the group. The marriage was contracted between spouses of two different generations. The children of the union (C6, C7, and C8), should they trace their relationships with their cousins (C1, C2, C3, C4, C5, C9 and C10) through their father, would be of the same generation as they. If, however, they traced their relationship through their mother, they would count themselves a generation below their cousins. Thus, when a marriage is between spouses of two different generations, the offspring have a choice of relating themselves as of equal or of descending generation to a given number of kinsmen. In a particular situation a man may manipulate his kinship ties to suit his interest. Such ambiguity allows flexibility among relationships which are supposedly fixed.

Second, the children of the four siblings (B1, B2, B3 and B4) are related to one another in a number of different ways as a result of the marriages of their parents. The children of Sabha and Muhammad (C9 and C10) are seminal half siblings while the child of Sabha and Imfathi, (C5) and the children of Sabha and Muhammad (C6, C7, and C8) are uterine siblings. The children of Fatma and Muhammad (C9 and C10) and the child of Sabha and Imfathi (C5) are linked in step relationship. That is, the latter counts the former as his mother's husband's children. The child of Sabha and Imfathi (C5) and the children of Maryam and Adbullah (C1 and C2) on the other hand, have no sibling relationships, but they are cross cousins. The children of Fatma and Abdullah

(D1 and D2) and the child of Sabha and Imfathi are, however, not only cross cousins but also affines, the former counting the latter as father's sister's husband's child.

Structural complication can occur not only as a result of leviratic and polygynous marriages but also when several types of marriage are found relating the same group of kinsmen. For example, the descendants of Mas'ood (A2 on Chart 14) and the descendants of Hamad (A1), subdivisions of the Abd al-Rahman section of Mass'adi, are related in a number of ways as a result of the conjunction of polygynous, sister-exchange, and close parallel cousin marriage among their members. Ibrahim al-Mas'ood (B4) and his sister (B3) married Uqla Abd al-Rahman (C3) and his sister (C2)—(see Chart 14). This sister-exchange marriage was followed by a second exchange in the next generation when the children of Ibraham (C14, C15) married the children of Uqla (D1, D2) producing the sort of two-family alliance I have just discussed.

The children of Ibrahim al-Mas'ood by his wife, Sarah (C5, C6, C7, C8) can trace relationship to Uqla in three ways. First, he is their *ibn 'amm*, their grandfather's brother's grandson. Second, he is their khal or mother's brother. Third, he is their *naSîb* or affine, being the husband of their father's sister by fact of sister-exchange marriage.

Polygynous marriage, then, provides the initial factor of complication, resulting in the distinction of full siblings from half siblings and mothers from stepmothers. If the male in the polygynous marriage takes a patrilateral parallel cousin as one of his spouses, certain patrilineal kinsmen are marked out as matrilateral relatives as well.[24] If, in addition, the close cousin marriage is a sister-exchange marriage, then the children of the two marriages are related as affines as well as agnates and matrilateral kinsmen.

The children of Ibrahim al-Mas'ood by his first wife, Fatma, however, would regard Uqla only as a patrilineal kinsman and an affine. And the children of this wife by a previous husband not of the clan could trace relationship to Uqla only through a series of affinal ties, i.e., mother's husband's sister's husband.

Close parallel cousin marriage along with polygyny and sister-exchange marriages complicate the structure of a patrilineal descent group providing the basis for intensification of ties as well as division among kinsmen in a given situation.[25] With each successive complication of the structure (by polygyny, close-cousin marriage, or sister exchange) the intensification becomes greater but so does the possibility of division. When a dispute occurs within such a group, the basis of alignment is already set in terms of the ties created by the marriages of the members of the group in previous generations (see Case 7, pp. 78–87).[26] But the very fact of structural complication—of double and triple linking between the members of the same lineage— creates strong pressures for settling the dispute. I have demonstrated this fact in Case 7. In the case of sister exchange (see Case 9, pp. 134–39), the pressures for settlement are given a particular poignancy by the peculiar structural interdependency established by such marriages.

I would suggest here that if the dispute occurs among the members of a single lineage, the complication serves initially to define the lines of division and only later to produce solidarity—if at all. If, however, the dispute involves two or more lineages, the complication serves to bind the group more closely against its opponent (see Case 7).

I wish to make clear here that my argument is not merely an exemplification of the peculiar nature of groups involved in "multiplex" relationships—relationships serving many interests. With or without these complicating marriages the groups are multiplex, being caught up in relationships which are at one and the same time economic, political, social, and recreational. I am concerned with marriage here simply to show the new ties it creates or the old ones it strengthens or converts and to demonstrate the structural complication thus introduced regardless of the interests linked to these ties. Structural ties are important, per se, and need not be coupled with explanations in terms of economic or political factors.[27]

Thus far the analysis of marriage patterns has been mainly within a synchronic framework. When viewed diachronically, however, a pattern of marriage may assume quite a different form. For instance, what may appear to be "scatter" in marriages when viewed synchronically (at a moment in time) presents quite another picture when viewed diachronically (over several generations). To say that the men and women of a lineage have at a given moment in time married into a number of different lineages in and out of the village is a true statement, as far as it goes. If one examines the incidence of marriage over several generations, however, such seemingly haphazard ties may follow previous affinal or kinship links. For instance, of fifteen marriages contracted by the youngest adult generation of the Beni Ghanim lineage, nine followed marriage links made in previous generations while two were with first patrilateral parallel cousins (who were already patrilineal kinsmen). Three marriages were with individuals related through the father's sister. Five were with individuals related through the mother while one was traced through an affinal tie made by the father's brother. Yet, viewed synchronically, these marriages were scattered among ten lineages.

Another instance is even more striking. Of fifteen marriages contracted by the last two adult generations of the Jabali lineage, twelve followed pre-existing ties (see Chart 15). Four were with first patrilateral parallel cousins and seven were with individuals related through women either in the parental or grandparental generations (that is, mother, stepmother, or grandmother). Yet, viewed synchronically, the marriages were scattered among seven lineages. While therefore, close parallel cousin marriage may not intralink a lineage in a given generation, analyses of the marriages of previous generations may reveal the families of the group to be related through kinship and marriage as well as descent. In this last illustration, seven of the marriages followed previous matrilateral ties while only four followed patrilateral ties. Ties through women were, here, more significant for marriage than ties through men. Such a state of affairs is not uncommon, as I suggested in Case 7.

The analysis of patterns of marriage in this section reinforces and elucidates what has been said earlier regarding the functions of marriage in establishing a community of kinship within the village. The complexity of kinship ties created by overlapping patterns of marriage — sister exchange, close patrilateral parallel cousin, matrilateral cross cousin, leviratic, polygynous, two-family alliance— brings in its train ambiguity. On the one hand, villagers are not able to trace the exact relationship with any particular individual or group, or if the tie is known, the variety of ways by which it can be traced creates as much confusion as clarity. On the other hand, the very richness, complexity, and wide dispersion of known kinship ties creates the presumption that such ties do exist whether they are known or not. The son of the village shrugs off inquiries about affinal relationships in the grandparental and previous generations with an air of wonderment and slight impatience, as if to say, "Why inquire about such things when it is well known that we are all related in some way or another." It is the "some way or another" that is of importance to him— and also to the ethnographer— in the assessment of the structural cohesiveness of the village community.

4. SISTER-EXCHANGE MARRIAGE: ANALYSIS OF "TRENCH WARFARE"

The last two sections have described the mode of marriage and described and analyzed the distinctive patterns of marriage found in the village. In the next two sections the consequences of two of these patterns— sister-exchange and close parallel cousin marriage—for social relations will be examined first in a detailed analysis of a single case and second in a brief discussion of functional relations.

CASE NINE

This case began in the guest house of an elder of Beni Dumi. Hasan al-Deek, a landless peasant who worked as village watchman for a meager salary, was telling the elder a tale of woe concerning the unfortunate marriages which he had contracted for his children. In view of his economic status, Hasan (B5 on Chart 16) was not regarded as a village notable, but his deceased brother (B6), a member of the Diyaka lineage of Beni Dumi, had served as mukhtar of that clan. He had been a mukhtar noted for his generosity and integrity, and Hasan himself was quick to defend his family honor from what he deemed to be the insults towards it by others.

Hasan was saying that his daughter-in-law (A1) had gone off to her mother's house (which was in the same quarter of the village) and had not returned. He said that the mother of his daughter-in law (B3) had reprimanded his own daughter (A7) because she had laughed in the presence of her (Hasan's daughter's) husband. When Hasan's daughter had returned to her father's house after being beaten by her husband (A2), Hasan's daughter-in-law (A1) had returned to her mother's house. The two women were linked in sister-exchange marriage.

Hasan said that he did not order his daughter-in-law out of the house— that at the time, he had stated that if her second patrilateral cousin, Ahmed al-Naji (A4), wanted her, he would have to come and get her. Hasan said that his daughter-in-law didn't want to leave. Then her cousin, Ahmed, came and stood outside the door of the courtyard calling her, and she took fear and went to him. Ahmed then sent her back to his own house.

Hasan said that his daughter-in-law was a *qārūta*, an orphan, and it was clear from the tone of his voice that he. was using the term invidiously. Her father (B2) had died long ago, and she had been reared by her mother. Hasan said that his son should never have taken her for a wife. If she had had a father, one could always have gone and dealt with him and he (the father) would have sent her back.

Hasan was particularly incensed by his daughter-in-law's action after her return to her paternal cousin's house. She had not stayed there but had gone off to harvest in the fields of villagers only putatively related to her (they were members of her clan but not her lineage).

Hasan said that everything was available in his house. The well was in the *dār* (meaning house including the courtyard); the oven was in the dar. He had even prohibited his own daughters from filling from the well set aside for his daughter-in-law. Why was it then that his daughter-in-law went to the well of her cousin, Ahmed al-Naji? Exasperated with his daughter-in-law's behavior, Hasan told his son Ahmed (A5) to move into a separate room in the dar with his wife, i.e., to set up his own independent household. According to Hasan, Ahmed told his father that he would never move away from him or set up his own household and he (Ahmed) had made this clear to his wife. A few days later both wives returned to their husbands' houses.

My attention was called to the case again only after a lapse of two months. I learned that Hasan's son-in-law, Muhammad al-Fallah "Abu Soof" (A2) had been put in jail for ten days in the next town. He had been charged by Hasan with beating his wife, Hasan's daughter, without rightful cause and had been found guilty. Two weeks after his release I again chanced to be in the guest house of a man of Beni Dumi who was lending a sympathetic ear to Hasan's description of his offspring's marital difficulties. Both girls had again returned to their natal homes.

Hasan described his irritation with his daughter-in-law when she had refused to go out to the fields and collect weeds that would be suitable as fodder for the animals. There had been three successive seasons of drought and numbers of animals had been slain or sold due to lack of fodder.

Hasan told the elder how he had managed to get his son-in-law's brother (A3), the "orphan" as he termed him, a job shepherding in a nearby village; how the boy through carelessness had broken the legs of three sheep by leading them over treacherous terrain; how he, Hasan al-Hamad, got the owner of the sheep to agree to supply the boy with a coat, a jacket, and five sacks of wheat at the end of the year; how, when the boy's paternal uncle, Duwayhis (B1), claimed the wheat for himself it was through his (Hasan's) intervention that the boy got his rightful share.

Hasan declared that as a result of these marital troubles the two lineages of Shehem and Diyaka were not on speaking terms; his affines even refused to greet him with the salutation, "Peace be upon you," when they passed him in the street. He was angry at his daughter-in-law's kinsmen for coming and taking her away He had, after all, not beaten her. And his own daughter had been beaten three times by her husband.

Hasan told of his daughter's objecting when her husband's brother, the young shepherd (A3), had taken grain from the grain store and traded it in the village shop for a nylon belt and candy.

Hasan's affines told him that his daughter had torn her long dress (*thawb*) as a manifestation of displeasure when her husband unexpectedly invited his mother for a supper for which Hasan's daughter was not prepared. His affines told him that his daughter had forbidden the feeding of guests.

Hasan said that his son-in-law beat his daughter over a trivial matter and over Hasan's alleged quarrel with his affine, Ahmed al-Naji. Then the son-in-law strode in on the spur of the moment with his mother and demanded that she (his wife) prepare supper. While she was making the dough, he hit his wife for objecting to his (Abu Soof's) pursuing and cursing her father. The girl jumped up to leave but was blocked at the door by her mother-in-law. She ran down the path after her father and told him what her husband had done. Hasan said that his insides boiled but he maintained his composure and told his daughter, "You know that men beat their wives." He tried to calm her but to no avail, and so he took her home with him.

On his arrival home, Hasan went directly to his daughter-in-law's room and told her, "Turn your face away from here," sending her back to her natal home. Soon after, Duwayhis and Ahmed al-Naji, the paternal uncle and cousin of the girl, came and told him that his daughter had just previously torn her dress to shreds, so great was her disrespect of her mother-in-law. Hasan went into the inner rooms and fetched his daughter's dress and told them, "Show me the tear." Hasan told them that divorce was better than the present situation. He described the black and blue bruises his daughter carried and the condition of her swollen face. He said of his son-in-law, "This man does not appreciate goodness. We treat his sister with kindness and this is what we get in return." Duwayhis, the girl's uncle, then said he would go off to see why his nephew hit her. Subsequently, Hasan raised a charge in the civil court against his son-in-law, who was then imprisoned.

Hasan then went on to review the circumstances that led to the first beating of his daughter and her return to her father's house "in a state of anger" (za'alane). He said that his daughter's husband was a shepherd who roamed with his flocks in the lands of an adjoining village and would stay with his flocks eleven or twelve days at a time before returning home to his wife. One day, he came home and, at the instigation of his mother, asked his wife why she had not gone to the forest and collected wood. She replied that there was plenty of kerosene available. The husband said, "No, you must go and get wood." She replied that she would go out and get the wood when the winter season approached. Then, he ordered his wife into the house. He forced her in and beat her—a beating which, for its severity, the neighbors heard and commented upon. In the morning, her husband threatened her with dire consequences if she told her father what had happened. But she went off to her father's house. Duwayhis then came to Hasan and told him it was unfair to take out a quarrel of one married couple on another. Hasan let his daughter-in-law stay on. Then her mother came to Hasan's house and made deprecatory remarks about the state of the furniture in the house. After she swore at Hasan he told her to leave the house and take her daughter with her. This had all happened after the first beating. Hasan, at that time, had told his son-in-law's paternal uncle, Duwayhis, "divorce is better [than this state of affairs]. Better a curtained setback now than a scandalous defeat later." But the wives were returned to their respective husbands.

Then Hasan returned to the immodest behavior of his daughter-in-law. She went off harvesting with neighbors, all the while telling them her troubles instead of remaining in her uncle's house. He praised his own daughter's exemplary behavior, by contrast. He said that she had never entered the house of her own first paternal cousin (who lived within the compound). Hasan said that his wife always stayed home. Even if she wished to spend an evening visiting her relatives, she would not know how—this as opposed to the conduct of his daughter-in-law. Hasan said that, in any case, he could always marry his son (who drew a regular army salary) to another wife. As if to sum up the whole affair, Hasan said, "Orphan children are not fit to be given in marriage."

Two weeks later, Muhammad Abu Soof, Hasan's son-in-law, went with a number of his clansmen to the house of the mukhtar of Beni Yasin (this though Muhammad was a member of Beni Dumi which had its own mukhtar). They asked the mukhtar to intercede on Muhammad's behalf and to recruit a deputation for the purpose of approaching Hasan al-Deek. The move was made only after two months had elapsed with both wives living "in a state of anger" in their natal homes.

That night the delegation left for Hasan's house. Besides Muhammad Abu Soof and the mukhtar, it included two members of Beni Dumi and Shaykh Luqman, the imam. It did not, however, include Muhammad's closest patrilineal kinsmen, his paternal uncle and cousin. At first, the deputation was unable to win Hasan's consent to return his daughter to her husband. But after much urging and a brief scuffle between Hasan and his son (A6, who opposed sending back his sister until they had confronted her uncle and cousin face-to-face and extracted from them a guarantee of her future good treatment), Hasan promised to send the girl back to her husband the next day.

Later that same night after the deputation had departed, Abu Soof returned to Hasan al-Deek's house where father-in-law and son-in-law had a long heart-to-heart talk about the conditions of the return of Hasan's daughter. In the morning Hasan's daughter went back to her husband's house while Hasan's daughter-in-law returned to her father-in-law's home.

Later, in reply to my question, the mukhtar told me that it was clear that Hasan's daughter had wanted to return to her husband, but that she had been afraid of her brother and that was the reason she had not readily returned to him.

The mukhtar said that he had pointed out to Hasan several days before the sending of the deputation that remarriage was a distinct improbability for both girls after a double divorce.

The case just described has important structural implications. The marriages contracted by Hasan al-Deek's children are examples of the fourth pattern described in the preceding section—the exchange pattern. The families connected by sister-exchange marriage are locked in a peculiar type of structural interdependency. Each set of actions by one of the conjugal pairs becomes a standard for the behavior of the other conjugal pair. Violation of norms by one of the pairs is followed by violations of the same norms by the other pair. Indeed, Hasan al-Deek was condemning himself for treating his daughter-in-law too kindly in light of the treatment of his own daughter. A break off of relations between one pair is followed by a break off of relations between the other pair. Hasan brought his beaten daughter home and was about to send his daughter-in-law on her way when her paternal uncle intervened and said it was unfair to let a quarrel in one family affect the other. Hasan gave way momentarily, but the mother-in-law's subsequent entry and disparaging remarks gave Hasan an excuse to expel both mother-in-law and daughter-in-law. On another occasion, the daughter-in-law's patrilineal kinsmen came and took her away. It is this constant feedback between families linked by sister-exchange marriages that makes the relations between them assume the character of "trench warfare."[28] Frequent skirmishes occur without such a serious confrontation as to result in a final break off of relations by divorce.

But the factor of locality also plays a part in permitting this state of affairs to continue. Ralph Linton pointed this out long ago when he said:

> The fact that a woman goes to live with her husband's people is less important, for practical purposes, than the degree of isolation from her own family which this entails. If she goes on living in the same village with her own brothers and sisters, the consanguine unit is not seriously disrupted.... At the first signs of trouble she can find shelter with her own male relatives, who probably do not like her husband's family anyway.[29]

Linton saw that the crucial factor was not locality but distance between the natal home and the conjugal home. In Case 4 I noted that the families linked in sister exchange were in fact next-door neighbors. In the present case, the families involved were in nearly the same position, although the entrances to the respective courtyards fronted on separate village paths. The state of "trench warfare" without divorce, therefore, depends not only on the peculiar character of the sister-exchange marriage but on the distance separating households.

Any single sister-exchange marriage, then, is a double link between two families. While the norm of equal treatment of spouse leads, almost inevitably, to discord between the members of each conjugal pair and between the pairs, the double link serves at the same time to restrain each side from irrevocable severance of relations.[30] In a sense, too much is at stake to permit complete breakdown.

Finally I would like to call attention to the critical importance of economic factors in many sister-exchange marriages. Hasan had spoken to the mukhtar several days before the attempted reconciliation and suggested that divorce was the only solution. The mukhtar had pointed out to him that the consequences of divorce would.be disastrous to all concerned. The families involved were in very poor economic circumstances. This was, perhaps, the principal reason for the contraction of the marriages in the first place. A sister-exchange marriage does not require the payment of mahr. Both girls would have stood very poor chances of remarriage in view of their poverty and in view of the failure of their first marriages with all the resultant unflattering publicity.

Such considerations regarding the social consequences of his actions must have (in addition to the structure of the sister-exchange link itself) influenced Hasan's decision to return his daughter in spite of his previous avowals that he would not do so under any circumstances.

5. THE FUNCTION OF PATRILATERAL PARALLEL COUSIN MARRIAGE

Marriage between close cousins (up to the fifth patrilateral parallel cousin) serves four functions in Kufr al-Ma.[31] All of these functions are with reference to the structural units I have termed luzum and lineage. Two of the functions are economic, the third is political, and the fourth is structural.

Economically, the first function of close parallel cousin marriage is to soften the effects of economic differentiation among close patrilineal kinsmen. Given the high degree of occupational mobility and the wide range of incomes among close kinsmen whose homes and families remain in the village, marriage relinks prosperous clerks, soldiers, and peasants with their poor kinsmen. The relinking may be resisted by the fortunate relative though unsuccessfully due to the consequences for social stability and the pressure of outsiders (e.g., Ahmed al-Ali in Case 3, pp. 63–65), it may be welcomed by him, or it may be resisted successfully by a man who has cut himself off from his own clan politically and residentially (e.g., Anhar al-Ibrahim in Case 6, pp. 74–77).

To contend that close cousin marriage softens economic differentiation assumes, in part, the inheritance and alienation of property by women. According to the rules of orthodox Islamic law wives inherit a certain portion of their husband's estate, daughter's a certain portion of their father's property, and sisters inherit equal portions corresponding to half the share of their male siblings.[32] In Jordan, the Islamic rules of inheritance are not applicable to cultivable land whose inheritance and disposal is governed by national law. This law stipulates that all siblings inherit equal portions regardless of sex. In addition to inheritance of property, Islamic law guarantees women the receipt of their marriage payment, or mahr. In receiving this property, whether by inheritance, purchase, or marriage payment, women are free to dispose of it as they wish.

In Kufr al-Ma, daughters and sisters who marry out of their clan and almost certainly those who marry out of the village are denied their shares in inheritance. Even if the woman marries within the village and within the clan, she often surrenders her right to property in favor of her male siblings. The imam's Friday sermons condemning the denial of property to wives, daughters, and sisters testifies to the prevalence of such customs.

On the other hand, my examination of the official land records shows land registered in the names of numerous women, whether as wives, sisters, or daughters. I have recorded a number of cases of women who did inherit property and passed on that property to their children; I have recorded instances of women controlling their property in the face of pressure from their elder male siblings (see Case 3, pp. 63–65); I have also witnessed instances of women charging their close patrilineal kinsmen with usurpation of the mahr in the religious court and noted that they won their cases. Moreover, I have been on hand at several divisions of movable property among the members of a family, male and female, by the imam according to Islamic law. The picture, then, is not all of one piece. Some women inherit movable property and alienate land while others are barred from their legal rights. Some women have property registered in their name but do not control it, while others own it officially and control it in actuality.

Yet, even when women do not inherit and are not able to pass on their property to their husbands and children, close parallel cousin marriage creates a link with a relative who is already a patrilineal kinsman. These kinsmen are those whose aid is requested during hard times. In addition, the obligation to extend generosity allows the individual to "sponge" off his relatives regardless of their propensity to offer such hospitality.

The second economic function of close parallel cousin marriage is to confine ownership of land within a small group of close kinsmen. In Kufr al-Ma alienation of land from the lineage group may take place in several ways. The land may be sold to a nonkinsman; it may be given to a bride not of the lineage as mahr; it may be inherited by sisters and daughters who marry out of the lineage and pass on their property to their children who are not members of it; or it may be inherited by a wife not of the group.

To take an example, in a polygynous household one plot of five acres was inherited in part by sons, in part by a daughter who married a third patrilateral parallel cousin, in part by a daughter who married out of the lineage, in part by a wife who was a close cousin, and in part by a wife who belonged to another lineage. The shares inherited by the sons, of course, remained within the group, as did the shares inherited by the daughter who married within the group and the share inherited by the wife who was of the group. The share inherited by the wife who was not of the lineage was only temporarily alienated since it would pass on to her children who were of the group. Thus, of the inheritors, only the share inherited by the daughter who married out of the group was permanently alienated. Of fifty shares in land, only six shares passed out of the group despite the rules of inheritance which disperse property among spouses, siblings, and offspring. Thus, close parallel cousin marriage confines ownership of land within a group of close kinsmen and, in part, nullifies the effects of Islamic and civil inheritance rules. It is true that property is alienated in the sense that it passes from one family to another through women at any given marriage. But the property remains in a pool on which ego or his descendants may draw in the future by taking advantage of the privileged position which Arab society gives to any male with respect to the possibility of marriage to his patrilateral parallel cousin.

The third function of close cousin marriage is political. It is to maintain close ties among cores of kinsmen who can still act together in moments of crisis even though many of the major political and economic activities which formerly attached to the agnatic group have lapsed. It is significant that in the instances I have recorded of men successfully defying the members of their own lineage and attaching themselves politically to another group, no close cousin marriages existed to reinforce the patrilineal bonds.

The fourth function of close cousin marriage (one that I have illustrated at some length above, pp. 125–34), is to complicate the structure of the lineage, providing the basis of division as well as intensification of ties. With each successive complication of the structure the intensification becomes greater, but so does the possibility of division. If the dispute be within the lineage, this complication serves to define the lines of division: if the dispute involves other lineages, the complication serves to intensify the bonds among close patrilineal kinsmen (see Cases 7 and 8).

So far in this section I have ignored the dysfunctional aspects of marriage, but a reading of Cases 5, 7, and 9 have made them apparent. Polygyny and sister exchange create relationships which are, by their structure, "conflictful." When these forms of marriage happen also to be close patrilateral parallel cousin marriages, the structural conflict is compounded. Even if such a coincidence of marriage forms is lacking, however, the norm of preferential patrilateral parallel cousin marriage in a situation of increasing economic differentiation in itself creates social strain: prosperous men wish to marry their daughters to the sons of other prosperous men rather than to the sons of their poor kinsmen.

Close cousin marriage is dysfunctional in another respect. Intensification of ties among patrilineally related relatives has a double edge. On the one hand, as the villagers see it, patrilateral parallel cousin marriages unite kinsmen—unite them by building up affective ties through women. But such intensification of ties exacerbates the antagonism over the very interests which serve to unite the group—land (see Cases 3, pp. 63–65, and 5, pp. 66–69) and women (see Case 4, pp. 65–66). In much the same way they do with matrilaterality, villagers stress the positive aspects of agnation and patrilateral parallel cousin marriage and completely overlook the tensions and animosities built into such principles of social relations.

Conclusion

In this monograph I have described the ties and cleavages prevailing among the significant and lasting social units in the village of Kufr al-Ma, Jordan. The units, discussed in order, were the subdistrict, the household, the close consultation group (luzum), the lineage, the clan, and the village. The ties and cleavages have been analyzed not only as they exist between these groups but also within them.[1] One conclusion that can be drawn from the analysis refers, perhaps, to a sociological truism; it is, nevertheless, worthy of mention—namely as the group becomes smaller in size and multiple in functions the pressures for cooperation and solidarity increase but so do the bases of dissension and the intensity of the conflict (see, particularly, Cases 3, pp. 63–65, 4, pp. 65–66, and 5, pp. 66–69).

Each section in the book has focused on a slightly different aspect of intergroup or intragroup relations. For instance, Chapter 1 demonstrated the limits placed on economic differentiation in the agricultural sector of the economy by unpredictable climatic conditions and an agricultural regime of a certain type—two-crop dry-cereal farming. Section A of Chapter 2 examined the relationship between ideology on the one hand and actual political cooperation on the other; sections C, D, and E focused on the consequences of increasing differences of wealth and occupational mobility for the solidarity of close kinsmen; section F focused on the relationship of the ideology of patrilineality and the existence of affinal and matrilateral ties; sections I and J examined the significance of social control for the maintenance of the clan and village as resilient social groups. Chapter 3 assessed the significance of marriage for the solidarity of the close consultation group, the lineage, and the village itself.

At all levels of the social structure, however, I have stressed a few general themes. First, it is clear that while patrilineality is the dominant ideology of intergroup and intragroup relations as well as the foundation for critical functions (e.g., authority in the household, inheritance, blood-money compensation), this ideology is adjusted to accommodate groups or individuals who would not qualify for membership or the exertion of authority if that principle were applied strictly. At the level of the household, several households are centered around women —widows or divorcées or "forsaken women" (women not divorced but no longer cohabiting or residing with their husbands)—who live separately with their children, dominate their sons, and deal with the other men of the village, albeit formally, through the men of their own family (see Case 2, pp. 55–56, and Chart 3, p. 57). At the level of the close consultation group, matrilateral and affinal relatives and close friends and neighbors may be members along with the core of patrilineal relatives (see Case 6). At the level of the lineage, families (e.g., Majadbi) are incorporated ideologically as well as functionally after generations of intermarriage, coresidence, and economic cooperation. Finally, at the level of the clan, lineages (e.g., Jabali, 'Ibadi, Basbus) are incorporated and referred to as "of the clan" even though their separate origins are recognized and their incorporation has not reached the stage of claimed genealogical relationship.

A second theme running through all the sections of the book is the critical importance of propinquity for village life. Because the idiom of peasant life in the Middle East (and other parts of the world) is an idiom of descent and because descent does in fact form the basis for the recruitment of particular groups and for the performance of critical functions, the importance of propinquity is often overlooked. This bias has a solid foundation in the structural complexity of Middle Eastern peasant life, for one's neighbors are, in most instances, one's kinsmen. Because of this structural coincidence and the analytical ambiguity that it fosters, I have paid particular attention to instances in which men have moved away from their kinsmen but remained within the village. That such movement is generally widespread is apparent from the spatial distribution of houses outside the original boundary of the village in 1940 (see Map 2B, p. 74). Wherever the individual moves within the village he must establish new ties of sociability (e.g., Mahmoud al-Salih, pp. 73–74), and economic and, perhaps, political cooperation (e.g., Anhar al-Ibrahim, Case 6, pp. 74–77) with his new neighbors, although his old ties of descent do not lapse (e.g., see Anhar's continued involvement with his lineage in Case 8, pp. 97–102). It is the necessity of forming economic, social, and political ties with one's neighbors that establishes any individual as a son of the village enjoying the services the community offers and susceptible to its controls. The importance of propinquity is obscured by the fact that the tie of the particular individual to his neighborhood, to his village, or to his district is very often expressed in an idiom of kinship or descent, e.g., "son" (resident) of the village, the "families" (peoples) of Tibne.

In his classic analysis of Bedouin social structure William Robertson Smith was the first to point out that among Arabs relations of propinquity are usually described in an idiom of kinship and descent (see William Robertson Smith, *Kinship and Marriage in Early Arabia*, pp. 43–46, 52–54, 57–62). All kinds of devices were available for attaching individuals and groups to the local camping unit (*Hayy*) and for establishing and maintaining the legal fiction of consanguineous relationship, e.g., adoption, blood brotherhood, alliance, clientship. But the idiom of kinship and descent did not change the fact that the fundamental social group among the Bedouin was the basic land-use unit that carried out the critical functions for group survival—the nomadic camp.

In a similar fashion it is possible to argue for the village of Kufr al-Ma that spatial propinquity whether in the settlement itself or on the land that surrounds it is the critical organizing factor of social relations. Thus propinquity in day-to-day relations may generate conflict among close kinsmen (Case 7, pp. 78–87) or it may necessitate their cooperation in spite of their deep-seated estrangement (Case 5, pp. 66–69). Thus, historically, the village, rather than the clan, was the social unit that constituted the ultimate inalienable unit of land division and administered "the flying of the pebble" under the musha' system. And it was village rather than clan leaders, as such, that presided over the dissolution of the musha' system in 1939 (see Chapter 1, pp. 19–24, and Chapter 2, pp. 90–91). The danger involved in following Smith's analysis in toto is that the peasant village may in fact be a genuine web of kinship and not merely a community described in an idiom of kinship. Thus, Kufr al-Ma, as stated in the previous chapter, has an extremely high rate of village endogamy (seventy-eight percent); there is, therefore, substantial structural validity for viewing the village as a deme— a community of kinsmen everyone of whom can trace a link of marriage or descent to some other individual and/or group within the village as a result of generation after generation of intermarriage. In addition, as Chapter 3 pointed out, the villagers themselves interpret and describe marriage ties in an idiom of kinship rather than marriage, thereby stressing the unity of the village rather than its division into descent groups or marriage alliances.

The case for the critical importance of propinquity in village life does, however, receive further substantiation from another direction. Just as the tie of agnation is reflected in an ideology that reappears at every level of the social structure so too is the tie of propinquity. At the lowest level of the social structure—the household—the tie of neighborhood was stressed by the imam of the village and given equal weight with the tie of kinship. At the highest level of the social structure, the subdistrict, the concept, "the peoples of Tibne," was rooted in the common experience of individuals who came together to live in the same locale, who were subject to the same historical vicissitudes, and who cooperated to achieve common solutions to their economic and political problems. And finally, at the level of the village, there was an explicit recognition of the existence of a village community which was the proper locus of competition for prestige, status, and political power and within which there was an ethical obligation—for every son of the village—to act with civility and toleration (see Case 7, pp. 78–87 and section J, pp. 103–13).

A third theme runs through this book, related to the two previous themes but, at the same time, separate from them. The patrilineal descent groups at any particular level of the village's social structure exhibit considerable diversity in structural attributes (e.g., size [see Table 9, p. 45], spatial relationships [see Maps 2A, 2B, and 3], genealogical depth, collateral segmentation, point of bifurcation, stage in the developmental cycle) and considerable flexibility in the performance of particular functions (e.g., control of marriage, joint control over land, political activity) and in the carrying out of particular ethical obligations toward their members (e.g., sociability—visiting, recitation of proper politeness formulas, hospitality—deference to elders, monetary aid). This flexibility and diversity is related to the fact (discussed above, pp. 59–62) that patrilineal descent groups reflect a continuum, structurally, functionally, and ethically rather than a set of discrete and easily identifiable social units. Flexibility and diversity is also accentuated by the fact that groups which meet structural criteria for classification as a certain social unit, e.g., the lineage, do not always meet the functional criteria and vice versa. The ambiguity created by such a situation is reflected in the terms of reference for descent groups, e.g., fandi, luzum, humula, 'ashira. These terms are used with varied and often contradictory meanings in Kufr al-Ma and in the Arab world at large. The flexibility and diversity of Arab descent groups is best exemplified in and has the most important consequences for political behavior. The subject of politics in Kufr al-Ma has not been treated within the compass of the present monograph whose orientation is towards social structure and ethnography rather than the analysis of the political process. However, the analysis of patrilineal descent groups in the present monograph is enough to suggest that far too little work has been done in the past on the nature of the "segments" which form the fundamental building blocks of political "systems." Indeed, I will go so far as to argue in a future work that any detailed analysis of these fundamental building blocks—certainly among Arab peasants—and probably among other types of communities (tribes, bands, cities) and in other cultures will necessitate a fundamental reassessment of the "political process" and the "segmentary system." concepts with which political scientists and political anthropologists have been so thoroughly absorbed in the past decade.[2]

CHART 9

MARRIAGES OF THE QARAQZI LINEAGE

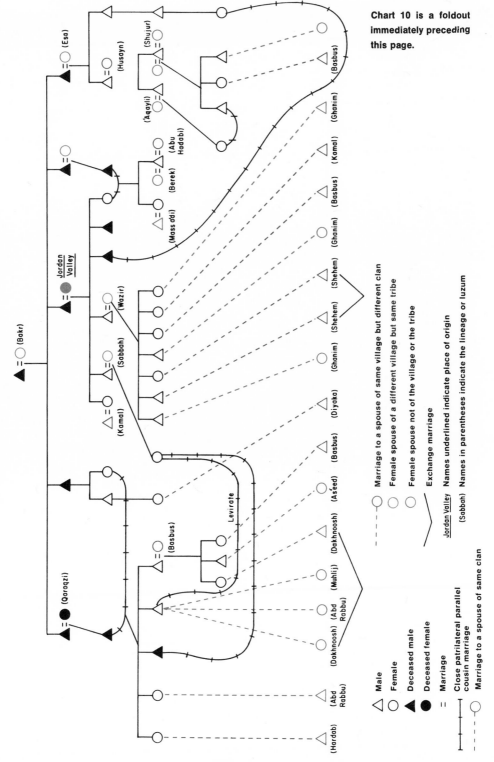

Chart 10 is a foldout immediately preceding this page.

△ Male
○ Female
▲ Deceased male
● Deceased female
= Marriage
⊥ Close patrilateral parallel cousin marriage

○ Marriage to a spouse of same village but different clan
○ Female spouse of a different village but same tribe
○ Female spouse not of the village or the tribe
--- Exchange marriage
Jordan Valley Names underlined indicate place of origin
(Sabbah) Names in parentheses indicate the lineage or luzum

○ Marriage to a spouse of same clan

147

CHART 11

MARRIAGES OF THE SHUJUR LINEAGE*

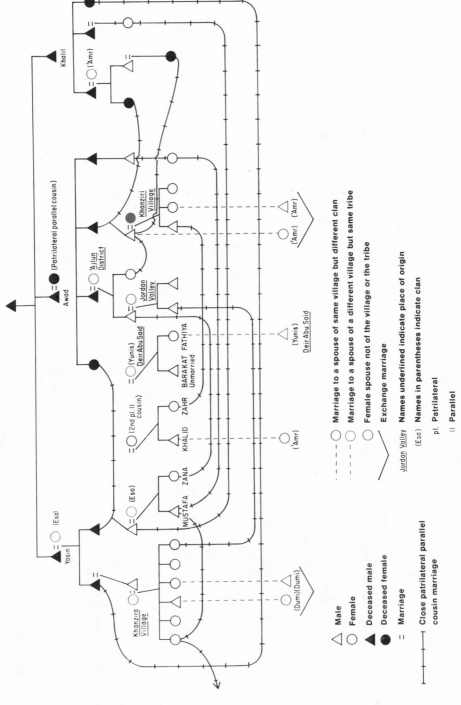

Male △

Female ○

Deceased male ▲

Deceased female ●

Marriage =

Close patrilateral parallel cousin marriage ——

Marriage to a spouse of same village but different clan

Marriage to a spouse of a different village but same tribe

Female spouse not of the village or the tribe

Exchange marriage

Jordan Valley — Names underlined indicate place of origin

('Esa) — Names in parentheses indicate clan

pl. Patrilateral

|| Parallel

*Not all recorded marriages are included, but all close-cousin marriages have been indicated.

148

CHART 12

TWO-FAMILY ALLIANCE PATTERN

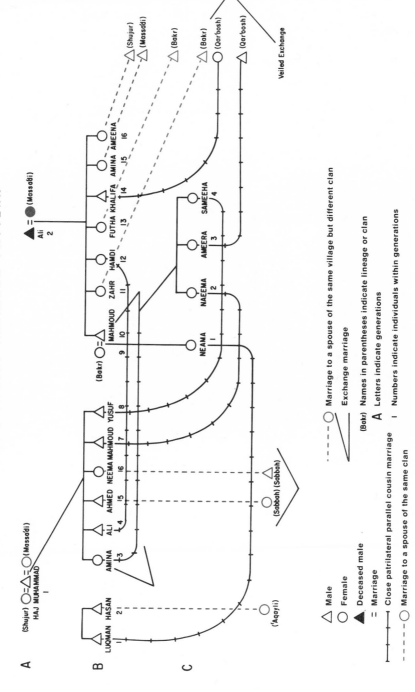

149

CHART 13

THE SISTER-EXCHANGE MARRIAGE PATTERN

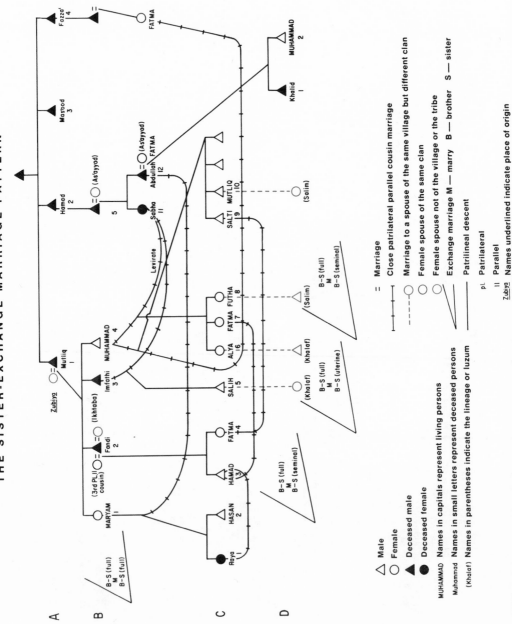

Male

Female

Deceased male

Deceased female

MUHAMMAD Names in capitals represent living persons

Muhammad Names in small letters represent deceased persons

(Khalaf) Names in parentheses indicate the lineage or luzum

$=$ Marriage

Close patrilateral parallel cousin marriage

Marriage to a spouse of the same village but different clan

Female spouse of the same clan

Female spouse not of the village or the tribe

Exchange marriage M — marry B — brother S — sister

Patrilineal descent

pl. Patrilateral

$\parallel$ Parallel

Zubiya Names underlined indicate place of origin

CHART 14

EXCHANGE MARRIAGE AND POLYGYNY AMONG CLOSE COUSINS*

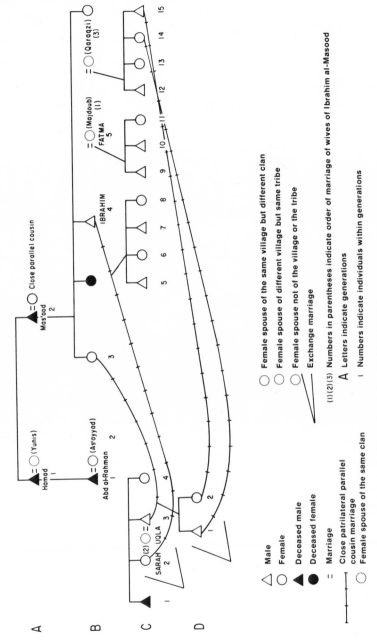

Male

Female

Deceased male

Deceased female

Marriage

Close patrilateral parallel
cousin marriage

Female spouse of the same clan

Female spouse of the same village but different clan

Female spouse of different village but same tribe

Female spouse not of the village or the tribe

Exchange marriage

(1)(2)(3) Numbers in parentheses indicate order of marriage of wives of Ibrahim al-Masood

A Letters indicate generations

1 Numbers indicate individuals within generations

*Not all marriages of the families concerned are here represented.

151

CHART 15

MARRIAGES OF THE JABALI LINEAGE

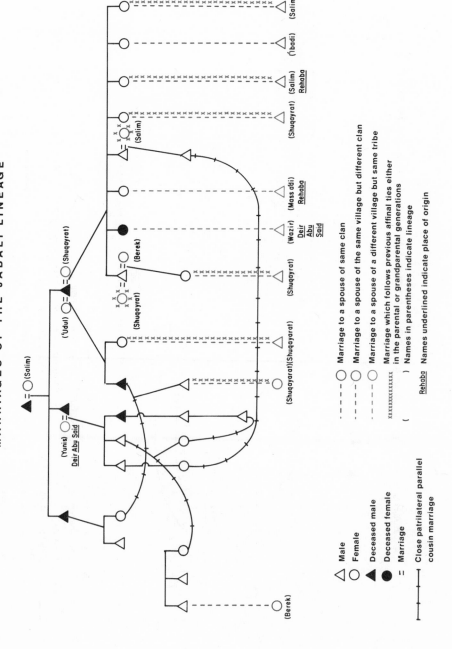

⊲ Male

○ Female

◀ Deceased male

● Deceased female

= Marriage

┤ Close patrilateral parallel
cousin marriage

○ Marriage to a spouse of same clan

○ Marriage to a spouse of the same village but different clan

○ Marriage to a spouse of a different village but same tribe

xxxxxxxxxxxx Marriage which follows previous affinal ties either
in the parental or grandparental generations

( ) Names in parentheses indicate lineage

Rehaba Names underlined indicate place of origin

152

CHART 16

FAMILIES LINKED IN SISTER EXCHANGE (Case 10)

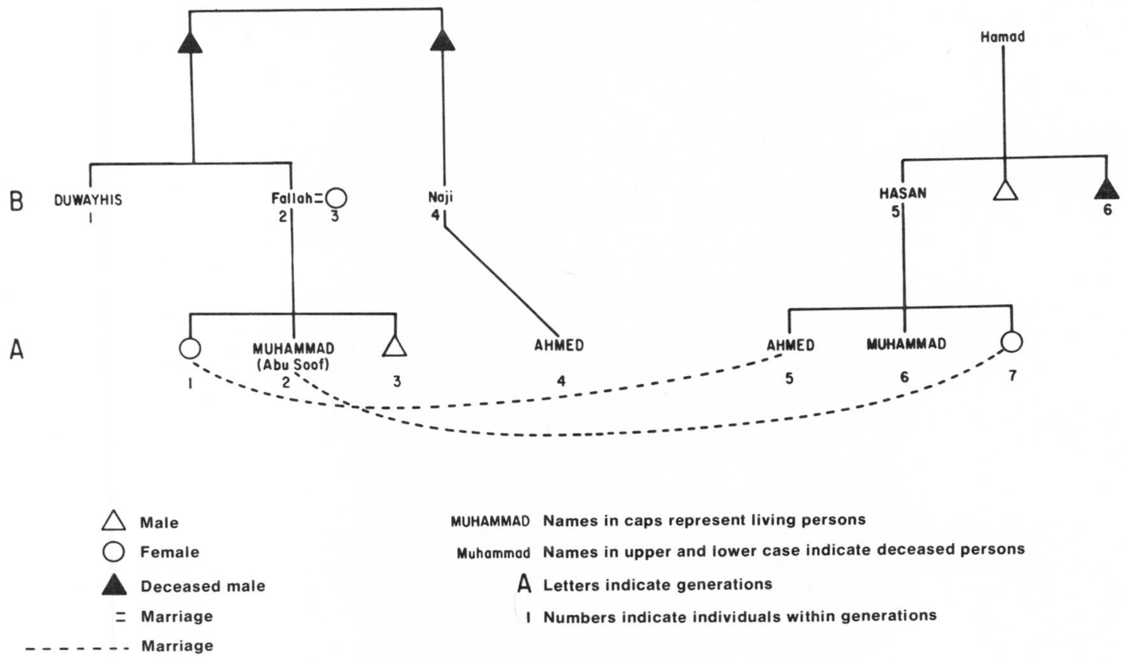

Male △
Female ○
Deceased male ▲
Marriage =
Marriage - - - - -

MUHAMMAD Names in caps represent living persons
Muhammad Names in upper and lower case indicate deceased persons
A Letters indicate generations
1 Numbers indicate individuals within generations

Notes

Preface

1. The works referred to above in order of publication are as follows: Hilma Granqvist, *Marriage Conditions in a Palestinian Village*, 2 parts, 1931 and 1935; *Birth and Childhood Among the Arabs*, 1947; *Child Problems Among the Arabs*, 1950; Abner* Cohen, *Arab Border-Villages in Israel*, 1965; Abdullah Lutfiyya, *Baytin: A Jordanian Village*, 1966.

2. See Conrad M. Arensberg and Solon T. Kimball, *Culture and Community*, pp. 9–10. An instance of such a discovery in my own research is as follows. I found in a simple census of households that only ten percent of all married men in Kufr al-Ma had more than one wife. Of these men (twenty in all) less than a quarter actually lived with more than one of their wives (the remaining wives had moved into the houses of their respective sons). Here, in a traditional rural Arab Muslim community in an area of the world that social scientists and orientalists alike classify as "polygynous" with respect to family structure, a census revealed an extremely high incidence of legal monogamy (ninety percent) and an overwhelming preponderance of de facto monogamy (97.5 percent)! While I have stressed the primary importance of the community as a thing-in-itself rather than as a sample or "mirror" of a wider social universe, Arensberg regards the study of the "nature" of the community as closely interrelated to its use as sample (p. 11). In some places Arensberg suggests that the study of the "nature" of the community is the real focus of the social anthropologist (pp. 18–20 and 100–103) and that the study of the "nature" of the community can be clearly demarcated from its use as sample and from the pursuit of particular theoretical problems (p. 34). In other places he suggests that community study is only a device, "a tool of science" (p. 30). For me and, I believe, for the great majority of social anthropologists, the study of the community is worthy in and of itself. Its use as a sample or to illuminate particular theoretical problems is legitimate and worthy, but strictly secondary.

Introduction

1. See, for example, the brilliant but, from this point of view, blameworthy works of Alfred R. Radcliffe-Brown (*The Andaman Islanders*, 1922), Edward E. Evans-Pritchard (*The Nuer*), and Edmund Leach (*Political Systems of Highland Burma*, 1954).

2. See, for example, Malinowski's" *Argonauts of the Western Pacific* (London: George Routledge and Sons, 1922), *The Sexual Life of Savages*, and *Coral Gardens and Their Magic* (New York: American Book Co., 1935),

and the attempts to reinterpret these works based on the evidence Malinowski himself furnished, e.g., by Meyer Fortes in *Man and Culture* (London: Routledge and Keegan Paul, 1957), edited by Raymond Firth; by Edmund Leach in *The Developmental Cycle of Domestic Groups* edited by Jack Goody; and by J. M. Singh Uberoi in *Politics of the Kula Ring.* See also the bulky and well-documented works of Malinowski's students, e.g., Raymond Firth, *We the Tikopea;* Audrey Richards, *Land, Labour and Diet in Northern Rhodesia* (London: Oxford University Press, 1939); and Douglas Oliver, *A Solomon Island Society.*

3. For this view I wish to acknowledge the influence of Paul Friedrich who introduced me to the intricacies of "kinship systems" by demonstrating that real men and women sweated through the crises posed by such systems; the influence of Emrys Peters who stressed the fact that man was the manipulator as well as the victim of any "system"; and the influence of Raymond Firth whose writings on "social organization" have analyzed the possibilities of human choice in given "structural" situations.

4. I am grateful to Clifford Geertz for bringing to my attention the critical importance of propinquity and land tenure for peasants in a series of lectures on cultural ecology delivered at Harvard University in the spring of 1957.

Chapter One

1. This estimate is quoted in Patai, ed., *Jordan,* pp. 21–27.

2. *Palestine and Transjordan,* pp. 73–75.

3. To my knowledge no soil analysis of the Al Kura subdistrict of northern Jordan had been made up to 1960.

4. *Palestine and Transjordan,* pp. 487–88.

5. *Proceedings of the Conference on Middle East Agricultural Development,* Report No. 6, p. 23.

6. Mustafa Shihabi, *Al-zirā' al-'ilmiyya al-Hadītha,* p. 64.

7. B. A. Keen, *The Agricultural Development of the Middle East,* p. 51.

8. Simpson, *Palestine Report on Immigration, Land Settlement, and Development,* p. 66.

9. Keen, p. 113.

10. Simpson, p. 66.

11. *Palestine and Transjordan,* p. 488.

12. The following account is a reconstruction of historical conditions based on three sources: Madi and Musa, *Tārikh al-irdun fi al-qarn al-'ashrin;* Frederick Peake, *The History of East Jordan;* and personal accounts collected by me from the villagers of Kufr al-Ma regarding the political leadership of the Wazir family of Tibne. Most men above the age of fifty were familiar with the district political structure before it collapsed in 1922 and the traditional land tenure system that disappeared only in 1939. But the details of their organization and operation are not clear. The account of this political structure and the account of the traditional land tenure system which follows it are frankly hypothetical at a number of points. The section constitutes an attempt to make sense out of

the facts available. I believe the account to be correct in its main points. In order to protect informants, names of certain individuals and families mentioned in the text are pseudonyms. Those interested in particular historical personages should consult the appropriate historical sources.

13. Madi and Musa, pp. 3–5.

14. A "shaykh," strictly speaking, is any elderly man. The term "shaykh" is also applied to any man of religious learning regardless of age. Shaykh Luqman, the imam of Kufr al-Ma (who led the prayers in the mosque), for instance, was only thirty years old and received this appelation. In this monograph, however, unless otherwise indicated, the term will be used to designate the political leader of a descent group or village or combination of descent groups or villages in a certain area. This man usually based his authority on his military prowess, his competence in settling disputes, and the size and distinction of his lineage. In Weber's terms, he was both a "traditional" and a "charismatic" leader (see Max Weber, *The Theory of Social and Economic Organization*, pp. 341–86). The shaykh supported his authority with the loyalty of his armed kinsmen, with semifeudal exactions in kind from peasants, and with the munificence of his hospitality to his followers (see below, and Section A). After 1922, with the establishment of the central government, the authority and the stature of the shaykh were reduced while the importance of another political leader, the mukhtar, grew. By comparison, the mukhtar was a dwarfish figure. Although he represented his own clan and his own village, he was tied to the central government as its functionary. He was selected by his clan and village not for the number of guns his kinsmen could command or the nobility of his pedigree but for his knowledge of town ways and his ability to manipulate government officials. When referring to the dominant shaykh of the "peoples of Tibne" the word "shaykh" is capitalized.

15. This in fact happened in Kufr al-Ma during World War I.

16. This information is based on the account of an elderly villager who reached maturity during the period of Kleb Wazir's dominance.

17. See Peake, p. 322.

18. More than one land division occurred. The one referred to was the final division. *Tayr al-Hiswa* means literally "flying of the pebble"; land was divided among different lineages by lot, each pebble representing a particular area of land.

19. Madi and Musa, p. 113.

20. This information was communicated to me by the land registry officer of Al Kura subdistrict.

21. A. Grannot, *The Land System in Palestine: History and Structure*, p. 213.

22. Jacque Weulersse, *Paysans de Syrie et du Prôche-Orient*, p. 104.

23. Ibid.

24. Grannot, p. 231.

25. The reconstruction of the musha' system presented here is based on written accounts such as Grannot and Weulersse as well as information collected from village informants who participated in this land tenure system before its abolition in 1939. Neither the authors who

have written about the system nor the present writer have observed it
in operation. Therefore all statements regarding the system must be
regarded as tentative.

26. The clan, or 'ashira, is the largest politically represented unit
within the village vis-a-vis the outside world. It is usually represented
by a mayor (mukhtar) selected by its members. In Kufr al-Ma there are
three clans, one of which is at present unrepresented by a mukhtar. The
clan is composed of a group of patrilineally related men with their
wives and children and excluding their outmarrying (that is, out of the
community) sisters and daughters. In other words, it is a localized
group. At the time of the musha' system, the clan exercised some degree of control over the land of its members. With the lapse of that
system, however, its corporate functions are limited to the exercise of
social control against erring or recalcitrant individuals among its own
members. The three clans of Kufr al-Ma are in order of size, Beni
Yasin with over 750 members, Beni Dumi with over 500 members, and
Beni 'Amr with over 300 members.

27. Grannot, p. 228. Of course, such a statement is conjectural
and assumes a minimum of buying or selling of shares since their original assignment at the time of the founding of the village.

28. Grannot, p. 246.

29. R. C. Tute, *Ottoman Land Laws*, p. 56.

30. Tute, p. 57.

31. See Richard T. Antoun, "Conservatism and Change in the Village Community: A Jordanian Case Study," *Human Organization*, 24 (spring
1965).

Chapter Two

1. The lineage, or fandi, is the minimal social unit demanding
political representation within the village. There are twenty-eight such
groups in Kufr al-Ma. Each lineage bears a distinctive name and consists of all locally resident patrilineally related men bearing that name
along with their wives and children. The lineage, then, is a locally defined descent group, a subdivision of one of the three larger descent
groups (clans) living in the village. The lineage is not a corporate group.
It does, however, exercise certain corporate functions, particularly social control. That is, its clearest crystalization occurs at certain critical moments when men are forced to define their positions and to take
one side or another during the course of a dispute.

2. Following native usage I am using the word "peasant" (fellah)
here to designate a man who is primarily engaged in subsistence farming, who owns and tills his land, or who sharecrops land for one-half of
the crop. The critical distinction between a peasant and other men who
till the soil is the amount of capital (land, seeds, animals) contributed
to the enterprise rather than land ownership. These economic distinctions are reflected in the occupational terminology used by the inhabitants themselves (see discussion below). Many of the men listed as
peasants, plowmen, or agricultural laborers spend a considerable part

of their time working as nonagricultural laborers particularly in years of drought. The definition of peasant used above is not meant to rule out a broader definition of peasant based upon cultural criteria. For certain purposes of analysis such a definition is more useful than the economic definition given above. (See, for instance, Richard T. Antoun, "The Social Significance of Ramadan in an Arab Village," *The Muslim World*, 58 [January, 1968]; see also Chapters 2 and 3 below.)

3. The first three categories of peasant are lumped under a single term by the villagers—fellah—but the other categories of cultivators are designated by distinctive terms (see discussion below).

4. Shepherds and agricultural pieceworkers tend to be younger men not heads of households. In fact, shepherding and piecework are generally regarded as a sort of apprenticeship before becoming a full-fledged peasant landowner or sharecropper.

5. The category of soldier includes men in the army, national guard, and police.

6. Local laborers seem to be recruited from older men who are heads of households while distant laborers are usually recruited from younger men not heads of households.

7. Kufr al-Ma "exports" masons to the surrounding villages. Most of these builders are, in fact, building outside Kufr al-Ma for most of the year.

8. Although a blacksmith is resident in the village, many peasants take their smithing trade to a neighboring village where a Christian blacksmith resides. He is regarded as being more skillful at the trade than his counterpart in Kufr al-Ma.

9. The tailor is a young man who, with his mother, works on a sewing machine recently purchased.

10. The imam is the religious specialist of the village. He is mainly supported by the villagers who pay him in grain on the threshing ground after harvest. But he is also recognized by the government which supplements his income with a meager monthly stipend. His primary duties are to lead the five daily prayers in the village mosque, to deliver the Friday congregational sermon, and to wash the dead and pray for them at their burial. One of the two imams listed is retired, but continues to wear the headdress of his occupation.

11. The mukhtar is the village mayor. There are two in Kufr al-Ma. They represent the village, although they are selected and paid by the members of their own clans on the threshing ground after harvest.

12. Like the mukhtar and the imam, the watchmen are paid in grain at the threshing ground after harvest.

13. Included among government employees are six law court clerks, two law court ushers, two teachers, a customs official, and an army officer.

14. The muezzin is the village crier. He calls believers to prayer on Friday from the roof of the mosque. He does not get a salary but often receives hospitality from the residents of the village.

15. The figures cited here represent approximately eighty-five percent of the employed men of the village. It had been my original in-

tention to census all employed men, but this proved to be impossible due to the high degree of occupational mobility. It is probable that the number of soldiers and laborers make up a larger percentage of the total employed force than indicated above.

16. The mukhtar is the village mayor. In Arabic the term mukhtar means "the one selected." He is selected by his own clan to represent it to the outside world including the central government and other clans of the village. There may be one mukhtar for every large clan. Thus a village may boast more than one mukhtar. In Kufr al-Ma there were two. Besides serving the local government by keeping records of births and deaths and meeting government officials who come to the village, the mukhtar is expected to serve the particular interests of his own clan or 'ashira as well as the interests of the village. This clan supports him economically by annual contributions in kind at the time of the harvest. The mukhtar bears the official seal of his office granted to him by the central government, a seal he affixes to all documents he is called on to witness or sign. In addition to representing his own clan to the government, he serves it by helping settle disputes among its members.

17. See pp. 88–113 for a discussion of the clan.

18. The term "lot viable" is used in the Simpson *Report* (p. 64).

19. The amount of land constituting the "lot viable" will vary with the class of land to which the holding belongs. A "lot viable" of irrigated land will be much smaller than a holding of nonirrigated land.

20. Simpson, p. 64.

21. See John B. Glubb, *A Soldier with the Arabs* (London: Hodder and Stoughton, 1957).

22. Simpson, p. 53.

23. These figures on agricultural income were collected in a year of poor agricultural production. But the greater income of salaried men, as opposed to farmers, remains significant.

24. See Chapter One, Section 4.

25. See pp. 16–19 for a discussion of the shaykhs.

26. As stated earlier, my reconstruction of historical events is based on three sources. The first is a historical account which provides information on the Ajlun District of Jordan in the late nineteenth and early twentieth centuries (Madi and Musa, *The History of Jordan*). The second is Frederick Peake's *History of East Jordan* which appears in slightly different versions in Arabic and English. The third is the collection of statements elicited from the senior generation of adult men of Kufr al-Ma regarding their past history some of which they themselves witnessed.

27. Madi and Musa, p. 181.

28. Peake's book has been translated into Arabic and at least one copy was available in Kufr al-Ma. This copy was probably passed around from hand to hand, as is the villagers' habit with interesting reading material. The possibility certainly exists that the villagers were merely recounting what was read to them in Peake's book. But the fact remains that Peake originally elicited the information from the heads of the descent groups in the area.

29. Peake, pp. 151–52.

30. See Oliver, *A Solomon Island Society*, p. 102, for the distinction of "aggregate" and "group" as applied to a Melanesian society.

31. Although I have translated *ahāli tibnah* as "the peoples of Tibne" thereby suggesting that the phrase refers to residence and propinquity, there is no doubt about the fact that the term, *ahāli*, has strong connotations of kinship. In fact, one of its dictionary meanings denotes family or household (see Hava's *Arabic-English Dictionary*). Among many Arab groups it refers to the extended family (see William J. Goode, *World Revolution and Family Patterns* [New York: Free Press of Glencoe, 1963], p.134).

32. Peake, p. 151.

33. Ibid.

34. "A norm . . . is an idea in the minds of the members of a group, an idea that can be put in the form of a statement specifying what the members or other men should do, ought to do, are expected to do, under given circumstances." See George Homans, *The Human Group*, p. 123.

35. I have assessed the significance of this case only in terms of a limited objective — the demonstration of the continued political importance of the subdistrict. I have completely ignored the significance of the case for social control and the sociology of dispute as well as for the norms governing modesty and sexual relations in Islamic law and local custom. The latter subject has been dealt with at length in another place. See Richard T. Antoun, "On the Modesty of Women in Arab Muslim Villages: A Study in the Accommodation of Traditions," *American Anthropologist*, 70 (December, 1968).

36. Since every family wished to receive its rightful share, and since the distribution of wheat was on a per capita basis, all families in the village were eager to register their members with the mukhtar. For this reason, the mukhtar's census can be regarded as fairly accurate.

37. In each case, only men above the age of fifteen were included in the genealogy — this was my decision and not my informant's — and counting of generations began from them. The decision to include only males above fifteen in the patrilineal genealogy is supported by ethnographic reality and native conceptions of maturity. Around the age of fifteen the male is expected to become a full time plowman and to begin regular attendance at the Friday congregational prayer service. (For details on the life cycle of the male see Richard T. Antoun, "Social Organization and the Life Cycle in an Arab Village," *Ethnology* [July 1967].) In each of the genealogies there are "areas of ambiguity" (see Emrys Peters, "The Proliferation of Segments in the Lineage of the Bedouin in Cyrenaica," *Journal of the Royal Anthropological Institute*, 90, [1960]). That is, different informants name different ancestors for the same structural position on the genealogy. In the case of Beni Dumi, this ambiguity begins in the fourth generation. That is, there is uncertainty about the name of the great-great-grandfather of the youngest men on the genealogy. (Peters found the "area of ambiguity" to be at the level of the fifth generation.) Each of the sibs traces their descent to a named ancestor. In only one case, that of Yasin, did the ancestor give his name to the aggregate. Beni Dumi traces their descent to Sirhan. The name "Dumi"

is believed by Peake to be related to their oasis of origin, Dumat al-Jandal. Beni 'Amr trace their descent alternatively to Uthman or 'Affan. Only in the case of Beni Yasin did all the subsibs claim genuine consanguineal relationship to the ancestor of the sib. As'eed, Assayad, Massa'di, Sabbah, Qar'oosh, 'Aqayli, and Shujur, the named subsibs of Beni Yasin, are all included in the genealogy. The Basbus of Beni Dumi, however, were not included in the main genealogy of that sib. I recorded them separately, although they claimed to be "of Beni Dumi." When I collected the Beni Dumi genealogy from its oldest elder, he entirely forgot to include a named subsib—Shehem. When I reminded him of this omission, he hastily added an ancestor, 'Id, at the top of the genealogy and traced their descent to him. No less than four subsibs of Beni 'Amr, while claiming to be "of Beni 'Amr," admitted that they were of separate stock. They were Jabali, 'Ibadi, Dakhnoosh, and Abu al-'Asali (see Table 10). I collected their genealogies separately.

38. The aggregates I have termed sibs differ in a number of respects from the sib described by Murdock (see George P. Murdock, *Social Structure*, Chapters 3 and 4). First, they are not exogamous. Marriage rules do not, therefore, serve as a precise social mechanism by which members of the sib can be distinguished from other like aggregates. Second, they have no totemic designations or ceremonial titles held in common. They do not worship at common shrines. There are a number of saint's tombs in the village but they are not the objects of pilgrimage by particular sibs or subsibs. Sibs do not act as units in life crisis situations nor do they regulate inheritance. Finally, they are not units of blood revenge.

39. For formal translations of Arabic words into English I have used J. G. Hava's *Arabic-English Dictionary*. Certain terms used in the village have strictly colloquial meanings. In these cases I have relied on my personal knowledge of the local meanings rather than the dictionary for translations.

40. Ibid.

41. The units I have termed clans and lineages are, like Murdock's "clan," characterized by a unilinear rule of descent, residential unity, and social integration. Yet few collective economic or political activities characterize these units. Moreover, it is questionable whether in-marrying spouses from other sibs and villages "are recognized as an integral part of the membership" (see Murdock, p. 68). In Kufr al-Ma, one of a woman's unbreakable ties is with her father and brothers. She may always—and often does—flee to them for refuge and support against her husband, her parents-in-law, or her husband's kinsmen. The woman marrying out of her village will always, as Granqvist has pointed out, remain a stranger in her husband's house unless she is a member of his sib (see Hilma Granqvist, *Marriage Conditions in a Palestinian Village*, II, 218—56).

42. Meyer Fortes, for instance, has distinguished between the "homestead," "domestic family," and "household." The important feature of all these units is their cooperation in production as work teams (see Fortes, *The Web of Kinship Among the Tallensi*, p. 47ff).

43. "The extended family includes two or more nuclear families united by consanguineal kinship bonds such as those between parents and child or between two siblings" (Murdock, p. 23). ". . . the nuclear family consists typically of a married man and woman with their off-spring, although in individual cases one or more additional persons may reside with them" (Murdock, p. 1).

44. See Emile Durkheim, *The Division of Labor in Society*, pp. 70–233, for an analysis of "organic solidarity."

45. The "parental" extended family is one in which the consanguineal tie uniting the two nuclear families is between parent and child. The "fraternal" extended family is one in which the consanguineal tie uniting the nuclear families is between brothers.

46. See Derrick J. Stenning, "Household Viability among the Pastoral Fulani" in *The Developmental Cycle in Domestic Groups*, ed. Goody, for a study of the developmental cycle of the family in response to ecological factors.

47. See Meyer Fortes, *The Web of Kinship Among the Tallensi*, Fortes, however, stresses the importance of affective and ritual ties (as well as economic factors) in bringing about reintegration of the domestic group.

48. See Jack Goody, "The Fission of Domestic Groups among the LoDagaba" in *The Developmental Cycle in Domestic Groups*, ed. Goody, for an analysis of family size and composition in terms of differential rules of inheritance and property control.

49. For an example of the family cycle reconstructed from a census of household composition see Fortes, "Time and Social Structure: an Ashanti Case Study" in *Social Structure Studies Presented to A. R. Radcliffe-Brown*, ed. Fortes.

50. Fission is "the process by which a social group divided into two or more distinct groups, so that the original group disappears as a social entity." (John Barnes, "Seven Types of Segmentation," *The Rhodes-Livingstone Institute Journal*, no. 17, p. 20.)

51. "A 'style of life' is a closely interwoven set of activities and possessions that are correlated with and become symbolic of membership in a social class" (Bernard Barber, *Social Stratification*, p. 138).

52. By "conflict" I do not mean dispute. Many disputes may not involve conflict in the sense specified here. By "conflict" I mean inherent social structural opposition. That is, the parties must, at some time, be drawn into opposition by the very fact of occupying the positions they do. Thus, for instance, in Islamic society the position of co-wife in a polygynous family is one involving conflict as is the position of the children of these mothers, being half siblings.

53. In his brief but insightful discussion of "larger kinship structures" William J. Goode has pointed out the ambiguity of the terms of reference specifying the middle levels of Arab social organization which are, according to Goode, the hamula, the *samiyah*, the *fendeh*, and the *fekhed* (in *World Revolution and Family Patterns*, pp. 132–34; see also Murphy and Kasden, "The Structure of Parallel Cousin Marriage," *American Anthropologist*, 61: 19, who noted the ambiguity in the terms of reference for the leaders of Arab descent groups, e.g., shaykh). Goode attributes

this ambiguity to the tendency of Arabs to interpolate terms according to an ideal six-level structure which has little reality in particular communities. At the higher levels of the social structure, the 'ashira and the humula (Goode is unsure whether to classify the latter on the middle or higher level), confusion is the result of the uneven growth and fission of family units and the opportunities for political amalgamation (see Goode, p. 137). The present monograph substantiates Goode's findings of ambiguity of terms of reference for descent groups but differs from his analysis in two important respects. First, ambiguity is found at all levels and not merely at the middle level of social organization. And second, the ambiguity of terms of reference is not related to regional differences in the use of terms or differences in growth and fission or political amalgamation as much as to the continuum of functions and ideology. This continuum allows particular descent groups within a single community to adopt a given function (e.g., political competition) and to adopt the ideology and terminology appropriate to it, and, at another time in another situation to revert to its original (strictly social or economic) functions and their concomitant ideology and terminology. For a fuller explanation see the following discussion and the conclusion at the end of the book.

54. The type of marriage whereby a brother marries with the mahr (marriage payment) provided by his sister's marriage resembles exchange and is termed by Granqvist "veiled exchange" (see Granqvist, *Marriage Conditions in a Palestinian Village,* I, p. 118). The villagers of Kufr al-Ma, however (as witnessed by this case) like the villagers of Artas, insist that such a marriage does not constitute exchange.

55. See A. R. Radcliffe-Brown's introduction to the book, *African Systems of Kinship and Marriage,* ed. Radcliffe-Brown and Forde, for a delineation of the principle of "the unity of the sibling group."

56. A "multiplex" relationship is one that serves many interests, e.g., economic, political, religious, recreational. See Gluckman, *The Judicial Process Among the Barotse of Northern Rhodesia,* p. 18.

57. This definition of lineage differs from Murdock's definition: "A consanguineal kin group produced by either rule of unilineal descent is technically known as a lineage when it includes only persons who can actually trace their common relationship through a specific series of remembered genealogical links in the prevailing line of descent" (see Murdock, p. 46). Murdock stresses actual consanguineal relationship in defining the lineage while I have stressed common residence. In Kufr al-Ma, the lineage, like the clan, is a local group, all of whose members reside in the village.

58. For the basic Islamic rules of inheritance, see J. N. D. Anderson, *Islamic Law in the Modern World,* Chapter 4.

59. See Antoun, "The Significance of Names in an Arab Village," *Ethnology,* 7 (April 1968), for an analysis of proper names and nicknames in relation to ethical evaluation and social control.

60. Gluckman, p. 18.

61. Victor M. Turner, *Schism and Continuity in an African Society,* p. 91.

62. This discovery is not my own. Emrys Peters of Manchester

University was the first to show the critical structural importance of women for Arab communities—nomadic and settled—which have traditionally been regarded as pervaded by the patrilineal principle. His article on "The Proliferation of Segments in the Lineage of the Bedouin of Cyrenaica" discusses the peculiar structural significance of both parallel and cross cousin marriage for the isolation of segments among a group of pastoral nomads. See also his analysis of marriage in "Aspects of Status and Rank in a Lebanese Village" in *Mediterranean Countrymen*, ed. Pitt-Rivers. In numerous discussions and seminars Peters drew my attention to the importance of matrilateral ties for my own analysis.

63. See the bibliography for a more complete listing of Peters's work.

64. In his recent book, *Pul Eliya* (Cambridge: University Press, 1961), Edmund Leach has argued that when anthropologists in tribal and peasant societies speak about kinship structure, they should, in fact, be speaking about the land and property relationships they have failed to analyze. The excellence of Leach's analysis of his own data does not compensate for the monistic strait jacket that Leach's exhortation imposes on anthropological theory. I can only say here that land tenure relationships in Kufr al-Ma are not determinative inasmuch as more than half of the employed men of the village are engaged in nonagricultural (and nonpastoral) employment. The dispute examined here was over land trespass but this fact had very little to do with the factors determining the alignment of groups. In any case, land ownership and use is only one factor with many others that enhances or diminishes the importance of particular structural ties. An analysis in terms of land tenure like an analysis in terms of the pattern of grudges does not replace a structural analysis of kinship but rather operates through it.

65. I am indebted for this insight to the reading of an early draft of an article on the feud among the Bedouin of Cyrenaica by Emrys Peters.

66. See Raymond Firth's *Elements of Social Organization*, particularly pages 75-79. For Firth, "social organization" involves coordination of activity based on foresight, assumption of responsibility, and compensation to the participants (whether material or nonmaterial). Of central importance to Firth's concept of social organization is the element of choice. Social organization comes into being to resolve conflicts of structural principles or to handle uncertainty which disrupts institutionalized procedures, e.g., marriage. In the social situation I have described, the actors have not acted in an ad hoc fashion, exercising a choice of possible alternatives. Rather, they have acted on the basis of clearly defined structural principles. See also Antoun, "Social Organization and the Life Cycle in an Arab Village," *Ethnology*, 6 (July 1967), for an analysis of "social organization" (rather than social structure) in Kufr al-Ma.

67. This view is clearly implied in Peters's analysis of peasant life in southern Lebanon. See his article, "Aspects of Rank and Status Among Muslims in a Lebanese Village," particularly p. 179, p. 189, and pp. 192-93.

68. This has been the traditional mode of economic support. In

1964 the central government passed a law stipulating that remuneration of the mukhtar would be according to services rendered. For each document he drew up and signed he was entitled to twenty-eight cents except documents of marriage for which he was entitled to one dollar and forty cents. This official change in the economic basis of the mayorship has created the potential for radical change in the traditional political institutions of the village. I hope to examine this potential in a detailed analysis of the political system of the village in a future publication.

69. This term was suggested to me by Frederick G. Bailey who found it appropriate in describing official political leaders in Indian villages.

70. This policy was first applied in Kufr al-Ma in 1955 at the time of the first formal elections for the position of mukhtar.

71. There is some historical evidence to indicate that from early times social control has been the critical function of Arab kinship groups in both nomadic and agricultural circumstances. When Muhammad was invited to the oasis of Medina before his famous Hegira, he was invited in his capacity as arbitrator rather than ruler or prophet. (See articles 23 and 42 of the Constitution of Medina in William Montgomery Watt, *Muhammad at Medina* [Oxford: Clarendon Press, 1956], pp. 223-24.) Anthropologists have also made references, albeit in an oblique fashion, to the continued importance of descent groups for social control in Arab villages today. See Salim's remarks concerning the importance of the clan guest house as a court of justice in southern Iraq (Salim, *Marsh Dwellers of the Euphrates Delta,* p. 72ff.) and Ammar's concerning clans and social control in southern Egypt (H. Ammar, *Growing Up in an Egyptian Village,* p. 45 and pp. 58-60).

72. See Gluckman, p. 18.

73. However, it can be done. Fortes, for instance, was faced with the problem of defining boundaries for the Tallensi in the absence of linguistic, topographic, ethnic, or cultural criteria. He formulated the concept of society as a "socio-geographic region" (see Fortes, *The Dynamics of Clanship Among the Tallensi,* p. 231).

74. See Afif Tannous' characterization of Middle Eastern villages in "The Arab Village Community of the Middle East" in Smithsonian Institution's *Annual Report for 1943,* pp. 523-44. See also C. A. O. von Nieuwenhuijze, "The Near Eastern Village: A Profile," *The Middle East Journal,* p. 301.

75. The analysis of continuity and change in the village's political institutions is too complex a subject to be dealt with in the compass of this monograph whose focus is primarily social structural and ethnographic. I plan to devote a separate monograph to the subject of village politics based upon fieldwork done in 1966 and 1967 as well as that done in 1959 and 1960.

76. By ties of descent, I refer to affiliation to particular patrilineal descent groups (e.g., clans and lineages). By kinship ties I refer to all consanguineal ties traced through any line and traced through males and/or females. Marriage within the community, if carried on genera-

tion after generation, results in relating all the members of the community to each other in one way or another.

77. The village does not conform, however, to all the criteria laid down by Murdock (see Murdock, pp. 62–63) for the existence of the "deme." Kufr al-Ma is segmented into unilineal consanguineal groupings of kinsmen (unlike the classic deme which is not) and, after the family, the strongest identification of the individual is with his clan (not with the entire community as in the classic deme). Furthermore, while endogamous village marriage is both an ethical and a strong statistical norm, a significant percentage of the population (twenty-two) still marries outside of the village.

78. See Part II, Chapter 9, of Granqvist, *Marriage Conditions*, for a discussion of the position of the "stranger" wife.

79. By functions, here, I simply mean activity. For clarification of the use of the term function, see Joseph H. Greenberg, *Essays in Linguistics* pp. 75–85.

80. See *Reports on Palestine Administration July 1920, December 1921*, p. 10.

81. "A network . . . is always egocentric: it exists only and is defined with reference to a particular individual. As Barnes remarks, each person sees himself at the centre of a collection of friends. It follows therefore that the network is always 'personal,' for the set of links that make it up is unique for each individual. . . . A network is made up of persons who interact with one another . . . and who regard each other therefore as approximate social equals. . . . Together these persons represent a selection—in all likelihood a fairly limited one—of the total range of his social contacts. . . ." (See A. L. Epstein, "The Network and Urban Organization," *The Rhodes-Livingstone Institute Journal*, no. 29, p. 56.) Although Epstein developed his conception of the network in relation to urban societies, his remarks are pertinent for the study of peasant villages. Instead of being a collection of friends, however, the network in Kufr al-Ma is largely a collection of kinsmen, affines, and neighbors. The major point still holds: the network is a selection of certain kinsmen and neighbors out of a large possible number. These are the individuals with whom any person interacts most frequently. See also John Barnes, "Class and Committees in a Norwegian Island Parish," pp. 39–58, and Elizabeth Bott, *Family and Social Network*. In the past much too little attention has been paid to the importance of propinquity and friendship and much too much to the importance of kinship and descent in the description of village life in the Middle East. The concept of the social network may help to right this imbalance (see concluding discussion below).

82. Even then, he remains subject to the community's social control if he continues to have relatives or land within it. For an example of pressure successfully applied against a villager who resided elsewhere for eleven months out of the year see Antoun, "Conservatism and Change," *Human Organization*, 24 (1965), and Case 8, pp. 97–102.

83. The term, *ibn al-balad*, literally means "son of the town," but is used in Jordan and other Arab countries to designate the individual born and bred in a particular village. The plural *awlād al-balad*, "sons of the

town" is also used to refer to residents of the village. In certain areas another term may designate the village, e.g., *Day'a* in Lebanon, *nazla* in Egypt. I have seldom heard villagers in any part of the Arab world use the classical Arabic term, *qarya*, to refer to the village. In Kufr al-Ma villagers do not use the phrase, *ibn al-balad*, with great frequency but they often use the term, *balad*, to designate the village. For example, one man distinguished individuals who lived in the village for many years but were not born and bred in it by saying, "They are in the village but not of it" (*fil balad wa lakin mush minha*). Another man who lived at a point equidistant from Kufr al-Ma and Deir Abu Said refused to make a contribution to Kufr al-Ma's village improvement fund, claiming that his house was not located within its boundaries. The mukhtar refused to accept his claim, saying, "He is of us; his lands are here, and he lives here." The "us" may be construed as having two references: the residents of Kufr al-Ma or the "peoples of Tibne" from whence the man had come four years previously. Common historical origin can be interpreted here quite literally as signifying covillageship since, originally, the ancestors of the mukhtar and the ancestors of the man in question did live together in one village—Tibne. Thus the ideology of subdistrict unity carries within it as part of the cultural past the ideology of common villageship. In this sense all of the "people of Tibne" are "sons of the village." A final example elucidates quite clearly the explicitly recognized distinction between the lineage and the subsib as well as the native view of their relative importance vis-a-vis village membership. I asked the elders of one lineage for their genealogy. They gave me a genealogy which omitted the names of their patrilineal kinsmen in other villages. I asked them why they had done so. They replied, "What do we know about them? We are living in one village and they are living in another."

84. This case is much more complex than suggested above, and its full analysis would necessitate an examination of the attitude of orthodox Islam towards the practice of magic in a village milieu. Of more immediate pertinence is the fact that the hometown magician had not committed serious violations of modesty as had the stranger nor was he so unsophisticated in his *modus operandi* as to be easily unmasked as an imposter. The differential treatment of the hometown magician and the stranger is, however, to a large degree a reflection of their different local origins.

Chapter Three

1. They are not entirely so, however. As pointed out in the last section, an individual's "social network" is made up not only of his lineage mates and affines but also of his friends and neighbors.

2. This description of marriage should not be construed as an attempt at comprehensive structural analysis. Besides overlooking the structural significance of two patterns of marriage described in section three, this chapter does not deal with the structural conflict inherent in

the Islamic code of marriage. To do so would necessitate introducing a considerable body of case material, an undertaking beyond the scope of the present monograph.

3. By mode, here, I mean the manner or way of doing.

4. For an analysis of the initial stage of marriage (wasita) that demonstrates the possibilities of choice in selecting both mediators and eligible marriage mates see Antoun, "Social Organization and the Life Cycle," *Ethnology* 6 (1967).

5. See Granqvist, *Marriage Conditions in a Palestinian Village*, Part I, Chapter I, for details of child betrothals in Palestine.

6. The pertinent passages in the Quran are as follows: "And give unto the women [whom ye marry] free gift of their marriage portions; but if they of their own accord remit unto you a part thereof, then you are welcome to absorb it [in your wealth]" (Chapter 4, Verse 2). "Lawful unto you are all beyond those mentioned, so that you seek them with your wealth, not debauchery. And those whom ye seek content [by marrying them], give unto them their portions as a duty" (Chapter 4, Verse 24). See Mohammed M. Pickthall's *The Meaning of the Glorious Koran*.

7. These figures represent only a small percentage of all marriages in the village. Moreover, the information was solicited from household heads who might wish to conceal the fact (for reasons of prestige) that they had given their daughters little or no part of the marriage payment. Yet I believe, on the whole, that the information given to me is accurate. In the two cases in which I suspected deceit I was able to check the accuracy of the information by consultation with close kinsmen of the individual involved.

8. Here, my findings are not in agreement with those of Rosenfeld who reports that in an Arab village in Israel women invariably surrender their rights to property to their fathers and brothers in order to gain their social support in critical situations. See Henry Rosenfeld, "On Determinants of the Status of Arab Village Women," pp. 66−70.

9. This was the sum stipulated in 1960. By 1966 the expected mahr payment for a bride from the village was 700 dollars.

10. Salim maintains that giving women as compensation in cases of elopement and honor was a customary means of settling serious grievances among the Marsh Arabs of Iraq. See Salim, *Marsh Dwellers of the Euphrates Delta*, pp. 52 and 58.

11. See Granqvist's discussion of the significance of "bride-purchase" in Palestine in *Marriage Conditions in a Palestinian Village*, Part I, Chapter 4.

12. Ibid.

13. All marriages are officially, by Islamic law, settlements of wealth on the bride by her husband. This fact is stated in the written marriage contract. In many cases the bride receives all or a large portion of the mahr. Yet, all marriages are in some sense passages of bridewealth too, since the money or property constituting the mahr passes from the bridegroom or, more often, the bridegroom's father to the father or legal guardian of the bride, who, in turn, disposes of it as he sees fit. (This is so, even though some women—conscious of their

rights under Islamic law—have appealed to the Islamic court against the "eating" of the mahr by their legal guardian.) In other words, passage of wealth is from one family head to another family head and not from the bridegroom to the bride. On the other hand, the mahr payment is not the same type of bridewealth transaction that anthropologists have described for many African tribes. Large numbers of agnatic and matrilateral kinsmen are not involved in the collection of the marriage payment and its subsequent distribution. The maternal and paternal uncles receive cloaks and the members of the bride's immediate family (mother and sisters) may be the recipients of gifts and the givers of gifts. But marriage does not establish a wide network of rights and obligations among the members of corporate descent groups. The villagers of Kufr al-Ma do not distinguish between the passage of bridewealth between family heads (signifying the transfer of legal rights over women) and the Islamic marriage settlement on the bride according to the written marriage contract. (The Somali of the horn of East Africa, as reported by Lewis, distinguish the Islamic mahr which they term as such from the bridewealth payment to which they assign a separate term, *yarac*; see Lewis, *Marriage and the Family in Northern Somaliland*, pp. 14–17). The two are regarded as synonymous and are referred to by the term mahr. In the past, however, and to some extent at present, the term *fayd* is used to describe the property passing from one family head to another. Thus, the term mahr has kept its Islamic meaning while encompassing the meaning formerly reserved for the term fayd. It is only from context, then, that the reference can be distinguished. In a case where the father of the girl in fact gives her the whole mahr the reference is to the Islamic meaning, except for the fact that it is still the father who controls and disposes of the marriage payment.

14. See the *Shorter Encyclopaedia of Islam*, s. v. "nikah."

15. See Fyzee, *Outlines of Muhammadan Law*, Chapter 13, for the requirements of a legal Muslim marriage.

16. Ibid., p. 98.

17. Pickthall, pp. 81–82.

18. Granqvist explains the absence of relatives and friends at the drawing up of the marriage contract in terms of traditional beliefs regarding the imminent threat of black magic on this occasion (*Marriage Conditions*, Part II, pp. 27–28). I did not record any such beliefs in Kufr al-Ma.

19. This was the situation up to 1960. By 1966, however, the imam of Kufr al-Ma, who had been appointed ma'thun over four villages in the area, had begun to encourage villagers to stipulate deferred mahr payments as being more in accordance with Islam and as offering more protection to the bride.

20. By pattern I mean structural pattern—that is, the arrangement of parts in a given universe of social relations. Here, the parts are the marriages contracted by the individuals of particular social units—the family, the luzum, or the lineage. I am not suggesting that these patterns are "basic" in the sense of being relatively immune to the vicissitudes of time. See Alfred Kroeber, "Structure, Function, and Pattern in Biology and Anthropology" in *The Nature of Culture*, pp. 85–94.

21. In her article "What is Caste" (*The Economic Weekly Annual* [January 1958]), Irawati Karve follows this procedure to distinguish three patterns of marriage in certain Indian communities.

22. See Granqvist, *Marriage Conditions,* Part I, pp. 118–19.

23. Conversations with Abner Cohen and Emrys L. Peters have elucidated this point for me.

24. I wish to thank Emrys L. Peters for calling my attention to the necessary conversion of patrilineal to matrilateral ties as a result of patrilateral parallel cousin marriage. See Peters' article, "Aspects of the Family Among the Bedouin of Cyrenaica" in *Comparative Family Systems,* ed. Nimkoff, particularly, p. 133. See also Barclay on the same point (Harold B. Barclay, *Buurri al Lamaab,* pp. 118–19).

25. Peters has pointed out the complication of structural ties through close parallel cousin marriage (with resultant incident division within the group) in his article "The Proliferation of Segments in the Lineage of the Bedouin in Cyrenaica." Here, I am stressing the fact that complication of structural ties can increase group solidarity as well as provide the basis for division in particular situations.

26. The protracted dispute between Meyer Fortes and Edmund Leach over the significance of affinal as opposed to matrilateral ties (see *Man,* 1953 and 1954) is resolved, for me at least, by remembering that each marriage establishes simultaneously affinal and matrilateral ties — the first mainly for those of the generation actually contracting the marriage and the second for their descendants. In each situation one must consider these ties and weigh them. Thus in the Trobriand Islands the affinal tie — a man and his brother-in-law—establishes certain rights and obligations as does the matrilateral tie—a man and his mother's brother. To assign one overriding significance does not deny the existence of the other. The fact that ties of kinship are described in one idiom (matrilaterality) rather than another (affinity) is not, however, an insignificant fact. On the contrary, the whole discussion of matrilaterality in the first section of this chapter suggests that the use of an idiom of matrilaterality has very definite consequences for the structure of the community.

27. In his recent book, *Pul Eliya,* Leach has argued that when anthropologists in tribal and peasant communities speak about kinship structure, they should, in fact, be speaking about the land and property relationships they have failed to analyze. In another place ("The Structural Implications of Matrilateral Cross-Cousin Marriage") Leach has analyzed matrilateral cross cousin marriage in terms of its establishment of status differences and political and economic control. I do not mean to suggest that explanations of particular ties of kinship and marriage in terms of political and economic factors are to be avoided; on the contrary, they enrich every analysis. However, land ownership and political control are only particular factors among many others that enhance or diminish the importance of particular structural ties. An analysis in terms of land tenure or status differences does not replace a structural analysis of kinship and marriage. Rather, it builds upon it.

28. See Ralph Linton, *The Study of Man,* p. 166.

29. Ibid., p. 164.

30. Granqvist's description of the structural interdependence of families linked in sister exchange is excellent. She failed to see, however, the other side of the coin—the strength of the sister-exchange tie which, in a sense, contains its weakness.

31. In this section I am using the term "function" as internal function on the organic analogy (see Greenberg, *Essays in Linguistics*, pp. 75–85), that is, internal to the unit under consideration—the lineage. I wish to trace the consequences—political, economical, and structural—of patrilateral parallel cousin marriage for the families composing a lineage or luzum. Insofar as such a pattern of marriage maintains in being a closely interacting group of patrilineal relatives who at a given moment may act as a united political group, my use of the term function is similar to that of Radcliffe-Brown. But, mainly, I am concerned with the effects of such a series of marriages internally—within the lineage. Unlike Radcliffe-Brown, I am not making statements about the unity or solidarity of larger social units such as the clan, the village, or the society itself, nor am I postulating the "social necessity" of this form of marriage. (See Radcliffe-Brown, *Structure and Function in Primitive Society*, particularly p. 43 and pp. 45–47.) Moreover, I am not using the term "function" in a mathematical sense to suggest relationships of concomitant variation.

32. See Fyzee, *Outline of Muhammadan Law*, Chapter 13.

Conclusion

1. Strictly speaking, as I have already pointed out (pp. 37–39), the subdistrict constituted by "the peoples of Tibne" is not a group but rather an aggregate. Also, although the relations between lineages and between clans have been touched upon in every chapter, a full analysis and understanding of intergroup relations can only come with a study of village politics, a subject beyond the scope of the present work.

2. Important work along these lines has already been undertaken by Frederick G. Bailey and Emrys L. Peters. Each in his own way and in his own area of interest (Indian villages and Arab tribes respectively) has pioneered in the analysis of basic structural units (microcastes and patrilineages) from the point of view of their participation in a wider political arena. See Bailey's *Caste and the Economic Frontier*, and *Tribe, Caste and Nation*, and Peters' "The Proliferation of Segments in the Lineage of the Bedouin in Cyrenaica"; "Aspects of the Family Among the Bedouin of Cyrenaica"; and "Some Structural Aspects of the Feud Among the Camel-Herding Bedouin of Cyrenaica." In a general theoretical statement one political anthropologist, M. G. Smith, has advocated the study of political systems and political processes through the analysis and comparison of the fundamental units that compose them. For Smith these units are "publics" or corporate groups of one kind or another (see M. G. Smith, "A Structural Approach to Comparative Politics" in *Varieties of Political Theory*, ed. David Easton). The difficulty of applying Smith's approach to the study of village politics is that the competing

units are often factions.   They do not necessarily or even usually coincide with the corporate groups based on principles of descent, age, or
propinquity that are so fully described in the literature of social and,
recently, political anthropology.

Bibliography

BOOKS

Ammar, Hamed. *Growing Up in an Egyptian Village.* London: Routledge and Kegan Paul, 1954.

Anderson, James N. D. *Islamic Law in the Modern World.* London: Stevens and Sons, 1959.

Arensberg, Conrad M., and Kimball, Solon T. *Culture and Community.* New York: Harcourt, Brace and World, 1965.

Bailey, Frederick G. *Caste and the Economic Frontier.* Manchester: Manchester University Press, 1957.

_____. *Tribe, Caste, and Nation.* Manchester: Manchester University Press, 1960.

Barber, Bernard. *Social Stratification.* New York: Harcourt, Brace and Company, 1957.

Barclay, Harold B. *Buurri al Lamaab.* Ithaca: Cornell University Press, 1964.

Bott, Elizabeth. *Family and Social Network.* London: Tavistock Publications, 1957.

Cohen, Abner. *Arab Border-Villages in Israel.* Manchester: Manchester University Press, 1965.

Durkheim, Emile. *The Division of Labor in Society.* Translated by George Simpson. Glencoe, Illinois: The Free Press, 1949.

Evans-Pritchard, Edward E. *The Nuer.* Oxford: The Clarendon Press, 1940.

Firth, Raymond. *Elements of Social Organization.* New York: Philosophical Library, 1951.

_____. *We the Tikopea.* London: George Allen and Unwin, 1957.

Fortes, Meyer. *The Dynamics of Clanship Among the Tallensi.* London: Oxford University Press, 1945.

_____. *The Web of Kinship Among the Tallensi.* London: Oxford University Press, 1949.

Fyzee, Asaf A. A. *Outlines of Muhammadan Law.* London: Oxford University Press, 1960.

Gluckman, Max. *The Judicial Process Among the Barotse of Northern Rhodesia.* Manchester: Manchester University Press, 1955.

Goode, William J. *World Revolution and Family Patterns.* Glencoe, Illinois: The Free Press, 1963.

Grannot, A. *The Land System in Palestine: History and Structure.* London: Eyre and Spottiswoode, 1952.

Granqvist, Hilma. *Marriage Conditions in a Palestinian Village.* Parts I and II. Commentationes Humanarum Litterarum, vol. 8. Helsinki: Societas Scientiarum Fennica, 1931; 1935.

_____ . *Birth and Childhood Among the Arabs.* Helsinki: Söderstrom, 1947.

_____ . *Child Problems Among the Arabs.* Helsinki: Söderstrom, 1950.

Greenberg, Joseph H. *Essays in Linguistics.* New York: Wenner-Gren Foundation for Anthropological Research, 1957.

Hava, J. G. *Arabic-English Dictionary.* Beirut: Catholic Press, 1951.

Homans, George C. *The Human Group.* New York: Harcourt, Brace, and Company, 1950.

Jaziri, Abd Al-Rahman. *Kitāb al fiqh ʿalā mathāhib al-arbaʿah* [The book of jurisprudence according to the four law schools]. Cairo: The Great Commercial Press, 1928.

Junod, Henri A. *The Life of a South African Tribe.* New York: Macmillan, 1927.

Keen, B. A. *The Agricultural Development of the Middle East.* London: His Majesty's Stationery Office, 1946.

Kroeber, Alfred J. *The Nature of Culture.* Chicago: University of Chicago Press, 1952.

Leach, Edmund. *Political Systems of Highland Burma.* London: G. Bell and Sons, 1954.

_____ . *Pul Eliva: A Village in Ceylon.* Cambridge: Cambridge University Press, 1952.

Lewis, I. A. *Marriage and the Family in Northern Somaliland.* Kampala: East African Institute of Social Research, 1962.

Linton, Ralph. *The Study of Man.* New York: Appleton-Century-Crofts, 1936.

Llewellyn, Karl N., and Hoebel, E. A. *The Cheyenne Way.* Norman, Oklahoma: University of Oklahoma Press, 1941.

Lutfiyya, Abdullah M. *Baytin: A Jordanian Village.* The Hague: Mouton and Company, 1966.

Madi, Munib, and Musa, Sulayman. *Tārīkh al-irdun fi al-qarn al-ʿashrīn* [The history of Jordan in the twentieth century]. Amman, 1959.

Malinowski, Bronislaw. *Crime and Custom in Savage Society.* London: Routledge and Kegan Paul, 1926.

_____ . *The Sexual Life of Savages in North-western Melanesia.* London: George Routledge and Sons, 1929.

_____ . *Argonauts of the Western Pacific.* London: G. Routledge and Sons, 1922.

_____ . *Coral Gardens and Their Magic.* New York: American Book Company, 1935.

Morgan, Lewis H. *The League of the Ho-de-no sau-nee or Iroquois.* New York: Dodd, Mead and Co., 1901.

Murdock, George P. *Social Structure.* New York: The Macmillan Company, 1949.

Oliver, Douglas L. *A Solomon Island Society.* Cambridge, Mass.: Harvard University Press, 1955.

Palestine and Transjordan. Geographical Handbook Series. British Naval Intelligence Publication, 1943.

Patai, Raphael, ed. *Jordan.* New Haven: Human Relations Area Files, 1956.

Peake, Frederick G. *The History of East Jordan.* Jerusalem, 1935.

_____ . *A History of Jordan and its Tribes.* Coral Gables, Florida: University of Miami Press, 1958.

Phillips, Paul G. *The Hashemite Kingdom of Jordan: Prolegomena to a Technical Assistance Program.* Chicago: University of Chicago Press, 1954.

Pickthall, Mohammed M. *The Meaning of the Glorious Koran.* New York: Mentor Books, 1959.

Radcliffe-Brown, Alfred R. *Structure and Function in Primitive Society.* Glencoe, Illinois: The Free Press, 1956.

_____, and Forde, Daryll, eds. *African Systems of Kinship and Marriage.* London: Oxford University Press, 1950.

_____. *The Andaman Islanders.* Glencoe, Illinois: The Free Press, 1922.

Rivers, William H. R. *The Todas.* London and New York: Macmillan and Co., 1906.

Salim, Mustafa S. *Marsh Dwellers of the Euphrates Delta.* London School of Economics Monographs on Social Anthropology, no. 23. London: The Athlone Press, 1962.

Shihabi, Mustafa. *Al-zirā'a al-'ilmiyya al hadītha* [Modern practical agriculture]. Damascus: Moderation Press, 1935.

Smith, William R. *Kinship and Marriage in Early Arabia.* Boston: Beacon Press, 1966.

Turner, Victor W. *Schism and Continuity in an African Society.* Manchester: Manchester University Press, 1957.

Tute, R. C. *The Ottoman Land Laws,* 1927.

Uberoi, J. P. S. *Politics of the Kula Ring.* Manchester: Manchester University Press, 1962.

Watt, Montgomery. *Muhammad at Medina.* Oxford: Clarendon Press, 1956.

Weber, Max. *The Theory of Social and Economic Organization.* Edited by Talcott Parsons and translated by A. M. Henderson and Talcott Parsons. Glencoe, Illinois: The Free Press, 1947.

Weulersse, Jacque. *Paysans de Syrie et du Pròche-Orient.* Paris: Gallimard, 1946.

ARTICLES

Antoun, Richard T. "Conservatism and Change in the Village Community: A Jordanian Case Study," *Human Organization* 24 (Spring 1965): 4–10.

_____. "Social Organization and the Life Cycle in an Arab Village," *Ethnology* 6 (July 1967): 294–308.

_____. "The Social Significance of Ramadan in an Arab Village," *The Muslim World* 58 (January 1968), 36–42; (April 1968), 95–104.

_____. "On the Significance of Names in an Arab Village," *Ethnology* 7 (April 1968): 158–70).

_____. "On the Modesty of Women in Arab Muslim Villages: A Study in the Accommodation of Traditions," *American Anthropologist* 70 (December 1968): 671–97.

Barnes, John A. "Class and Committees in a Norwegian Island Parish." *Human Relations* 7 (1954): 39–58.

_____. "Seven Types of Segmentation. *Rhodes-Livingstone Institute Journal,* no. 17 (1955), pp. 1–22.

Epstein, Arnold L. "The Network and Urban Social Organization," *Rhodes-Livingstone Institute Journal,* no. 29 (1961), pp. 29–62.

Fortes, Meyer. "Time and Social Structure: An Ashanti Case Study." In *Social Structure Studies Presented to A. R. Radcliffe-Brown,* edited by Meyer Fortes, pp. 54–84. Oxford, 1949.

Goody, Jack. "The Fission of Domestic Groups Among the LoDagaba." In *The Developmental Cycle in Domestic Groups,* edited by Jack Goody, pp. 53–91. Cambridge Papers in Social Anthropology, no. 1. Cambridge: At the University Press, 1958.

Karve, Irawati. "What Is Caste," *Economic Weekly Annual,* January, 1958, pp. 125–42.

Leach, Edmund. "The Structural Implications of Matrilateral Cross-Cousin Marriage." *The Journal of the Royal Anthropological Institute of Great Britain and Ireland* 81 (1951): 23–55.

Murphy, Robert F., and Kasden, Leonard. "The Structure of Parallel Cousin Marriage." *American Anthropologist,* 61 (1959): 17–29.

Nieuwenhuijze, C. A. O. von. "The Near Eastern Village: A Profile." *The Middle East Journal* (Summer 1962), 295–308.

Oliver, Douglas L. "An Ethnographer's Method for Formulating Descriptions of Social Structure." *American Anthropologist* 60 (1958): 801–26.

Peters, Emrys L. "The Proliferation of Segments in the Lineage of the Bedouin in Cyrenaica," *The Journal of the Royal Anthropological Institute of Great Britain and Ireland* 90 (1960): 29–53.

_____. "Aspects of Rank and Status among Muslims in a Lebanese Village." In *Mediterranean Countrymen,* edited by Julian Pitt-Rivers, pp. 159–202. Paris: Mouton and Company, 1963.

_____. "Aspects of the Family Among the Bedouin of Cyrenaica." In *Comparative Family Systems,* edited by M. F. Nimkoff, pp. 121–46. Boston: Houghton Mifflin, 1965.

_____. "Some Structural Aspects of the Feud Among the Camel-Herding Bedouin of Cyrenaica." *Africa* 37 (1967): 261–82.

Richards, A. *Land, Labour and Diet in Northern Rhodesia.* London: Oxford University Press, 1939.

Rosenfeld, Henry. "Processes of Structural Change Within the Arab Village Extended Family." *American Anthropologist* 60 (1958): 1127–39.

_____. "On Determinants of the Status of Arab Village Women," *Man* 60 (1960): 66–70.

Smith, M. G. "Segmentary Lineage Systems," *The Journal of the Royal Anthropological Institute of Great Britain and Ireland* 88 (1956): 39–80.

_____. "A Structural Approach to Comparative Politics." In *Varieties of Political Theory,* edited by David Easton, pp. 113–28. Englewood Cliffs, N.J.: Prentice-Hall, 1966.

Stenning, Derrick J. "Household Viability Among the Pastoral Fulani." In *The Developmental Cycle in Domestic Groups,* edited by Jack Goody, pp. 92–119. Cambridge Papers in Social Anthropology, no. 1. Cambridge: At the University Press, 1958.

Tannous, Afif I. "The Arab Village Community of the Middle East." *The Smithsonian Report for 1943.* (Washington: United States Government Printing Office, 1944), pp. 523–44.

REPORTS

Government of Palestine. *Reports on Palestine Administration July 1920, December 1921.* London: His Majesty's Stationery Office, 1922.

The Proceedings of the Conference on Middle East Agricultural Development. Agricultural Report no. 6. Cairo: Middle East Supply Center, 1944.

Simpson, John H. *Palestine Report on Immigration, Land Settlement and Development.* London: His Majesty's Stationery Office, 1930.

UNPUBLISHED MATERIAL

Peters, Emrys. "The Sociology of the Bedouin of Cyrenaica." Ph.D. dissertation, Oxford University, 1951.

_____ Draft of article (above) on the feud among the Bedouin of Cyrenaica. Manchester, 1961.

Index